Tourism and Development Southeast Asia

C000313722

This book analyses the role tourism plays for development in Southeast Asia. It seeks to assess tourism's impact on residents and localities across the region by critically debating and offering new understandings of its dynamics on the global and local levels.

Offering a myriad of case studies from a range of different countries in the region, this book is interdisciplinary in nature, thereby presenting a comprehensive overview of tourism's current and future role in development. Divided into four parts, it discusses the nexus of tourism and development at both the regional and national levels, with a focus on theoretical and methodological foundations, protected areas, local communities, and broader issues of governance. Contributors from within and outside Southeast Asia raise awareness of the local challenges, including issues of ownership or unequal power relations, and celebrate best-practice examples where tourism can be regarded as making a positive difference to residents' lives.

It is the first edited volume presenting a comprehensive analysis of tourism in Southeast Asia as both an economic and social phenomenon through the lens of development — useful to students and scholars of tourism, development, Southeast Asian culture and society, and Asian Studies more generally.

Claudia Dolezal is a Senior Lecturer in Tourism and Development at the University of Westminster, UK, with a background in tourism, development studies and social anthropology.

Alexander Trupp is an Associate Professor in Tourism and Hospitality Management at the School of Hospitality, Sunway University, Malaysia, and previously worked at the School of Tourism and Hospitality Management at The University of the South Pacific, Fiji.

Huong T. Bui is an Associate Professor, and a Field Leader of the Tourism and Hospitality Program of the College of Asia Pacific Studies, Ritsumeikan Asia Pacific University, Japan.

Routledge Contemporary Southeast Asia Series

For more information about this series, please visit: https://www.routledge.com/Routledge-Contemporary-Southeast-Asia-Series/book-series/RCSEA

Tourism and Development in Southeast Asia

Edited by Claudia Dolezal, Alexander Trupp and Huong T. Bui

Routledge
Taylor & Francis Group

LONDON AND NEW YORK

First published 2020
by Routledge
2 Park Square, Milton Park, Abingdon, Oxon OX14 4RN

and by Routledge
605 Third Avenue, New York, NY 10017

First issued in paperback 2022

Routledge is an imprint of the Taylor & Francis Group, an informa business

British Library Cataloguing in Publication Data
A catalogue record for this book is available from the British Library

Library of Congress Cataloging-in-Publication Data
Names: Dolezal, Claudia, editor. | Trupp, Alexander, editor. |
Bui, Huong T., editor.
Title: Tourism and development in Southeast Asia / edited by Claudia Dolezal, Alexander Trupp and Bui T. Huong.
Description: NY : Routledge, 2020. | Includes bibliographical references and index.
Identifiers: LCCN 2019053649 | ISBN 9780367209254 (hardback) |
ISBN 9780429264191 (ebook)
Subjects: LCSH: Tourism--Social aspects--Southeast Asia. |
Economic development--Southeast Asia. |
Economic development--Sociological aspects.
Classification: LCC G155.S585 T67 2020 |
DDC 338.4/79159--dc23
LC record available at https://lccn.loc.gov/2019053649

ISBN 13: 978-1-03-240029-7 (pbk)
ISBN 13: 978-0-367-20925-4 (hbk)
ISBN 13: 978-0-429-26419-1 (ebk)

DOI: 10.4324/9780429264191

Typeset in Times New Roman
by Taylor & Francis Books

Contents

Illustrations

Figures

Maps

Tables

Contributors

Tracy Berno is an Associate Professor at AUT University in Auckland, New Zealand. Her research interests include the relationship between agriculture, tourism and cuisine, sustainable food systems, and food politics. Tracy has lectured and researched in Thailand for many years, and it was during this time that her interest in Thai food and culture started. Tracy has researched and published widely on culture, cuisine, and tourism and has co-authored two international award-winning books in this area, including one which won the best cookbook in the world in 2010. Email: tracy.berno@aut.ac.nz

Huong T. Bui is an Associate Professor at Ritsumeikan Asia Pacific University (APU), Japan. She holds a PhD in Tourism Management from Griffith University (Australia). She has received research grants from the Japan Foundation and the Japan Society for the Promotion of Science (JSPS) on the topics of heritage tourism in Southeast Asia, and disaster risk management for the tourism sector in Asia. Her research interest is special interest tourism in Southeast Asia including backpacking, dark tourism and heritage tourism. Prior to her career in academia, she worked in the tourism industry and was a consultant for tourism development projects in Southeast Asia. Email: huongbui@apu.ac.jp

Heidi Dahles is Adjunct Professor at the Griffith Institute for Tourism (GIFT), Griffith University, Brisbane (Australia). Her research interest is at the interface of development, business and tourism in Southeast Asia. She published over 40 chapters in edited volumes and 60 articles in peer-reviewed journals (such as Annals of Tourism Research, Journal of Sustainable Tourism, Asia-Pacific Journal of Tourism Research, Journal of Developmental Entrepreneurship, Journal of Enterprising Communities, Journal of Contemporary Asia). Dahles actively engages with journals in the field of tourism and business as editorial board member and book review editor. Email: heidi.dahles@gmail.com

Fahrurozy Darmawan is a Lecturer at the Faculty of Tourism at the Universitas Pancasila, Jakarta, Indonesia. He holds a Master's Degree in Tourism Planning from Bandung Institute of Technology. His research focuses on community-based tourism, tourism impacts and sustainable tourism. He currently engages in the SOSIS (Save Our Small Island) project, a collaborative project to empower communities to take part in addressing environmental issues in a bid to achieve sustainable tourism in the Islands. Email: fahrurozy@univpancasila.ac.id

Glenn Dentice is a Senior Lecturer at AUT University where he lectures in Contemporary Cuisine Aotearoa and in Patisserie in the Bachelor of Culinary Arts. His interests are in the history of Thai gastronomy and culture. Glenn has worked as a lecturer in Thailand as well as in New Zealand. He has also worked as a lecturer at South Australia Regency College. Email: glenn.dentice@aut.ac.nz.

Claudia Dolezal is a Senior Lecturer in Tourism and Development at the University of Westminster and is on the editorial board of the Austrian Journal of South-East Asian Studies (ASEAS). Her background is in tourism, international development and social anthropology, with a geographical focus on the region of Southeast Asia, and most recently London and Latin America. Claudia's research interests focus on tourism and social inequalities, tourism for development, community-based tourism and the anthropology of tourism. She is specifically interested in the ways marginalised groups use tourism for empowerment, as well as the multifaceted power dynamics that shape the tourism encounter in tourism settings of both the developed and developing world. Email: c.dolezal@westminster.ac.uk

Riza Firmansyah is a Lecturer at the Faculty of Tourism, Universitas Pancasila, with specialisation in ecotourism and sustainable tourism. He earned his Master's Degree in Natural Resources and Environmental Management at Bogor Agricultural University, Indonesia, in 2014. His research interests are sustainable tourism development, tourism suitability and tourism carrying capacity. He is also involved as an expert consultant in tourism development with the Ministry of Tourism in Indonesia in formulating and assessing rural and urban tourism databases. In 2017–2019, he acted as the Head of the Research and Community Services Unit at the Faculty of Tourism, Universitas Pancasila. Email: rfirmansyah@univpancasila.ac.id

Nicole Häusler has worked for more than 25 years as a Responsible Tourism Consultant, mainly in Southeast Asia and with a focus on Responsible Tourism Management and Training, the implementation of CSR and Tourism & Poverty Reduction. She holds a Master's Degree in Social Anthropology and a PhD in Responsible Tourism. Nicole is a licenced change management consultant focusing especially on cultural due diligence and holds an honorary professorship at the University for Sustainable Development in Eberswalde (Hochschule für nachhaltige Entwicklung-HNEE). Since 2013 Nicole has been living in Myanmar, working mainly for the Deutsche Gesellschaft für internationale Zusammenarbeit - GIZ; the International Trade Center and the Hanns-Seidel Foundation in close cooperation with Ministry of Hotels and Tourism and the Myanmar Tourism Federation; furthermore she supports the NGO Myanmar Responsible Tourism Institute as an adviser. Email: nhaeusler.consult@gmail.com

Thomas E. Jones is an Associate Professor of Ritsumeikan Asia Pacific University, Japan. His research revolves around the human dimensions of natural resource management, focusing on national parks and protected areas. Originally from the UK, Jones completed a PhD at Tokyo University in 2010, carrying out fieldwork at Mt Fuji and the Japan Alps. He has published on themes related to nature-based tourism and regional revitalization. Email: 110054tj@apu.ac.jp

Devi Roza Kausar is an Associate Professor and Dean of the Faculty of Tourism, Universitas Pancasila. Her research interests are cultural heritage tourism, sustainable tourism, rural development, and disaster mitigation in tourism. She has a PhD in International Development from Nagoya University, Japan, a Master's Degree in Tourism Management from Curtin University, Australia, and a Bachelor of Economics from Padjadjaran University, Indonesia. She has been involved in various projects in the Ministry of Tourism, particularly in the field of rural tourism, tourism planning and tourism education. Email: devikausar@univpancasila.ac.id

Frauke Kraas is Professor for Human Geography at the Institute of Geography, University of Cologne, Germany. In 1991 she finished her PhD (University of Münster) and in 1996 her Habilitation (University of Bonn). Her research focuses on (mega)urban and regional development, transformation processes, urban governance, urban heritage, urban health, risk/disaster research, migration and ethnic minorities in Southeast Asia, India and China. Since 1996 Frauke has been conducting research in Myanmar with colleagues from the Universities of Yangon and Mandalay, the Department for Urban and Housing Development, Ministry of Construction, and the Yangon City Development Committee. She is International Advisor of the University of Yangon. Email: f.kraas@uni-koeln.de

Aldi Lasso is a Lecturer and the Head of the Tourism Destination Study Programme at Universitas Kristen Satya Wacana, Indonesia. He finished his PhD at the Griffith Institute for Tourism, Griffith University, Brisbane, Australia. He published a peer-reviewed conference paper in 2017 and an article in a peer-reviewed journal in 2018. He focuses his research on tourism, sustainable development and local livelihoods in South East Asia. Email: aldilasso@gmai.com

Prasit Leepreecha is an Assistant Professor at the Department of Social Science and Development, Faculty of Social Sciences, Chiang Mai University. He earned his doctoral degree in Cultural Anthropology from the University of Washington, Seattle. His research interests include ethnic tourism, indigenous peoples' movement, citizenship and ethnic responses to development and globalization. Email: prasit.lee@cmu.ac.th

Pham Hong Long is an Associate Professor and Dean of the Faculty of Tourism Studies, University of Social Sciences and Humanities, Vietnam National University (Hanoi). He graduated from Vietnam National University in Hanoi before receiving his Master's Degree in Malaysia and PhD from Rikkyo University in Japan. His research areas are ecotourism, community-based tourism, sustainable tourism development, tourism policies and governance in Southeast Asia. He is a leading consultant in sustainable tourism, community-based tourism and ecotourism in protected areas in Vietnam for international organisations such as the British Council Vietnam, KOICA, GIZ, USAID, ILO and JICA. Email: longph@vnu.edu.vn

Jitka Markova is the Cambodian Country Director for Conscious Tourism International, a UK-based NGO that uses community-based tourism as a tool for the implementation of Sustainable Development Goals (SDGs) and the UN 2030 Agenda. Her main areas of expertise include community-based tourism, women-run social enterprises, financial modelling and diversity. She also a co-founder of Impact Explorer, an online marketplace for community-based tourism projects that bridges the gap between rural communities and independent travellers. Email: jitka@camconscious.org

Dieter K. Müller is a Professor at the Department of Geography, Umeå University, Sweden. His research interest and specialty is second home tourism. He is Deputy Vice-Chancellor, Umeå University, Chairperson of the Arctic Research Centre at Umeå University, Chair, IGU Commission Geography of Tourism, Leisure and Global Change, book series editor for Geographies of Tourism and Global Change, resource editor at the Scandinavian Journal of Hospitality and Tourism, editorial board member for Current Issues in Tourism, Tourism Geographies, Matkailututkimus – The Finnish Journal of Tourism Research, and Hrvatski Geografski Glasnik – Croatian Geographical Bulletin. Email: dieter.muller@umu.se

Sabine Müller is Lecturer and Project Manager at the Institute of Tourism at Lucerne University of Applied Sciences and Arts in Switzerland. Her main areas of expertise include community-based tourism, destination competitiveness and sustainable tourism development. Sabine is involved in teaching and leading consulting projects in a variety of topics with tourism businesses and political institutions. Prior to her work at the Institute of Tourism in Lucerne, she has worked for the German Development Cooperation in Asia. Email: sabine.mueller@hslu.ch

Zin Nwe Myint gained her Master's Degree in geography in 1998 and PhD in 2004 from the University of Yangon. Her fields of specialisation are urban geography and tourism geography. She was appointed as a tutor in Yangon University of Distance Education in 1997 and transferred to the University of Yangon in 1999. In 2006, she started to work as an Assistant Lecturer at Sittway University. Since then her research has focused on tourism, especially related to the Rakhine State. Currently, she is a Professor at the Department of Geography, University of Yangon. She has been awarded a Georg Forster Research Fellowship for Experienced Researchers by the Alexander von Humboldt Foundation, Germany, in 2017. Email: zinnwemyint@gmail.com.

Saithong Phommavong is a Lecturer in the Faculty of Social Sciences, National University of Laos, Vientiane, Lao PDR. He holds a Bachelors degree in Political Sciences from the National University of Laos, a Master in Economics from Kobe University in Japan and a PhD in Social and Economic Geography from Umeå University, Sweden. His research interests are economic development, pro-poor tourism, political economy, sustainable development, gender relations and land use planning. Some recent publications are in the International Journal of Culture and Tourism Research, Current Issues in Tourism, Springer, Global Social Welfare, Routledge and IntechOpen. Email: sai7512@yahoo.com.

Sindhuri Ponnapureddy is a Digital Marketing and Analytics consultant in Switzerland and previously worked as a Tourism Research Associate in Lucerne University of Applied Sciences. She also holds a PhD in sustainable tourism and communication from the University of Zurich. Her research interests include marketing, consumer behavior, and sustainable tourism. Email: sindhuri.ponnapu@gmail.com.

Natalia B.M.T. Syura is currently working in Malaysia. She completed a Master's Degree in Public Policy in 2014 at the Graduate School of Governance Studies in Meiji University, Tokyo. She has an interest in the tourism industry, including nature-based tourism, and conducted field work in Langkawi, the case study site for her Master's Thesis. Email: synlaqua@gmail.com.

Alexander Trupp is an Associate Professor in Tourism and Hospitality Management at the School of Hospitality, Sunway University, Malaysia. He previously worked at the School of Tourism and Hospitality Management at The University of the South Pacific, Fiji, Mahidol University, Thailand, and the University of Vienna, Austria. Alexander has extensive fieldwork experience in the Asia Pacific Region. His research is nested in the broad fields of tourism studies and human geography. He has conducted research on host-guest encounters in ethnic and cultural tourism, rural-urban migration, urban street vending, Asian outbound tourism, immigrant entrepreneurship, tourism microbusinesses, and migration and natural disasters. Alexander is also the editor-in-chief of the Austrian Journal of Southeast Asian Studies and a former Associate Editor of the Journal of Pacific Studies. Email: alexander.trupp@univie.ac.at

Jutamas (Jan) Wisansing is a founder and managing director, leading an innovative team at Perfect Link Consulting Group "A Consortium of Experts" in Thailand. She specialises in community innovation and transformative empowerment programs, creative tourism, and sustainable culinary supply chain management. Jan has had a leading role in establishing the ASEAN Gastronomy Tourism Network and representing ASEAN voice as a board member of IGCAT (International Institute of Gastronomy, Culture, Arts and Tourism). Email: Perfectlink1@yahoo.com

Yukio Yotsumoto is a Professor of Asia-Pacific Studies at Ritsumeikan Asia Pacific University in Japan. He received a Bachelor's Degree in economics (Soka University, Japan), a Master's Degree in agricultural extension education (University of Georgia, USA) and a PhD in rural sociology (University of Kentucky, USA). He is interested in rural development and tourism and his most recent publications are two chapters entitled "Revitalization of the Ainu Language: Japanese Government Efforts" and "Place Names and Natural Disasters in Japan" in the Handbook of the Changing World Language Map, edited by S.D. Brunn and R. Kehrein. Email: yotsumot@apu.ac.jp

Foreword

Kathleen Adams

A little over 60 years ago, the Pacific Area Trade Association (PATA) and the US Department of Commerce commissioned a study tour of nations in Asia and the Pacific to assess their potential for tourism development (Wood, 1979, p. 274). Their ultimate report declared tourism sorely underdeveloped in the region and urged Asian and Pacific nations to embrace tourism as an avenue for achieving job growth and expanding economies. Characteristic of this early era, tourism was optimistically celebrated as "a new kind of sugar," a smokeless industry that would usher in an array of benefits—modernization, development, infrastructural improvements, well-being, and fiscal security—without the negatives associated with plantations and factories (see Finney, 1975). As jumbo jets and advertising campaigns brought mushrooming numbers of tourists to Asian and Pacific nations in the 1960s and 1970s, some scholars began questioning the veracity of these bold Pollyanna-ish claims (e.g. Finney, 1975; de Kadt, 1984). Around the same time, similar concerns were starting to be raised for tourism in Southeast Asian nations (e.g. Wood, 1980). Yet, as sociologist Robert Wood soberly observed in 1979, thirty years after the tourism study tour, "international tourism now constitutes an increasingly important aspect of the development strategy of almost every non-socialist government in Asia [yet] apart from technical project evaluations…almost no studies of its spread and its economic, social and political consequences have been carried out" (Wood, 1979,p. 274).

Since that time, tourism's complex entanglements with development have become a topic of growing interest to Southeast Asia scholars, consultants, activists, and local stakeholders. Today, many tourism scholars and practitioners have come to recognize the Janus-faced character of tourism as a path to development (e.g. Cohen, 2000, pp. 26–27; Sanchez & Adams, 2008; Avond et. al., 2019). While tourism may bring Southeast Asian governments new income streams, tax revenues and infrastructural improvements, we know that tourism development does not always yield the promised "multiplier effect" enhancing the well-being of local-level stake-holders (who often lack the economic or political clout to have a say in the transformations of their environments). Although some Southeast Asian minority groups such as the Toraja have successfully lassoed tourism to enhance their image on the national stage, demonstrating a degree of agency in the face of externally-imposed development (Adams, 1995;

2006), others have found themselves excluded from tourism-generated rewards, be they material (in the form of economic revenues) or immaterial in the form of ethnic prestige, as evidenced by Koh Samui fishers in Thailand, whose once-easy sea access was blocked by beach-front hotels (Green, 2005).

As critical tourism studies have taken root, classic Western-generated tourism-as-development paradigms are increasingly questioned, critiqued, and/or reformulated. There has been a palpable need for a compendium of ethnographically grounded case studies that shed light on the complexities of lassoing tourism for "good" in Southeast Asia. What can be learned from how tourism has unfolded in different regions in Southeast Asia? What challenges have been encountered in Southeast Asia's varied environments and nations? What scenarios are to be avoided? What might a more genuinely sustainable tourism look like? Are there any successful formulas that can lead to locally led tourism projects that foster assured livelihoods and local empowerment?

Although we have a growing array of individual case studies on tourism in the region, far too often these studies are not in dialogue with one another, appearing in different languages, in varied disciplinary journals, or buried in hard-to-access dissertations and technical reports to government bodies and granting agencies. Until now there has been no single volume that offers both a systematic theoretical interrogation of tourism-as-development paradigms in Southeast Asia and insights from case studies. Claudia Dolezal, Alexander Trupp and Huong T. Bui's *Tourism and Development in Southeast Asia* addresses this palpable gap, bringing us valuable theoretical and case study-based insights into the complexities of the nexus of tourism and development in the region.

Not only does this thought-provoking volume enhance our awareness of existing local-, regional- and national-level challenges, but it also offers best-practice examples wherein tourism has been effectively used to enhance local community members' lives. Together, the theoretical discussions, reflections on the complexities of doing tourism ethnography, and rich case studies presented in the book enhance our understanding of why careful ethnographically informed tourism research attuned to, even guided by, local stakeholders is so essential. In short, the publication of this book represents an important new resource for critical tourism scholars, tourism practitioners, and local stakeholders hoping to lasso tourism to play a more uniformly positive role in Southeast Asians' lives.

References

Adams, K.M. (2006). *Art as Politics: Re-crafting Identities, Tourism and Power in Tana Toraja, Indonesia*. Honolulu: University of Hawai'i Press.

Adams, K.M. (1995). Making up the Toraja: The appropriation of tourism, anthropology and museums for politics in upland Sulawesi, Indonesia. *Ethnology* 34(2), pp 143–153.

Avond, G., Bacari, C., Limea, I. et. al. (2019). Overtourism: A result of the Janus-faced character of the tourism industry. *Worldwide Hospitality and Tourism Themes* 11(5), pp. 552–565.

Cohen, E. (2000). Thai tourism: Trends and transformations. In E. Cohen, *Thai Tourism: Hill Tribes, Islands and Open-Ended Prostitution*. Bangkok: White Lotus Press, 2nd edition, pp. 1–28.

de Kadt, E. (1984). *Tourism: Passport to Development? Perspectives on the Social and Cultural Effects of Tourism on Developing Countries*. Washington, D.C.: World Bank Group.

Finney, B.R. (1975). *A New Kind of Sugar: Tourism in the Pacific*. Honolulu: East-West Center, University of Hawaii.

Green, R. (2005). Community perceptions of environmental and social change and tourism development on the Island of Koh Samui, Thailand. *Journal of Environmental Psychology* 25, pp. 37–56.

Sanchez, P.M. and Adams, K.M. (2008). The Janus-faced character of tourism in Cuba: Ideological continuity and change. *Annals of Tourism Research* 35(1), pp. 27–46.

Wood, R.E. (1979). Tourism and underdevelopment in Southeast Asia. *Journal of Contemporary Asia* 9(3), pp. 274–287, DOI: doi:10.1080/00472337985390251.

Wood, R.E. (1980). International tourism and cultural change in Southeast Asia. *Economic Development and Cultural Change* 28(3), pp. 561–581.

Part I

Introduction

Theoretical and methodological foundations

1 Mapping tourism, sustainability, and development in Southeast Asia

Alexander Trupp, Claudia Dolezal and Huong T. Bui

Introduction

This book is aimed at understanding the contested role that tourism plays in achieving development in Southeast Asia. In this context, Southeast Asia represents a diverse region with different historical, political, and socioeconomic developments and a broad range of natural and cultural tourist attractions. These assets, along with favourable tourism policies, have meant that over the last three decades, international tourist arrivals in the region sky-rocketed from 21.2 million in 1990 to 129 million in 2018 (UNWTO, 2019). While Southeast Asian countries feature diverse socioeconomic and political developments, all have – to different extents – embraced tourism as a vehicle for income generation and job creation (Trupp, 2018). Simultaneously, however, different forms of (mass) tourism development have led to unequal distribution of economic benefits, overexploitation of resources, and uncontrolled tourism development.

In putting together this book, we aim to create a forum for critical discussions on the ever-growing sector and social phenomenon of tourism, which is increasingly used as a tool for poverty alleviation, residents' empowerment, and livelihood diversification across the region. Collections in this volume critically debate and deepen the understanding of the dynamics of tourism on both global and local levels and the impact it has on residents and localities in Southeast Asia. Arguably, tourism has not only contributed to economic growth but also caused increasing socioeconomic inequality and vast disruptions to local ecosystems, societies, and cultures. The expansion of an industry that often exceeds local carrying capacity limits, supported through injections of capital by external funding bodies with little room for local initiative has often led to residents' marginalization and the widening of socioeconomic gaps within local communities. In reconsidering the relationship between tourism and development in this volume, we highlight several dimensions of this nexus.

First, tourism's relationship with nature is contested. Erb (2001) argues that the environment is often perceived as a resource to be exploited, even though the kind of tourism under study here in the Indonesian context was aimed at sustainable development. In some cases, such as Boracay Island (Philippines) and Maya Bay (Thailand), problems of overtourism and the degradation of natural resources have led to government decisions to temporarily close popular island destinations (Koh & Fakfare, 2019). While such shutdowns can help the natural environment to recover, they also lead to the loss of jobs and revenue, strongly affecting small businesses and the badly protected informal sector. In addition to environmental impacts that compromise sustainability in Southeast Asia, tourism leads to changing socio-cultural dynamics, including transformations in gender relations (Trupp & Sunanta, 2017), cultural commodification (Cole, 2007), identity (Adams, 2006), inequalities within the resident population (Dolezal, 2015a), economic leakages (Lacher & Nepal, 2010), and the use of heritage for economic and political ends (Hitchcock, King, & Parnwell, 2010; Bui & Lee, 2015). All of these studies demonstrate that, after all, striking the balance between the various pillars of sustainable development still remains challenging.

Second, it is also acknowledged that tourism connects people (Dolezal, 2015b) – not only the Western tourist and their 'hosts', but also those local to the region, resulting in a rise in domestic and intra-regional travel. This domestic travel has the power to stimulate disadvantaged economies and slowly make changes to the travel patterns that have been dominating development of the region (Singh, 2009). Domestic tourism also has grown to be a driving force for developing economies, such as Vietnam (Bui & Jolliffe, 2011). Hence, although tourism's repercussions are well known, it is often seen as a panacea for prevailing issues in developing countries.

Third, while the scale and scope of tourism development differ across Southeast Asia's national boundaries, growing awareness of a more sustainable tourism exists, particularly of the value of grassroots tourism projects that are led by local communities and have the potential to diversify local incomes with the use of residents' skills and available assets (Dolezal & Burns, 2014). It seems that politicians, activists, academics, local decision makers, and community members themselves increasingly discover ways of how to 'do development correctly' in terms of increasing local capacity, creating linkages to other sectors, or 'empowering' those that are affected most by tourism: locals themselves.

However, development itself remains a highly contested term and one that this book attempts to trace and critique particularly in Chapter 2 (by Bui & Dolezal). The notion of development has largely been influenced by capitalist thinking from the early beginnings onwards and while efforts of modernisation and neoliberal politics advancing Western interests soon faced critiques by dependency theorists and alternative development thinkers, many argue that there still is an inherently unhealthy power dynamic at play (Sciortino, 2017). In times of the Sustainable Development Goals (SDGs), which perpetuate a strong focus on a sustainable development that includes the Global North as much as South, it is argued that 'the SDGs still centre contemporary capitalism as a mechanism to deal with persistent poverty, growing inequality and ecological ruin' (Klein & Morreo, 2019, p. 3). Reaffirming Escobar's early critiques of the development machinery, what is really needed therefore is not 'development alternatives but alternatives to development' (Escobar, 1995, p. 215). This book thus sheds light on the grassroots and realities on the ground not only to decolonize development in Southeast Asia but also to create a space to enable an alternative development discourse in line with post-development thinking.

The following sections provide an overview of the nature and development of tourism in Southeast Asia, followed by an outline of the status quo on tourism and development research in Southeast Asia through a systematic quantitative literature review which draws on the Scopus research journal article database, covering the years 2000–2019. The final section of this chapter will position the present collection in relation to other books, introduce the structure of this edited volume and give a synopsis of the individual contributions.

The development of tourism in Southeast Asia

Tourism in Southeast Asia traces back many years, with early forms of travel including pilgrimage, and travel for trade, land, resources, missions and warfare. Tourism is thus a long-established economic, religious, and social activity in the region though mass tourism is a rather recent phenomenon which largely began to expand in the 1970s (Hitchcock, King, & Parnwell, 2008).

In the past decades, tourism in Southeast Asia has seen unprecedented growth (Figure 1.1), while the region has also undergone major changes in relation to markets, mobility and integration between countries in economic

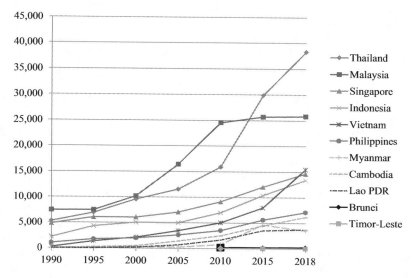

Figure 1.1 International tourist arrivals in Southeast Asia (1990–2018) (in thousands)
Source: UNWTO 2016, 2019

and political terms. The creation and expansion of the Association of Southeast Asian Nations (ASEAN) from a defence alliance to a political and economic relationship between member countries is significant in the formation of the Southeast Asian identity. Founded in 1967 as a non-communist block of East Asian countries, ASEAN plays a major role in the region's economic, social and political development. In 1976, the organisation created a Sub-Committee on Tourism for the development of coordinated tourism projects and their enhanced marketing and, four years later, the ASEAN Tourism Forum was established as an annual event. Later, in 2015, the 10 members of ASEAN signed a declaration on the formal establishment of the ASEAN community, a broad framework of regional integration made up of three pillars: the ASEAN Economic Community (AEC), which focuses on economic integration; the Political-Security Community, which aims to link up regional foreign affairs and security interests; and the Socio-Cultural Community, which seeks to build people-to-people connections (Hall & Page, 2017).

Moreover, the opening of political systems and international borders accompanied by improvements in infrastructure led to further economic cooperation and mobility within the region and had substantial implications for tourism, both at the regional and international level. Tourism growth has also been spurred on by the birth of a range of regional low-cost airlines, spreading mass tourism beyond already established honeypots (Duval & Weaver, 2017). The recent financial crisis and economic instabilities have encouraged many Southeast Asian tourists previously travelling to North America and Europe to take their holidays in their own countries or the region, thereby driving regional tourism development.

As seen in Figure 1.1, the patterns of tourism development seem to concentrate on several 'centres' both in terms of the distribution of market and space. Thailand receives most international tourists within the region and has undergone a transformation in recent years as new source markets such as China, India, and Russia have boosted international arrivals dramatically (Trupp, 2017). Concurrent to this growth, tourism planners in Thailand have attempted to counter the growth of more conventional (4-S) forms of tourism by promoting alternative tourism, which is 'more personalized, novel and authentic' (Kontogeorgopoulos, 2017, p. 160). Malaysia's strategy is to target high-yield tourists, including MICE participants and tourists from Middle Eastern countries; the country also promotes ecotourism, and medical tourism (Musa & Thirumoorthi, 2017). Vietnam has experienced significant growth in tourist arrivals in recent years and has also experienced diaspora tourism, with overseas Vietnamese returning to their former homes (Nguyen & King, 2002). Tourism development in Vietnam is state-led, demonstrating features such as an emphasis on quantity over quality and multiple barriers concerning product diversification and service quality (Truong & Le, 2017). Indonesian tourism is diverse in its nature owing to the country's resource abundance, however, the economic revenue from tourism is highly concentrated in Bali (Connell, 2018) and natural disasters and terrorism in the past few years have affected tourism development in Indonesia (Hampton & Clifton, 2017). Having the highest ratio of tourists to residents in the region, Singapore's key tourism plans have expanded from the emphasis on local culture and nature sites in the 1980s to a regional agenda in the 1990s, with global ambitions (Chang, 2017) and the introduction of integrated resorts where casinos are part of a larger tourist attraction (Henderson, 2016).

The Philippines were isolated from airline connections for many years but experienced tourism growth as access options improved. Laos opened its gates for international tourism in the 1990s and since then has focused on tourists seeking new nature-based and cultural experiences and places. Cambodia too has grown steadily in the wake of peace in this century, but tourism in the country is mainly focused around the area of Angkor Wat/Siem Reap and the capital city Phnom Penh. In the country of Myanmar where only a decade ago ethical concerns were raised over any travel to the country, tourism is also growing faster than ever. However, recent violence in Rakhine state led to the current downturn of tourism arrivals. Isolated Timor-Leste is the newest nation in Southeast Asia. Despite the effort of the government and various international organisations to develop tourism in the country (Tolkach & King, 2015), Timor-Leste only has a token tourist economy because of poor communications and infrastructure (Connell, 2018). Experiencing a similarly small number of tourist arrivals, Brunei, by contrast, shows an image of a high cost destination and travel constraints related to 'unfamiliar cultural constraints' such as 'lack of knowledge and experience with Brunei's cultural heritage and religion' (Chen, Chen, & Okumus, 2013, p. 205).

The Southeast Asian states do not only vary in terms of tourist numbers and the kind of tourism they pursue though. When looking at other indicators relating to tourism and development, one can see great variances (Table 1.1). Member countries range economically from prosperous Singapore and the oil-rich sultanate of Brunei, the relatively developed economies of Malaysia, Thailand, and Indonesia, to the much lower rated developing nations of Laos, Cambodia, Timor-Leste and Myanmar. It is also interesting to note that those countries that do not score particularly high in the HDI-based socioeconomic development are most dependent on tourism, such as Cambodia and the Philippines – two countries where tourism plays a key role in development. Moreover, a higher HDI seems to somewhat translate also into low levels of gender inequality, with Singapore, Brunei and Malaysia occupying the top ranks of the Southeast Asian nations. The same does not apply to environmental sustainability though, where Brunei is the top polluter in terms of carbon dioxide, followed by Singapore and Malaysia, while Laos is at the very opposite end of the spectrum. It is not surprising that the most populated country is Indonesia, a country that gets a fair share of Southeast Asia's tourist arrivals. However, Thailand remains at the top in terms of tourist arrivals and receipts and also sees strong improvements to its HDI ranking. Thailand now ranks 83rd, besides Brunei, Malaysia and of course Singapore which score even higher.

Table 1.1 Tourism and development characteristics in Southeast Asia

	Population 2017 (in millions)	Int. tourist arrivals 2018 (in millions)	Int. tourism receipts 2018 (USD million)	Total contribution of tourism to GDP in % in 2018	Total contribution of tourism to employment in % in 2018	HDI rank	Gender Inequality Index	Carbon dioxide emissions per capita in 2014
Brunei	0.4	0.28	190	6.7	8.1	39	0.236	22.1
Cambodia	16	6.20	4352	32.8	31.6	146	0.473	0.4
Indonesia	264	13.40	14110	6.0	10.3	116	0.453	1.8
Laos	6.9	3.77	734	12	10.5	139	0.461	0.3
Malaysia	31.6	25.83	19143	13.3	11.9	57	0.287	8.0
Myanmar	53.4	3.55	73 (2017)	6.8	5.9	148	0.456	0.4
Philippines	104.9	7.13	7461	24.7	26.4	113	0.427	1.1
Singapore	5.4	14.67	20528	10.0	8.8	9	0.067	10.3
Thailand	69	38.28	63042	21.6	15.9	83	0.393	4.6
Timor-Leste	1.3	0.08	73 (2017)	N/A	N/A	132	N/A	0.4
Vietnam	95.5	15.50	10080	9.2	7.4	116	0.304	1.8
Southeast Asia	648.4	128.68	142314	12.6	12.2			

Source: UN, 2019; UNWTO, 2019; WTTC, 2019

In addition to the above tourism developments and development indicators, changes are also seen in terms of tourism markets. Tourism markets in Southeast Asia have transformed from hosting primarily European, Western tourists to being more dominated by tourists from East Asia, particularly from China, in addition to a growing number from South Korea and from established markets such as Japan (Hall & Page, 2017). This transformation has reshaped patterns of tourism development in the region. Inbound tourists to ASEAN generally come from Asia, with about half travelling between ASEAN states, and more than a quarter coming from other Asian states (China, Korea, Japan, India, and Taiwan).

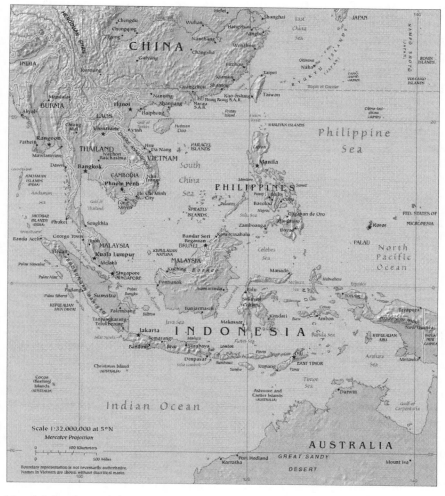

Map 1.1 Southeast Asia
Source: https://commons.wikimedia.org/wiki/File:Southeast_asia.jpg

These developments are not surprising, after all tourism has been recognized as a powerful engine of growth and a creator of employment, prompting greater ease for visa requirements, i.e. visa exemption for ASEAN citizens travelling within the region (Connell, 2018). The total contribution of travel and tourism in Southeast Asia to the gross domestic product of the region is 12.6% and 38 million jobs (12.2% of total employment) are related to the travel and tourism industry (WTTC, 2019). It is the most important sector and a major source of foreign exchange earnings in Thailand; it ranks second in Malaysia and the Philippines; and it is the third most important sector in Singapore and Indonesia. The tourism sector in the Greater Mekong Sub-region (Cambodia, Laos, Myanmar, Vietnam, Thailand, and parts of South China), for example, was the main leading sector for economic growth from 2006 to 2013 (Connell, 2018).

Considering the above, it is therefore without doubt that Southeast Asia is now regarded as both a major generator and recipient of tourism, and as a place for significant international tourism, regional tourism (within ASEAN) and domestic tourism. With tourism steadily on the rise, increasingly more research is dedicated to understanding the fascinating and complex facets of tourism and the role it has to play in development in the region. However, little is known about which countries within Southeast Asia are thereby the prime focus of existing tourism and development research, and, above all, which thematic areas prevail. The next section therefore offers an overview of tourism and development research through a systematic literature review analysis.

Mapping tourism and development in Southeast Asia

Over the years, tourism for development has become an essential research field in its own right (Burns & Novelli, 2008; Mowforth & Munt, 2016; Novelli, 2016; Sharpley & Harrison, 2019; Telfer & Sharpley, 2008), also in Southeast Asia, where negative socioeconomic and ecological impacts of (mass) tourism have become increasingly visible (Dolezal & Trupp, 2015). While definitions of development can be debated, most scholars would probably agree that as a broad concept it encompasses diverse though partly overlapping dimensions such as economic (e.g. wealth creation or access to resources), social (e.g. gender equality or participation), cultural (e.g. strengthening of indigenous communities or cultural identities), political (e.g. asserting good governance or human rights), and environmental (e.g. conservation or responding to climate change) components. Such components of development have also been reflected in the eight Millennium Development Goals (MDGs) (2000–2015) and – in greater detail – in the subsequent 17 SDGs (2015–2030), which shape the current development agenda (see UN, 2019).

This section provides an overview of the status quo on tourism and development research in Southeast Asia through a systematic quantitative literature review by drawing on the Scopus research journal article database for the years 2000–2019. By mapping the geographical distribution of keywords and concepts relating to tourism and development research, we envisage not only which countries have been the centre of attention of research, but also which thematic areas.

The systematic quantitative literature review has received increasing attention in tourism studies and has been praised for its more objective approach in examining research themes and variables (Mura & Sharif, 2015; Pickering & Byrne, 2014). The mapping process is quantitative because research papers and topics are identified, selected, counted and then further analysed. The analysis is inspired by the work of Yang, Khoo-Lattimore, and Arcodia, (2017) as well as by Khoo-Lattimore, Mura, and Yung (2019) who suggest a five-level analytical process in their mappings of 'risk and gender in tourism research' and 'mixed methods on tourism': First, researchers establish the aims and questions of the review; second, they identify search terms, scholarly databases, and literature selection criteria; third, they search the database and screen search outcomes against the identified search terms or concepts; fourth they structure a summary table which represents the basis for the fifth and final step, which is the analysis.

The review analyses the status quo on tourism and development research across all eleven countries in Southeast Asia and for the region as a whole. The authors developed a list of 11 keywords that aim to broadly reflect the different dimensions and ongoing discourses of development, particularly in tourism contexts. Of course, this is not an exhaustive list of terms, however these keywords were chosen as they were deemed important when it comes to development discourse (Cornwall & Eade, 2010), specifically influenced by how development is understood by the UN SDGs, which set the current development agenda. In addition, these also reflect the focus of the contributions in the present edited volume. The following 11 concepts and related search terms were therefore used to search the database (Table 1.2).

Each of these 11 (sets of) terms were used in conjunction with the terms 'tourism AND development' and were applied to all countries in Southeast Asia and the region at large, using the geographical search terms shown in Table 1.2.

All these developmental and geographical key terms were searched in the Scopus database fields of 'article title', 'abstract', and 'keywords'. Relevant literature for these terms were purposefully used from 2000 up to the time of analysis and write up of the chapter (July 2019). Authors selected the year 2000 as the starting point for analysis since this marks the launch of the MDGs, 'a historic and effective method of global mobilization to achieve a set of important social priorities worldwide' (Sachs, 2012, p. 2206). The selected database is Scopus which represents one of the largest academic databases consisting of more than 5,000 publishers and over 22,800 serial titles (Elsevier, 2019). Scopus also proved to be the more comprehensive database when compared with other databases such as Emerald or EBSCO (Khoo-Lattimore, Mura, & Yung, 2019). It is important to emphasise though that many journals are not (yet) indexed in Scopus but publish valuable and relevant work. This may relate to rather newly established journals or those which predominantly publish in non-English languages. Furthermore, the Scopus database search was limited to peer-reviewed journal articles, thus

Table 1.2 Thematic and geographical search terms

Thematic search concepts	Used search terms	Searched countries/region
(1) MDGs (tourism and development era 2000–2015)	MDGs OR millennium development goals	(1) Brunei
(2) SDGs (tourism and development era 2015–2030)	SDGs OR sustainable development goals	(2) Cambodia
(3) Sustainability (broad reference to sustainable or responsible tourism)	Sustainability OR sustainable OR responsible	(3) East Timor OR Timor-Leste
(4) CBT/Ecotourism (more specific reference to forms of sustainable tourism)	CBT OR Community-based OR ecotourism OR eco-tourism	(4) Indonesia
(5) Pro-poor (more specific reference to poverty and inequality issues in tourism development)	Pro-poor OR poor or poverty OR inequality	(5) Laos OR Lao PDR
(6) Participation (tourism and participation)	Participation	(6) Malaysia
(7) Empowerment (tourism and empowerment)	Empowerment	(7) Myanmar OR Burma
(8) Gender (tourism and gender)	Gender	(8) Philippines
(9) Governance/NGO (tourism and governance)	Governance OR NGO	(9) Singapore
(10) Human Rights (tourism and human rights)	Human rights	(10) Thailand
(11) Environment (tourism, climate change and environmental sustainability)	Environment OR climate change	(11) Vietnam
		(12) Southeast Asia OR South-East Asia

Source: Self-elaborated

excluding editorials, book reviews, conference papers, and book chapters. While the selection of journal articles through Scopus generally captures a comprehensive volume of relevant articles on tourism and development research in Southeast Asia, the authors are aware that this method is unable to reflect all relevant research within the field, which needs to be acknowledged.

The initial search in the Scopus database for all countries and the region resulted in 1,323 results. After screening and reading all metadata of the appearing articles, 100 results were removed mainly for the following two reasons: First, a Southeast Asian country name appeared in the metadata but the focus of the paper was on another region or country; second, terms were captured in the results but did not meet the context of tourism and development (for example the term poor was used for poor service quality). Moreover, it has to be noted that the total number of all keywords and all countries includes many duplications since one and the same article may appear under the search terms 'sustainable', 'ecotourism', and 'participation'. Other articles, for example, pursued a comparative study discussing different countries within the region, thus appearing in more than one country search result. These duplications however were not removed since the aim is to provide an overview of captured development topics and not of the number of articles.

Topical and geographical distribution of tourism and development research

Based on the selection and analytical criteria explained in the previous paragraph, Table 1.3 shows the topical and geographical distribution of tourism and development research across different countries in Southeast Asia. The two most researched countries of the region in this context are Malaysia (308) and Thailand (269), which are also the countries with the highest number of international tourist arrivals as shown in Table 1.3. Indonesia, the region's fourth most visited destination and the biggest country in terms of population showed 215 results in the Scopus analysis. With 792 results in total, these three countries clearly receive most attention from scholarly work in Southeast Asia. Less research has been conducted on the region of Southeast Asia at large (123), Vietnam (84), and the Philippines (78). The least researched countries in the field of tourism and development are Cambodia (49), Lao PDR (40), Singapore (26), Myanmar (18), Timor-Leste (11) and Brunei (2). These countries, with the exception of Singapore, are also the least visited countries in the region and feature (with the exception of Singapore and Brunei) comparatively low human development indices.

There are further interesting aspects to note in terms of the spread of thematic areas on which research in the region focuses. What emerged from the analysis is that most tourism and development research centres around sustainability. This is not surprising given that sustainable development has become a global agenda, one that Southeast Asia also needs to adopt in all its dimensions (Savage, 2006). ASEAN, for example (as well as most governments), states that it seeks to actively promote sustainable tourism and that this is the only way forward for the region (Thomas, 2019). At the same time, however, sustainability has become a catchphrase, a buzzword just like 'participation' and 'empowerment' (Cornwall & Eade, 2010). Most research on sustainable tourism is conducted in the Malaysian, Thai and Indonesian context – the three countries that also score highest in terms of tourist arrivals and hence urgently need to mitigate the negative impacts of tourism. One way of doing so is through adopting community-based or ecotourism, forms of tourism that, if based on real values of participation and

Table 1.3 Topical and geographical distribution of tourism and development research across Southeast Asia

	MDGs/ SDGs	Sustainability	CBT/Eco- tourism	Pro-poor	Participa- tion	Empow- erment	Gender	Governance	Human rights	Envir- onment	Total
Brunei	0	1	1	0	0	0	0	0	0	0	2
Cambodia	0	17	15	11	1	1	1	3	0	0	49
East Timor/ Timor-Leste	0	2	3	3	1	1	0	1	0	0	11
Indonesia	0	81	46	21	34	12	4	10	2	5	215
Lao PDR	0	18	5	8	3	1	1	1	0	3	40
Malaysia	0	145	64	18	43	5	7	13	0	13	308
Myanmar	0	9	0	3	1	0	0	2	1	2	18
Philippines	0	29	21	5	6	0	2	12	0	3	78
Singapore	0	16	2	4	0	2	0	1	0	1	26
Thailand	0	111	55	24	37	5	5	18	2	12	269
Vietnam	0	38	14	10	7	2	3	5	0	5	84
Southeast Asia	0	52	29	13	10	4	2	7	0	6	123
Total	0	519	255	120	143	33	25	73	5	50	1223

Note: search terms as fully formulated in Table 1.2 were used for this analysis

conservation, can indeed be viable engines for sustainable development. Indeed, these forms of tourism are ranked second in terms of thematic research areas in the region, again with Malaysia, Thailand and Indonesia at the fore. This is followed by a discourse on pro-poor tourism, poverty and participation, all terms which relate to tourism's increasing developmental role in Southeast Asia, improving the role it plays in society. While the environment and climate change still see a good level of research contribution, topics like gender, human rights issues and empowerment are at the bottom of the list of topics researched in the region. As Table 1.3 above has demonstrated, gender inequality and environmental pollution are indeed important issues to be addressed and hence need to be researched more to make sure tourism incorporates all aspects of sustainability. Interestingly, what further emerges is that no research was found on either the MDGs or SDGs as part of the sample. The SDGs still constitute a new terrain, one that also receives much well-deserved criticism; however, they are essential in driving the current post-2015 development agenda. More research on the region, particularly critical in nature, is therefore needed, not least because ASEAN claims to actively work towards the SDGs, even though more progress is needed to make sure Southeast Asia does not lag behind in their achievement (IMF, 2018; Lu, 2019).

However, of course, the SDGs are not the only way to understand Southeast Asia's progress towards sustainable development. Just like their predecessors, the MDGs, there is a danger that they 'could turn real development successes into imaginary failures' (Clemens & Moss, 2005, p.3) given their focus on indicators, attempting to measure areas of social life that are often difficult to measure. Of course, this also applies to the analysis above, in that numbers and indicators do not fully represent reality. Oftentimes, these are essentially Eurocentric, based on Western values and hence still part of the capitalist machinery that are often critiqued. It needs to therefore become an utmost priority to imagine 'different ways of measuring "development" in the sense of "positive social change"' (Ziai, 2007, p. 8). Despite these limitations, however, the above represents a valuable overview of the Southeast Asian nations, their great variances, facets, and basic characteristics, which can be used as a starting point for further analysis and critique.

Another challenging aspect for the completion of this book is related to the current forms of authoritarianism across Southeast Asia (Einzenberger & Schaffar, 2018) and how political systems oppress freedom of expression in general and academic freedom in particular. Authors of two chapters of this edited volume were not able or willing to fully address the reviewers'/editors' queries for a more critical analysis. Reasons provided included current political sensitivities on the specific issue in the country where research was conducted and where chapter authors are based or affiliated and fears of one's job being affected in a negative way. Academic freedom should provide scholars with protection from state interference and retaliation (Bartel, 2019) so that no academic compromises need to take place. Scholars in Southeast Asia sometimes face different realities, making authors of these particular chapters opt for a balancing act where certain critical issues are raised but not further critically analysed. Editors took the conscious decision though to include these chapters in the present volume, given the quality of research conducted and to enable their research to become part of the broader academic discourse and open debate.

Positioning and structure of the book

While several books on more general issues regarding tourism development in Southeast Asia (or more broadly on Asia, see for example Hall & Page, 2017) exist, no coherent monograph or edited volume has yet analysed tourism as both an economic and social phenomenon through the lens of development. *Tourism in South-East Asia*, edited by Hitchcock, King, and Parnwell (1993), provided a first comprehensive analysis of the nature and development of tourism in the region. This pioneering work has been followed by a number of edited volumes covering different aspects of tourism in the region. For example, *Tourism in Southeast Asia: A New Direction* (Chon, 2000) discusses selected aspects of ecotourism, impacts of tourism on local communities, and collaborative tourism marketing. At around the same time, *Tourism in South and Southeast Asia: Issues and Cases* (Hall & Page, 2000) debated tourism development from a variety of perspectives (historical, social, cultural, economic, policy-based, ecological, planning, etc.) in order to determine the evolution of development patterns across countries and regions in Southeast Asia. *Tourism in Southeast Asia: Challenges and New Directions* (Hitchcock, King, & Parnwell, 2008) provides a wide range of thematic as well as geographical areas of tourism development in the region. Further books on tourism and Southeast Asia have examined political dimensions, globalization and interconnectedness in Southeast Asian tourism (Teo, Chang, & Ho, 2001), heritage tourism (Hitchcock, King, & Parnwell, 2010), relationships between tourism and migration (Husa, Trupp, & Wohlschlägl, 2014), and emerging research in special interest tourism (Handayani, Seraphin, & Korstanje, 2019).

The present collection features authors from within and outside the region – therefore creating a space not only to raise awareness of the local challenges that still exist, including issues of ownership or unequal power relations, but also to celebrate best-practice examples where tourism can be regarded as making a positive difference to residents' life. The 14 chapters of the book are divided into four parts discussing the nexus of tourism and development in Southeast Asia both at regional and national levels. The contributions to the current debate on tourism and development are made by a wide selection of case studies from across the region and therefore offer a wide-spanning view of tourism and development in Southeast Asia in regards to theoretical and methodological foundations (Part I), protected areas (Part II), local communities (Part IV), and issues of governance (Part IV).

Part I. Introduction: theoretical and methodological foundations

Part I discusses the theories and methods that are used to research tourism and development in Southeast Asia, particularly when engaging in fieldwork, as well as current issues on tourism and development, applying development theory to tourism in the region.

Chapter 2 provides a critical analysis of the tourism-development nexus in Southeast Asia with an overview of how tourism has been embracing development paradigms in the region. It traces the early beginnings of tourism in the region back to modernisation theory, dependency relationships, and unequal power relations. Alternative development paradigms and the sustainable development agenda also form part of the discussion, with reference to the UN Sustainable Development Goals (SDGs) and the post-development agenda.

Chapter 3 discusses the fieldwork challenges that arise when using ethnographic methods in Southeast Asia, focusing specifically on the insider-outsider debate, power relations, access to the field, and language. It is not only the cultural background that complicates the fieldwork process, but also gender, gatekeepers, and pre-existing field relationships, and time spent in the field cannot be neglected in Southeast Asia, a region so highly complex in terms of cultural variances, ethnic minorities and indigenous populations.

Part II. Tourism and development in protected areas

Chapter 4 analyses the economic contribution of ecotourism to sustainable financing of protected areas in Vietnam, such as self-generated income from entrance tickets, Payments for Forest Environmental Services (PFES), and ecotourism services. The authors argue that an inadequate legal and institutional framework for resources management impede the development of alternative mechanism for financing protected areas, reflecting a transitional period from a centrally planned economy to a market-based economy.

Chapter 5 discusses the search for sustainable tourism in Malaysia drawing on the empirical case study of Langkawi Geopark Rangers. Findings from interviews and ranger reports revealed three categories of potential obstacles related to i) human resources and job conditions; ii) ranger activities; and iii) inter-organisational collaboration. Thus, sustainable tourism development is argued to be a 'green wash' syndrome with Langkawi's development aligning towards a sustainable mass tourism trajectory.

Collaborative conservative projects (SOSIS) in the Kepulauan Seribu Islands, Jakarta, the capital of Indonesia, are covered in Chapter 6. The collaborative projects involve a non-governmental organisation serving as the project anchor responsible to the donors, several other non-governmental organisations, private operators, and academia in order to raise awareness of the environment and behavioural change in the community. Lessons learned from the project were how to overcome communication issues and build effective multi-stakeholder communication and cooperation between organisations involved in the sustainable tourism development on the Islands.

Part III. Tourism, development, and local communities

Having analysed the economic impact of ecotourism for the poor in Laos, researchers of Chapter 7 compared the economic impacts of two ecotourism projects, one privately owned and one publicly owned. While the publicly run companies often promoted by donors and academics do not necessarily contribute more to the local economy, private companies with limited resources, in fact, perform slightly better in this respect. It is recommended that strategies create backward linkages for local tourism development and to involve the poorest groups of society.

Chapter 8 examines the migratory movements of predominantly female Akha ethnic minority vendors into urban tourism micro-entrepreneurship. Their activities create employment for themselves and other members of their own ethnic group and – to a lesser extent – can support the livelihoods of their families left behind. Yet, the majority of Thailand's ethnic micro-entrepreneurs in the souvenir business come from socioeconomically marginalised regions and remain at the fringes of a business niche in urban and beach-sided tourism hotspots that do not offer sustainable career prospects.

The authors of Chapter 9 argue that although the transition to using tourism as a new livelihood enables former fishing communities in Labuan Bajo (Indonesia) to generate a relatively satisfactory income, it would be premature to conclude that tourism is an appropriate strategy to provide sustainable livelihoods for local people. Hence, tourism is a fickle industry and local communities depending on this industry are at risk of falling into extreme poverty if tourism declines.

Chapter 10 discusses Ifugao's (Philippines) cultural landscape change in relation to its underlying causes, that is, macro social processes of modernity and globalization. Tourism brings cash into the local economy, which, in turn, changes residents' lifestyle and landscape. However, it is not the only factor that plays into the process of socio-cultural transformation. Before the arrival of tourism, processes of modernity have transformed people's way of life especially through education. Tourism, then, provided an expanded opportunity to earn cash. Therefore, the formation of the Ifugao landscape and culture is not a linear process; rather, it is a product of multiple social processes that started at different time periods.

Part IV. Tourism, development, and governance

Chapter 11 looks at the dynamics, policies and challenges of tourism development and policy in Myanmar. As Myanmar opens up to the world, the growing options and opportunities are also leading to greater regional and societal disparities. A lack of transparency in the planning and development of new destinations may soon cause conflicts within and between communities, local authorities, and investors, thus making Myanmar less attractive for future investment. Future developments in Myanmar's tourism industry will need to take into account innovations and trends in the broader regional context of the growing competition for tourism in Southeast Asia.

Chapter 12 shifts the debate towards community-based tourism development and destination governance in the case of Cambodia and shows that entrepreneurial thinking, even in small businesses, can be a better driver for sustainable success compared to financing CB(E)T sites through donor aid. Authors contend that informal collaborative networks driven by local businesses seem to be more effective than CB(E)Ts driven by government and donor organisations with rigid administrative and hierarchical structures. However, CB(E)Ts need to follow a more strategic approach in terms of product development, marketing and site management.

Chapter 13 considers the potential for agritourism as a tool for sustainable community development in Thailand within the context of the nation's current economic development policy, Thailand 4.0. In order for agritourism to continue to be an effective tool for sustainable development, the way in which agritourism is conceptualised and operationalised in these rural areas needs to continue to be challenged. The authors argue that it is the relationships between agriculture, cuisine, local arts, and tourism, and the creative ways in which these can be harnessed collectively as 'creative agritourism' that has the potential to effect these changes.

Based on these contributions, the book therefore creates a forum that brings together contributors from a range of disciplines to debate the dynamics of tourism when used as a development engine in a strongly emerging region of the world. It covers some of the key debates relating to the role that tourism plays in development, while also pointing to future trends in the concluding remarks in Chapter 14.

References

Adams, K. (2006). *Art as politics: Re-crafting identities, tourism, and power in Tana Toraja, Indonesia*. Honolulu: University of Hawaii Press.

Bartel, R. (2019). Academic freedom and an invitation to promote its advancement. *Geographical Research* 57(3), 359–367.

Bui, H.T., & Jolliffe, L. (2011). Vietnamese domestic tourism: An investigation of travel motivations. *Austrian Journal of South-East Asian Studies* 4(1), 10–29.

Bui, H.T., & Lee, T.J. (2015). Commodification and politicization of heritage: Implications for heritage tourism at the Imperial Citadel of Thang Long, Hanoi (Vietnam). *Austrian Journal of South-East Asian Studies* 8(2), 187–202.

Burns, P.M., & Novelli, M. (2008). *Tourism and mobilities: Local-global connections*. Wallingford: CABI.

Chang, T.C. (2017). Singapore Tourism. In C.M. Hall & S. Page (Eds.), *The Routledge handbook of tourism in Asia* (pp. 139–148). Abingdon: Routledge.

Chen, H.-J., Chen, P.-J., & Okumus, F. (2013). The relationship between travel constraints and destination image: A case study of Brunei. *Tourism Management* 35, 198–208.

Chon, K.-S. (Ed.). (2000). *Tourism in Southeast Asia. A new direction.* New York: Haworth Hospitality Press.

Clemens, M., & Moss, T. (2005). *CGD brief: What's wrong with the millennium development goals?* Washington, DC: Center for Global Development.

Cole, S. (2007). Beyond authenticity and commodification. *Annals of Tourism Research* 34(4), 943–960.

Connell, J. (2018). 'Timeless Charm': Tourism and development in Southeast Asia. In A. McGregor, L. Law, & F. Miller (Eds.), *Routledge handbook of Southeast Asian development* (pp. 153–168). London: Routledge.

Cornwall, A., & Eade, D. (Eds.) (2010). *Deconstructing development discourse: Buzzwords and fuzzwords.* Warwickshire: Practical Action Publishing & Oxfam.

Dolezal, C. (2015a). *Questioning empowerment in community-based tourism in rural Bali.* Doctoral Dissertation, University of Brighton.

Dolezal, C. (2015b). The tourism encounter in community-based tourism in Northern Thailand: Empty meeting ground or space for change? *Austrian Journal of South-East Asian Studies* 8(2), 165–186.

Dolezal, C., & Burns, P. (2014). ABCD to CBT: Asset-based community development's potential for community-based tourism. *Development in Practice* 25(1), 133–142.

Dolezal, C., & Trupp, A. (2015). Tourism and development in Southeast Asia. *Austrian Journal of South-East Asian Studies* 8(2), 117–124.

Duval, D.T., & Weaver, A. (2017). Transport and infrastructure issues in Asian tourism. In C.M. Hall & S. Page (Eds.), *The Routledge handbook of tourism in Asia* (pp. 34–44). Abingdon: Routledge.

Einzenberger, R., & Schaffar, W. (2018). The political economy of new authoritarianism in Southeast Asia. *Austrian Journal of South-East Asian Studies* 11(1), 1–12.

Elsevier (2019). Scopus content at a glance. Retrieved August 1, 2019, from: https://www.elsevier.com/solutions/scopus/how-scopus-works/content.

Erb, M. (2001). Ecotourism and environmental conservation in western Flores: Who Benefits? *Antropologi Indonesia* 66, 72–88.

Escobar, A. (1995). *Encountering development: The making and unmaking of the Third World.* Princeton: Princeton University Press.

Lacher, R.G., & Nepal, S.K. (2010). Dependency and development in Northern Thailand. *Annals of Tourism Research* 37(4), 947–968.

Hall, C.M., & Page, S. (Eds.). (2000). *Tourism in South and Southeast Asia: Issues and cases.* Oxford: Butterworth Heinemann.

Hall, C.M., & Page, S. (Eds.). (2017). *The Routledge handbook of tourism in Asia.* Abingdon: Routledge.

Hampton, M., & Clifton, J. (2017). Tourism in Indonesia. In C.M. Hall & S. Page (Eds.), *The Routledge handbook of tourism in Asia* (pp. 181–190). Abingdon: Routledge.

Handayani, B., Seraphin, H., & Korstanje, M.E. (2019). *Special interest tourism in Southeast Asia: Emerging research and opportunities.* Hershey: IGI Global.

Henderson, J. (2016). Integrated resorts and tourism: A Singapore perspective. *Asia-Pacific Journal of Innovation in Hospitality and Tourism* 5(2), 191–208.

Hitchcock, M., King, V.T., & Parnwell, M. (2010). *Heritage tourism in Southeast Asia.* Honolulu: University of Hawaii Press.

Hitchcock, M., King, V.T., & Parnwell, M. (2008). *Tourism in Southeast Asia: Challenges and new directions.* Copenhagen: NIAS Press.

Hitchcock, M., King, V.T., & Parnwell, M. (1993). *Tourism in South-East Asia.* London: Routledge.

Husa, K., Trupp, A., & Wohlschlägl, H. (Eds.). (2014). *Southeast Asian mobility transitions: Issues and trends in migration and tourism.* Vienna: Institut für Geographie und Regionalforschung.

IMF (2018). *ASEAN progress towards sustainable development goals and the role of the IMF.* Retrieved Oct. 8, 2019, from: https://sustainabledevelopment.un.org/con tent/documents/28341101118aseanprogresstowadssustainabledevelopmentgoals.pdf.

Khoo-Lattimore, C., Mura, P., & Yung, R. (2019). The time has come: A systematic literature review of mixed methods research in tourism. *Current Issues in Tourism* 22 (13), 1531–1550.

Klein, E. & Morreo, C.E. (2019). Introduction. In E. Klein & C.E. Morreo (Eds.). *Postdevelopment in practice: Alternatives, economies, ontologies* (pp. 1–18). Abingdon: Routledge.

Koh, E., & Fakfare, P. (2019). Overcoming "over-tourism": The closure of Maya Bay. *International Journal of Tourism Cities.* doi:10.1108/IJTC-02-2019-0023.

Kontogeorgopoulos, N. (2017). Tourism in Thailand: Growth, diversification and political upheaval. In C.M. Hall & S. Page (Eds.), *The Routledge handbook of tourism in Asia* (pp. 149–163). Abingdon: Routledge.

Lu, J. (2019). *Asian Countries are off track to achieve the Sustainable Development Goals. UN Dispatch.* Retrieved Oct. 8, 2019, from: https://www.undispatch.com/asia-sdgs.

Mowforth, M., & Munt, I. (2016). *Tourism and sustainability: Development, globalisation and new tourism in the Third World.* Abingdon: Routledge.

Mura, P., & Sharif, S. (2015). The crisis of the 'crisis of representation'– Mapping qualitative tourism research in Southeast Asia. *Current Issues in Tourism* 18(9), 828–844.

Musa, G., & Thirumoorthi, T. (2017). Tourism in Malaysia. In C.M. Hall & S. Page (Eds.), *The Routledge handbook of tourism in Asia* (pp. 164–180). Abingdon: Routledge.

Nguyen, H.T., & King, B. (2002). Migrant Communities and Tourism Consumption. In C.M. Hall & A. Williams (Eds.), *Tourism and migration: New relationships between production and consumption* (pp. 221–240). Dordrecht: Springer.

Novelli, M. (2016). *Tourism and development in Sub-Saharan Africa: Current issues and local realities.* Abingdon: Routledge.

Pickering, C., & Byrne, J. (2014). The benefits of publishing systematic quantitative literature reviews for PhD candidates and other early-career researchers. *Higher Education Research & Development* 33(3), 534–548.

Sachs, J.D. (2012). From millennium development goals to sustainable development goals. *The Lancet* 379(9832), 2206–2211.

Savage, V.R. (2006). Ecology matters: Sustainable development in Southeast Asia. *Sustainability Science* 1, 37–63.

Sciortino, R. (2017). Philanthropy in Southeast Asia: Between charitable values, corporate interests, and development aspirations. *Austrian Journal of South-East Asian Studies* 10(2), 139–163.

Sharpley, R., & Harrison, D. (2019). *A research agenda for tourism and development.* Cheltenham: Edward Elgar Publishing.

Singh, S. (Ed.). (2009). *Domestic tourism in Asia: Diversity and divergence.* London: Earthscan.

Telfer, D., & Sharpley, R. (2008). *Tourism and development in the developing world.* London: Routledge.

Teo, P., Chang, T.C., & Ho, K.C. (2001). *Interconnected worlds: Tourism in Southeast Asia.* London: Pergamon.

Thomas, J. (2019). Towards sustainable tourism in ASEAN. *The ASEAN Post.* Retrieved from: https://theaseanpost.com/article/towards-sustainable-tourism-asean.

Tolkach, D., & King, B. (2015). Strengthening community-based tourism in a new resource-based island nation: Why and how? *Tourism Management* 48, 386–398.

Truong, D.V., & Le, A. (2017). The evolution of tourism policy in Vietnam. In C.M. Hall & S. Page (Eds.), *The Routledge handbook of tourism in Asia* (pp. 191–204). Abingdon: Routledge.

Trupp, A. (2017). *Migration, micro-Business and tourism in Thailand: Highlanders in the city.* London: Routledge.

Trupp, A. (2018). Tourismus in Suedostasien. Entwicklung und Trends. In K. Husa, R. Korff, & H. Wohlschlägl (Eds.), *Suedostasien* (pp. 274–291). Vienna: New Academic Press.

Trupp, A., & Sunanta, S. (2017). Gendered practices in urban ethnic tourism in Thailand. *Annals of Tourism Research* 64, 76–86.

UN (2019). *Sustainable Development Goals.* Retrieved from: https://sustainabledevelopment.un.org.

UNWTO (2019). *UNWTO Tourism Highlights.* Retrieved from: https://www.e-unwto.org/doi/pdf/10.18111/9789284421152.

UNWTO. (2016). *UNWTO Tourism Highlights.* Retrieved from: https://www.e-unwto.org/doi/pdf/10.18111/9789284418145.

WTTC (2019). *Travel & tourism economic impact 2019: Southeast Asia.* London: World Travel and Tourism Council.

Yang, E.C.L., Khoo-Lattimore, C., & Arcodia, C. (2017). A systematic literature review of risk and gender research in tourism. *Tourism Management* 58, 89–100.

Ziai, A. (2007). *Exploring post-development: Theory and practice, problems and perspectives.* London: Routledge.

2 The tourism-development nexus in Southeast Asia

History and current issues

Huong T. Bui and Claudia Dolezal

Introduction

Without doubt, the concept of development has changed over time and, equally so, tourism has experienced a steady evolution. Development theory has seen manifold application to tourism (Andriotis, 2018; Mowforth & Munt, 2016; Novelli, 2016; Scheyvens, 2002), particularly theories of modernisation, dependency, neoliberalism, alternative development, human development, and sustainable development. These have been applied to tourism in order to understand its complexities when used as an engine for development. However, an analysis is missing to date that not only relates tourism and development but puts this into a Southeast Asian context. This chapter thus reviews the history and current issues of tourism along with the evolution of development theories in the Southeast Asian context to ultimately understand how tourism in the region has been embracing various development paradigms.

Development theory and tourism

Development as a concept can be both prescriptive and normative and while its definition is open to debate, it is most commonly defined as a process moving society from one condition to another (Sharpley, 2000), implying positive transformations for the better (Thomas, 2000). Traditionally, it has been defined as western-style modernisation achieved through economic growth (Redcliff, 1987), a paradigm paramount in the 1950s and 1960s, when it was believed that the path from underdevelopment to development lay along a series of steps of economic advancement (Rostow, 1960). By the late 1960s it had become clear that economic growth was not only failing to solve social and political problems but was also causing or exacerbating them. As a result, the reduction of poverty and unemployment was integrated into the broader concept of development (Seers, 1969). Self-reliance as an important indicator of development was introduced in the 1970s, particularly through dependency theorists who implied that the dependency of a developing nation on the world's most powerful nations, rooted deeply in colonialism, needs to be reduced (Seers, 1977).

Having sketched the emergence of development paradigms, parallels to the evolution of tourism can be noted (Telfer & Sharpley, 2014) with 'tourism and development' having become its own field of study (Andriotis, 2018; Mowforth & Munt, 2016; Novelli, 2016; Scheyvens, 2002). During the 1960s, tourism was even equated with development as part of the modernisation paradigm, with a belief that tourism increased foreign exchange and employment, and generated multiplier effects, which in turn stimulated the local economy. However, over time, the benefits of tourism were questioned (Bryden, 1973), with lower multiplier effects and high levels of economic leakages being the reality. Similarly, the neoliberal economic paradigm and tourism studies focused on international markets and considerations of tourism as an invisible export (Mathieson & Wall, 1982). Parallels to dependency theorists' critique of modernisation can be noted, building on the argument that tourism does not foster independence, but rather creates dependencies on foreign exchange, capital, visitors and assistance (Britton, 1982; Holden, Sonne, & Novelli, 2011). Some argued that destinations in developing countries were becoming a 'pleasure periphery' for the West (Turner & Ash, 1975), thereby fostering a dependency relationship.

This influence by non-Western thinkers paved the pathway for a changing definition of development, with notions of 'alternative' and 'human' development emerging. Both of these centred around adopting a more people-centred approach, with the former gaining importance in the 1980s, notably with Chambers' (1983) 'development from below', introducing the notion of participation by arguing that 'putting the last first' was paramount. The latter was introduced by Amartya Sen, whose work later became the foundation of the human development index, which incorporated a social dimension into the measurement of development (UNDP, 1990). In this time, tourism was also mainly understood as a means for livelihood diversification and benefits for local residents, based on 'true' participation and empowerment and through alternative types of tourism (Scheyvens, 2002). These social aspects have become an essential pillar of sustainability, a concept that tourism had already embraced in its early beginnings. However, a more multidimensional view of sustainability that acknowledges more than just tourism's impact on the environment still had to wait at this time (Mowforth & Munt, 2016).

In particular, alternative development seemed to be the way forward when 'doing' development to enable true bottom-up participation. However, the discourse associated with it soon came to be criticised, with buzzwords such as 'participation' and 'empowerment' holding potential political power to create imposed consensus and often few practical implications (Cornwall & Brock, 2005). These words are part of the changing language of development that 'evoke[s] a world where everyone gets a chance to take part in making the decisions that affect their lives' (Cornwall & Brock, 2005, p. 1044). Whether this language translates into real differences on the ground remains questionable though. Criticism has come from post-development thinkers who argue that the entire machinery of development, including its institutions, discourse and the notion of development itself, are inherently western and hence unequal power relations are still at play (Sidaway, 2014). What are really needed therefore are not 'development alternatives but alternatives to development' (Escobar, 1995, p. 215).

Similar criticisms continued around the turn of the Millennium with the introduction of the UN Millennium Development Goals (MDGs). These were criticised as 'normative instruments' creating a neoliberal development discourse of participation and empowerment in order to establish 'a visionary goal towards which to strive' (Cornwall & Brock, 2005, p. 1055) – a criticism which can equally be applied to the Sustainable Development Goals (SDGs) that followed in 2015. Even the SDGs, which are supposed to challenge the way development has been perceived as a project aimed only at the Global South, are criticised for building again on the capitalist system which has been problematic for a long time (Klein & Morreo, 2019, p. 3). However, what both sets of goals stand for is a clear shift in how development is understood as multidimensional and more than the eradication of extreme poverty. Indeed, scholars have begun to address this debate and the contribution to the SDGs also in tourism (Boluk, Cavaliere, & Higgins-Desbiolles, 2019).

Sustainable development, therefore, faces equal criticisms as other notions of development did in the past, particularly for the non-binding nature of many of the declarations decided upon by supranational organisations. Nevertheless, the progress that has been made should not be forgotten – after all, sustainable development principles have found their way into government policies, business strategies and the general public's vocabulary (of course, with questionable consequences on the ground). Still, more is needed to address some of the most pressing environmental and social concerns of our times and turn sustainable development into more than yet another buzzword.

The question that arises therefore is what will be the next development paradigm, with some more recent trends including the de-growth agenda, which moves away from capitalist models of over-production and -consumption (Andriotis, 2018). The principle of de-growth as applied to tourism thereby is a de-commodifying approach that addresses issues of over-tourism not through sustainable development (whose principle is sustainable economic growth), but, rather, a more fundamental change away from competition and economic gain to the downscaling of production and consumption (Andriotis, 2018), for example through social enterprises in tourism (Sheldon & Daniele, 2017). Ecuador's or Nicaragua's 'buen vivir' concept is one such example which moves away entirely from the capitalist system towards community and environmental values (Fisher, 2019). Some even question whether the term 'development' has a future at all, or whether we are slowly reaching the end of an era that has too long been at the expense of the environment and those in need (Carmody, 2019). The idea of the 'de-development' of rich countries might be a useful one to deal with some of the most pressing problems such as the overuse of resources for example, therefore shedding light on the problems of developed nations (Hickel, 2015). Table 2.1 illustrates the evolution of those development paradigms discussed above that shape the history of development thoughts in tourism research.

Tourism and development paradigms in Southeast Asia

In the past decade, tourism in Southeast Asia has seen unprecedented growth, while the region has also undergone many changes in relation to markets, mobility and integration between countries in terms of the economy and politics. The following sections evaluate the key development paradigms which tourism in Southeast Asia has embraced.

Modernisation

Modernisation has been the implicit base for many studies on tourism in developing Southeast Asian countries. Tourism has long been promoted as a developmental strategy to increase employment, foreign exchange and gross domestic product (GDP), attract developmental capital, promote a modern way of life in line with Western values and generate transformations of traditional societies (Mathieson & Wall, 1982). Tourism is still considered a viable economic alternative for many countries and a tool for economic development (Moscardo, 2009). Mass tourism, providing sufficient economies of scale, was commonly regarded as the preferred model, having the greatest stimulus effect on development, especially for poverty-stricken regions where economic options are constrained (Weaver & Lawton, 2010).

Since the 1980s, the Southeast Asian region has achieved and sustained a remarkable rate of growth, and incomes increased well above the developing country average (Coxhead, 2014), with tourism being one of the most important sectors in ASEAN economies. In 2018, tourism contributed (in total) more than 20 percent to the GDP of Thailand and the Philippines, and 32.8 percent to the Cambodian GDP (WTTC, 2019).

Part of the success of modernisation was due to neoliberal politics in the 1970s and 1980s, underpinned by the belief that 'open, competitive, and unregulated markets, liberated from all forms of state interference, represent the optimal mechanism for economic development' (Brenner & Theodore, 2003, p. 2). ASEAN in particular has played a major role in the economic, social and political development and liberalisation in the region since 1967. Tourism was identified as one of the specific areas of cooperation within ASEAN general economic assistance because it is a trade activity common to all member countries. However, neoliberalism was a reality at a much more global scale. Western investment into developing countries was particularly supported by initiatives by the World Bank (WB) and the International Monetary Fund (IMF), which intensified inequalities between rich and poor (Harvey, 2005).

Table 2.1 Development theories and paradigms

Theories/ Paradigms	Key Characteristics	Key Outcomes
Modernisation/ Diffusion (1950s–1960s)	- Based on western experience - Reliance on imported expertise and technology - Ideas or built facilities spread from one location to another - Local elite acts as agent of change - Alterations in the structure and function of the social system - Stages of growth - Trickle down effects	- Regional inequalities - Disparities between socioeconomic classes - Elitist entrenchment - Negative environmental impact - Destinations lose their authenticity
Dependency (1960s–early 1980s)	- Underdevelopment - External control - Reliance of the periphery on the core - Tour operator dominance	- Structural inequalities between core and periphery - Benefits obtained by outsiders - Poverty of the local population - Adverse effects in economic, social and environmental terms
Neo-liberalism (Mid 1970s–1980s)	- Private sector dominance - Deregulation/privatisation - Minimum interference by government (free market) - Unlimited growth/exploitation of local resources	- Accumulation of vast wealth and powerful vested interests to the rich - Poverty of a major part of society - Uncontrolled tourism development - Detrimental effects on the environmental and sociocultural resources
Sustainable development (Late 1980s–1990s)	- People-centred development - Preservation of local resources - Respects the needs and aspirations of the local population - Environmental quality	- Depend on the level of environmental concern given towards the tourism/environment system - Often emphasises economic outcomes over environmental and social concerns
Towards a new paradigm (2000s)	- Endogenous anti-capitalistic model of development - Environmentally-friendly growth - Respects limits to growth - Rejection of Western travel amenities and commoditised tourism products - Downscaled tourism infrastructure	- Self-sustained growth - Richness of experience - Equitable distribution of tourism benefits - Focus on locality/Involvement of the local community in the development process - Better living standards - Equitable income distribution - Environmental and sociocultural preservation - Efficient use of local resources

Source: Andriotis, 2018

Much of the investment discussed above took place in Southeast Asian tourism, particularly mass tourism in the form of 3S, i.e. sun, sea and sand, which best illustrates the principles of modernisation. Southeast Asia possesses rich resources for coastal tourism – sandy beaches, coral reefs, thousands of islands and diverse cultural heritage to complement coastal tourism development. The region has a long history of beach resort development dating back to the colonial period, such as those in Bali known by Western tourists since the 1930s (Wong, 1998). Distribution of resorts have concentrated in Indonesia and the Philippines in the past, and expanded to Vietnam and Cambodia in recent years. The impact of 3S mass tourism includes unplanned development, with Pattaya representing one of the best examples (Wong, 1998). To avoid the consequences of unplanned development, resorts (both government-sponsored and private) adopt important principles in controlled development, such as in Nusa Dua in Bali, Indonesia, where the idea was that the 'physical isolation of the resort facilities and the institutional arrangements envisaged should ensure a controllable relationship between foreign visitors and local population' (World Bank, 1974, p. 5).

However, resort coastal tourism has been problematic in the region. For example, leakage is a key issue when it comes to mass tourism dominated by foreign influence. Further problems relate to coastal protection policies in Malaysia, particularly due to the lack of public support and awareness for environmental issues in the country, inadequate governmental agency coordination and a lack of funding which is necessary for the successful implementation of these policies (Lee, 2010). In particular, islands are highly sought after for resort development but also vulnerable, which leads to tourism causing problems with fresh water and waste disposal (Cole, 2012). Inefficient understanding of the costal environment, including monsoon effects and costal erosion, is another critical issue associated with costal resorts in Southeast Asia (Wong, 1998). Along with the growth in tourism development, especially an increasing demand for resorts, substantial changes have therefore occurred in the coastal areas in the region (Henderson & Smith, 2009).

What the above has demonstrated is the importance of tourism as a contributor to GDP and an engine for development in line with Western thinking, particularly in the early days of tourism development in the region. This has fostered mass tourism developments, often characterised by uniformity to offer tourists a standard in service. However, this is not to say that no other paradigms are embraced in the region, such as the alternative development paradigm, which will be discussed later.

While the traditional idea of mass tourism is that of resort destinations, an interesting development is taking place in Southeast Asia, which is that of alternative and more niche forms of tourism turning into mass phenomena. Two such examples are heritage tourism and backpacking. The early 1990s saw the beginnings of what were to become major developments in heritage conservation and an increasing interest among the national governments in Southeast Asia in exploiting the potential of heritage and history as an element in tourism-promotion policies (King, 2015). Heritage tourism is the most important form of tourism for Cambodia (Winter, 2010), while it is considerably significant for Thailand and no less important for Singapore (Henderson, 2009; Teo & Huang, 1995). For example, the majority of tourists visited Cambodia's cultural and heritage sites, including 1,000 ancient temples, but above all, the Angkor Wat's UNESCO World Heritage Site, making it increasingly commodified and touristified (Sharpley & McGrath, 2017).

In addition, the evolution of backpacking in Southeast Asia has dramatically changed the landscape of tourism destinations (Muzaini, 2006). Backpackers are the new mass tourists in Thailand, who oftentimes seek enclaves more than, as once argued, off the beaten track experiences (Spreitzhöfer, 2008). Owing to the low budget and long-stay notion of backpacking, there is an argument that backpacking generates a considerable negative impact on the local economy and society, and host governments may treat this type of tourism with caution (Hannam & Ateljevic, 2007). However, backpacking is significant for poverty alleviation and local development, since it has stronger linkages to the local economy and less leakage than conventional international tourism (Hampton, 2013). It therefore is not a type of tourism that embraces modernisation in a straightforward manner – this depends on the degree of local involvement, the amount of money that stays in the economy, and the importance of local culture and variance in the product offered. In addition, contemporary backpacking experiences changed with the introduction of services, accommodation and entertainments for a 'new generation' of Chinese, Japanese and other Asian backpackers (Bui, Wilkins, & Lee, 2014). Asian backpacking is a new social phenomenon which challenges the conventional notion of authenticity and otherness (Teo & Leong, 2006) and essentially questions the unequal power relations as propounded by modernisation.

Dependency

Dependency theory's most important contribution is the idea that reasons for underdevelopment can only be found outside rather than within a nation by embedding least developed countries (LDCs) into the capitalist world system and questioning the roots of colonialism (Frank, 1966; Wallerstein, 1979). The notion of dependency has been influential in the understanding of the tourism development process in less developed nations, particularly those with colonial legacies, including Southeast Asia. In this context, tourism was seen as 'leisure imperialism' which symbolized 'the hedonistic face of neo-colonialism' (Crick, 1989, p. 322).

Part of this dependency relationship is the European construction of Asia, which has been of great significance for a long time 'within the process of geographic, cultural and political "othering"' (Yapp, 1992, cited in Hall & Page, 2017, p. 6). The historical development of global tourism, and its links to voyages of discovery, conquest, sequestration and subjugation as part of European colonialisation and mercantilism, date back to Marco Polo's 13th century travel (Shackley, 2006). The colonial infrastructure has a key role to play in shaping modern-day tourism. For instance, the colonial legacy of discovery began with travel to the region by sea, on steamships, and continues today with cruise ships (Connell, 2018). Other advances in land-based transport, especially European-sponsored railways, have subsequently been turned into mass systems for domestic tourist travel. The growth of hospitality and hosting generated a new dimension to colonialism, for example the hill stations in Vietnam (Michaud & Turner, 2006). An early form of mountain resorts, established in high altitude areas for colonialists and elite locals, have remained and set a standard for the modern-day hospitality sector in Vietnam (DeWald, 2008).

The links between tourism and colonialism are clear, with tourism constructing stereotypical images often based on post-colonial representations of Asian culture, portrayed as 'primitive' and 'pre-modern' to satisfy Western desires and fantasies (Hall, 2009). These stereotypes are driven by Westerners' quest for authenticity (MacCannell, 1976) – in addition to communities themselves for their own empowerment (Dolezal, 2015). Ethnic tourism has largely emerged out of a colonial desire to portray the Other, such as ethnic tourism in highland areas in Southeast Asia, including Northern Thailand, Northwest Vietnam and Laos (Cohen, 2016). Critical views of tourism's impact on ethnic cultures as a new form of colonialism portray Southeast Asians as powerless and vulnerable – often even as human zoos (Trupp, 2011). At the same time though, it cannot be forgotten that residents have agency and that in many cases they are very much in control of the processes of commodification, staged authenticity and representation (Dolezal, 2015; Trupp, 2015).

Nevertheless, tourism in Southeast Asia is often characterised by key differences in wealth between visitors and residents and one cannot forget the limited choices that residents often have when deciding on what is sold as an attraction (Dolezal & Trupp, 2015). What the above shows is the influence of history on today's tourism in Southeast Asia and the creation of Asia as defined by the West, with many of the inequalities stemming from an unequal embeddedness in the capitalist world system. Dependency theory thereby acknowledges the agency of the East while arguing that this agency is not enough if inequalities in the capitalist system are maintained.

Sex tourism can be an example of the agency that women have to make choices in the selling of their bodies, while one needs to acknowledge the limited choices particularly for those living in poverty, and the dependency on the western consumer in the betterment of one's life (Law, 2000). Initiatives aimed at empowering sex workers, for example the NGO Empower in Thailand, give sex workers the necessary skills to ameliorate the dependency relationship that women often experience with male clients. Of course, a yet more problematic and even criminal component of sex tourism is child sex tourism, notably in Cambodia, where the trafficking of orphaned children continues to be a serious issue (Carpenter, 2015).

Despite increasing acknowledgement of residents' agency in tourism, it is still very much a reality that tourism 'as an institution and economic policy is part of an externally oriented approach to development which includes reliance on foreign aid and investment, imported technology, and many other links with advanced capitalist countries' (Wood, 1980, p. 566). Tourism, after all, started off in Southeast Asia as an industry not only dependent on international visitors, but also financial and technical assistance with strong foreign influence. Indeed, it was found that even community-based tourism (CBT) in Bali, one of the alternative forms of tourism, repeats similar dynamics to mass tourism, creating dependency on help from the outside (and even abroad) for promotion, training, and investment by the tourist (Dolezal, 2015). At the same time though, changes need to be acknowledged, such as increasing inter-regional travel, residents' skills and local ownership of tourism businesses.

Alternative development and human development

Alternative and human development are subsumed here given that both are rooted in more people-centred and bottom-up approaches to development, empowering people through participation (Chambers, 1983) and 'enlarging people's choices' (UNDP, 1990, p. 10). Southeast Asian tourism has embraced these paradigms to an extent, with an emphasis on alternative forms of tourism as well as the diversification of livelihoods through tourism to create more opportunities, particularly for rural communities. However, this is not always as straightforward as it may seem. For example, tourism initiatives in the Calamianes Islands (the Philippines) do not offer social benefits and an alternative source of livelihoods for fisherman (Fabinyi, 2010). Similarly, inclusive growth from tourism in Ha Long Bay (Vietnam) is not yet evident because of the combination of weak backward linkages and significant economic leakage, in concert with low tourism expenditure (Hampton, Jeyacheya, & Long, 2018).

Without doubt, Southeast Asia incorporated alternative tourism into its tourism policies early on (Hall & Page, 2011), including, amongst others, ecotourism, community-based tourism, homestays, agritourism or, formerly, backpacking. Reasons and motivations for this growth are manifold but include: the negative impacts of more orthodox and conventional tourism (mass tourism) (Hall & Page, 2011); the abundancy of natural and cultural attractions on which to capitalise (Yamashita, 2003); to spread the benefits of tourism to more rural areas (Byczek, 2011); to benefit women (Scheyvens, 2000); to increase residents' participation and empowerment (Cole, 2005); to foster local entrepreneurship (Trupp, 2016); to diversify livelihoods (Lasso & Dahles, 2018); and to satisfy the needs of the authenticity-seeking tourist (Picard, 1992).

As highlighted in the introduction to this edition, ecotourism and community-based tourism specifically have experienced much attention in the literature on Southeast Asia, with studies focusing, amongst many others, on locals' perception of the impact of ecotourism in the Philippines (Jalani, 2012), the success factors for CBT in Thailand (Kontogeorgopoulos, Churyen, & Duang-saeng, 2014), critical discussions of the role of authenticity (Dolezal, 2011), the environmental impact of ecotourism in Indonesia (Butarbutar & Soemarno, 2013), and community participation in Malaysia (Kayat, 2007). While CBT and eco-tourism in the region are often praised, these alternatives to mass tourism experi-ence equal criticism, including unequal power relations within communities, the impact on social capital and culture, as well as intrusion into privacy and environ-mental issues through greenwashing. Particularly, the two buzzwords 'empower-ment' and 'participation' have experienced much debate in tourism (Dolezal, 2015; Cole, 2005), just like in alternative development.

The contribution that alternative tourism, specifically CBT, makes to devel-opment is a contested issue (Goodwin, 2009), given the controversy over whose and what kind of development CBT should contribute to. Advocates of pro-poor tourism (PPT) criticise CBT based on the idea that it is generally associated with small-scale tourism initiatives and often does not have a significant enough impact for sustainable developmental change (Ashley & Mitchell, 2005). This is not to say that CBT ignores the wider developmental context, and the Respon-sible Ecological Social Tours Project Thailand (REST, 2003, p. 11) argues that CBT seeks 'to address a different, developmental question: "[h]ow can tourism contribute to the process of *community* development [our italics]?"'. Therefore, CBT can indeed improve the lives of a group of people, even though it may not yield developmental benefits at a macro level. At the same time, though, Kontogeorgopoulos' (2003) work on ecotourism in Phuket and Bali has shown that ecotourism essentially links to the structures that are created through mass tourism and can happen in mass tourism places, creating a form of 'mass eco-tourism', where both kinds of tourism co-exist and blur into one another.

While the boundaries between mass and alternative tourism are not always clear, both can be used as a means for poverty alleviation in the region, where a substantial proportion of the population live below the poverty line. In parti-cular, the human development approach is concerned with the livelihood of locals at a time when the economies of Southeast Asian countries are increas-ingly dependent on tourism. PPT is often used to help empower the poor (Holden, 2013; Truong & Hall, 2015). PPT initiatives by NGOs in Laos, for example, have generated positive economic impacts and retain the earnings among the local community (Harrison & Schipani, 2007; Hummel, van der Dium, & Ritsma, 2013). Improving the quality of life for disadvantaged groups in society is another outcome of PPT in Cambodia (Brickell, 2008); however, the income from tourism remains extremely low because the poor do not have financial resources, business knowledge or access to markets (Mao, DeLacy, & Grundfield, 2014). Unequal distribution of the profits from tourism is found in Sapa, Vietnam, where a large proportion of income accrued goes to the tour operators, leaving a very small proportion for poor local streets vendors who do not have the capital and language proficiency to establish homestays (Truong, Hall, & Garry, 2014).

Sustainable development

'Sustainability' has penetrated the public consciousness over the past three decades, also in tourism. This development can be led back to the increasing awareness of the negative impact of tourism on destinations, environment and people (Saarinen, 2006). In many destinations, tourism has adopted a 'triple-bottom line' approach that aims to address economic, environmental and socio-cultural impacts, with the SDGs offering an even more complex understanding of sustainability.

Sustainable tourism, however, has also experienced much criticism, amongst others that it is just a marketing ploy (Lansing & De Vries, 2007). Sharpley (2000) even argues that tourism development remains embedded in early modernisation theory whilst the principles of sustainable tourism overlook the characteristics of the production and consumption of tourism, suggesting that sustainable development cannot be transposed onto the specific context of tourism. The accompanying ambiguity on matters of implementation and context is reflected in the evolving relationship between sustainable tourism and mass tourism. The latter was initially and widely regarded as the antithesis of the former, but this simplistic dichotomy was soon challenged by the understanding that large- or small-scale (alternative) tourism could be sustainable or unsustainable depending on the destination and planning/management context (Weaver & Oppermann, 2000).

One of the best examples to illustrate how Southeast Asia addresses sustainable tourism is ecotourism, which appears to have great potential, however, its growth encounters various issues of planning, development and management for sustainability. Resonating with Sharpley's (2000) argument on the significant differences between the concepts of sustainable tourism and sustainable development, Kontogeorgopoulos' (1999) early study found that the sustainability of tourism, defined as the ongoing growth and survival of the tourism industry, has compromised the ecological sustainability of key tourism destinations in Southern Thailand, and that ecotourism is just a 'green label' for cashing in. The example of Cambodia, on the other hand, reveals a range of challenges in pursuing sustainable tourism, such as the lack of consideration of the impact of the socio-economic and cultural context, as well as the limited practical guidance on how to realize a vision of sustainable tourism (Carter, Thok, O'Rourke, & Pearce, 2015).

At least, however, Southeast Asia increasingly recognizes unsustainable practices and takes action. Having acknowledged the environmentally and socially unsustainable development in Boracay, for example, the 'number one beach' of the Philippines, a number of programmes have been implemented since the late 1990s aiming to improve Boracay's sustainability (Ong, Storey, & Minnery, 2011). However, these programmes have not been very successful, which is why Boracay became known as one of the first examples where overtourism and the degradation of natural resources have led to government decisions to temporarily close the popular island destination.

Moving on to sustainable tourism in Indonesia, the example of ecotourism is again an interesting one. Both culture and particular perceptions of a more 'authentic' nature of Indonesia draw increasingly more tourists from China and Japan (Yamashita, 2009), in addition to international tourists. Amongst Southeast Asian natives with disposable income, however, relatively few tourists seek out rural pleasures other than those of the 'regimented and sanitized' form (Michaud & Turner, 2006, p. 793). Despite having great potential for development, ecotourism in Indonesia is facing numerous problems of governance, awareness and commitment to sustainability; in other words, genuine ecotourism remains beyond reach (Cochrane, 2006).

Having reviewed the development of ecotourism in five Southeast Asian countries (Malaysia, Thailand, Vietnam, Laos, and Cambodia), Ly and Bauer (2016) compared theory and practice of ecotourism management in each country. The authors found that the lack of communication and cooperation between policymakers and other tourism stakeholders contribute to widening the gap between theory and practice. The government is significant in leading sustainable development, and an official and national sustainable tourism strategy is required in planning and operating ecotourism and other forms of tourism in the region.

A range of other problems in addition to the above can be identified as obstacles to a more sustainable tourism in the Southeast Asian region. These include 'cultural erosion and dislocation, damage to fragile coastal and mountain ecosystems, exploitation and exclusion of local populations, inflation and conspicuous consumption, pollution and resource shortages, fickleness and insecurity' (Parnwell, 2008, p. 238). At the same time, however, it needs to be acknowledged that the region does embrace the sustainable development paradigm – at least to an extent. Indeed, in the Plan of Action on ASEAN cooperation in tourism, sustainable tourism finds strong mentioning (ASEAN, 2012), however, it remains to be seen just how far the negative impacts of tourism in the region can sufficiently be managed in the future.

Conclusion

This chapter provided a critical analysis of the tourism-development nexus in Southeast Asia with an overview of how tourism has been embracing development paradigms in the region. It has traced the early beginnings of tourism in the region back to modernisation theory, which pursued a form of tourism boosting economies and seeking progress, with little long-term understanding of the impact. Most importantly, it was shown that while this paradigm was one of the first to shape tourism development in the region, it is still dominating despite the growing importance of a more alternative and sustainable approach. Mass tourism in resort destinations is still a reality and will always be part of the identity of Southeast Asian tourism. The way forward for destinations is therefore most likely not to move entirely towards the alternative side of the spectrum, but rather, to apply sustainability principles to all kinds of tourism in the region. This is to say that none of the paradigms debated here are a thing of the past – tourism in Southeast Asia also continues to create strong dependency relationships and unequal power relations between destinations and Western countries, however, again, these relationships are much more complex than often presented. Simultaneously, and reflecting geopolitical realignments within the Asian region, Southeast Asian countries have become increasingly dependent on tourist arrivals from China, for example.

With some of the Southeast Asian countries regarded as strong emerging economies (e.g. Indonesia) and intra-regional travel, local collaboration and investment on the rise, dependency's black and white image of the global system of power does not fully hold true. At the same time, the region sees strong positive efforts when it comes to alternative tourism, particularly with community-based and ecotourism creating alternative livelihoods holding the power to contribute to many of the SDGs. Again, though, success depends on a wide range of factors, including local awareness of tourism's impacts, how tourism is managed on the ground, the resources available, local involvement, governments' support through policies, and more. If not planned and managed well, alternative tourism can equally experience similar criticisms to those of mass tourism in the region.

One of the key issues this chapter identified is the economic gain of tourism still remaining at the forefront when it comes to its planning and management on the ground. It is questionable therefore whether tourism growth in the region can be sustained, with some first signs of tourists moving to less crowded and polluted areas. The region still embraces paradigms of modernisation and neoliberalism, with foreign investment, GDP growth and service-orientation (i.e. the customer) prioritised over residents' needs and environmental protection. With changing new markets visiting the region (including the Chinese market), the tourism-development nexus will yet keep evolving further. The question therefore remains what importance local people's needs and the environment will take in these more recent developments. Both future tourism development and research needs to therefore not only focus on the above-mentioned trends, but also identify viable alternatives to development originating from the Southeast Asian region itself.

References

Andriotis, K. (2018). *Degrowth in tourism: conceptual, theoretical and philosophical issues.* Wallingford: CABI.

ASEAN (2012). Plan of action on ASEAN cooperation in tourism. Retrieved from: https://asean.org/?static_post=plan-of-action-on-asean-cooperation-in-tourism.

Ashley, C., & Mitchell, J. (2005). Can tourism accelerate pro-poor growth in Africa? *ODI Opinion* 60.

Boluk, K.A., Cavaliere, C.T., & Higgins-Desbiolles, F. (2019). A critical framework for interrogating the United Nations Sustainable Development Goals 2030 Agenda in tourism. *Journal of Sustainable Tourism* 27(7), 847–864.

Brenner, N., & Theodore, N. (2003). *Spaces of neoliberalism: Urban restructuring in North America and Western Europe* (Vol. 4). Oxford: Wiley-Blackwell.

Brickell, K. (2008). Tourism-generated employment and intra-household inequality in Cambodia. In J. Cochrane (Ed.), *Asian tourism: Growth and change* (pp. 299–310). Oxford: Elsvier.

Britton, S.G. (1982). The political economy of tourism in the third world. *Annals of Tourism Research* 9(3), 331–358.

Bryden, J.M. (1973). *Tourism and development*. Cambridge: Cambridge University Press.

Bui, H.T., Wilkins, H.C., & Lee, Y.-S. (2014). The social identities of Japanese backpackers. *Tourism Culture & Communication* 13(3), 147–159.

Butarbutar, R., & Soemarno, S. (2013). Environmental effects of ecotourism in Indonesia. *Journal of Indonesian Tourism and Development Studies* 1(3), 97–107.

Byczek, C. (2011). Blessing for all? Community-based ecotourism in Bali between global, national and local interests – a case study. *Austrian Journal for South-East Asian Studies* 4(1), 81–106.

Carmody, P. (2019). *Development theory and practice in a changing world*. Abingdon: Routledge.

Carpenter, K. (2015). Childhood studies and orphanage tourism in Cambodia. *Annals of Tourism Research* 55, 15–27.

Carter, R., Thok, S., O'Rourke, V., & Pearce, T. (2015). Sustainable tourism and its use as a development strategy in Cambodia: A systematic literature review. *Journal of Sustainable Tourism* 23(5), 797–818.

Chambers, R. (1983). *Rural development: Putting the last first*. London: Longman.

Cochrane, J. (2006). Indonesian national parks: Understanding leisure users. *Annals of Tourism Research* 33(4), 979–997.

Cohen, E. (2016). Ethnic tourism in mainland Southeast Asia: The state of the art. *Tourism Recreation Research* 41(3), 232–245.

Cole, S. (2012). A political ecology of water equity and tourism: A Case Study from Bali. *Annals of Tourism Research* 39(2), 1221–1241.

Cole, S. (2005). Cultural tourism, community participation and empowerment. In M. Smith & M. Robinson (Eds.), *Cultural tourism in a changing world: Politics, participation and (re)presentation* (pp. 89–103). Clevedon: Channel View Publications.

Connell, J. (2018). 'Timeless Charm' Tourism and development in Southeast Asia. In A. McGregor, L. Law & F. Miller (Eds.), *Routledge handbook of Southeast Asian development* (pp. 153–168).Abingdon: Routledge.

Cornwall, A., & Brock, K. (2005). What do buzzwords do for development policy? A critical look at 'participation', 'empowerment' and 'poverty reduction'. *Third World Quarterly* 26(7), 1043–1060.

Coxhead, I. (Ed.) (2014). *Routledge handbook of Southeast Asian economics*. Abingdon: Routledge.

Crick, M. (1989). Representations of international tourism in the social sciences: Sun, sex, sights, savings and servility. *Annual Review of Anthropology* 18, 307–344.

DeWald, E. (2008). The development of tourism in French Colonial Vietnam, 1918–1940. In J. Cochrane (Ed.), *Asian tourism: Growth and change* (pp. 221–232). Amsterdam: Elsevier.

Dolezal, C. (2015). *Questioning empowerment in community-based tourism in rural Bali*. Doctoral Dissertation, University of Brighton.

Dolezal, C. (2011). Community-based tourism in Thailand: (Dis)illusions of authenticity and the necessity for dynamic concepts of culture and power. *Austrian Journal of South-East Asian Studies* 4(1), 129–138.

Dolezal, C., & Trupp, A. (2015). Tourism and development in South-East Asia. *Austrian Journal for South-East Asian Studies* 8(2), 117–124.

Escobar, A. (1995). *Encountering development: The making and unmaking of the Third World.* Princeton: Princeton University Press.

Fabinyi, M. (2010). The intensification of fishing and the rise of tourism: Competing coastal livelihoods in the Calamianes Islands, Philippines. *Human Ecology* 38(3), 415–427.

Fisher, J. (2019). Nicaragua's Buen Vivir: A strategy for tourism development? *Journal of Sustainable Tourism* 27(4), 452–471.

Frank, A.G. (1966). The development of underdevelopment. *Monthly Review* 18, 17–30.

Goodwin, H. (2009). Reflections on 10 years of pro-poor tourism. *Journal of Policy Research in Tourism, Leisure and Events* 1(1), 90–94.

Hall, C.M. (2009). Heritage tourism in the Pacific: Modernity, myth and identity. In D.J. Timothy & G.P. Nyaupane (Eds.), *Cultural heritage and tourism in the developing world* (pp. 73–92). Abingdon: Routledge.

Hall, C.M., & Page, S. (2017). Introduction: Tourism in Asia – region and context. In C.M. Hall & S. Page (Eds.), *Routledge handbook of tourism in Asia* (pp. 3–24). Abingdon: Routledge.

Hall, C.M., & Page, S. (2011). *Tourism in South and Southeast Asia.* Abingdon: Routledge.

Hampton, M. (2013). *Backpacker tourism and economic development.* Abingdon: Routledge.

Hampton, M.P., Jeyacheya, J., & Long, P.H. (2018). Can tourism promote inclusive growth? Supply chains, ownership and employment in Ha Long Bay, Vietnam. *The Journal of Development Studies* 54(2), 359–376.

Hannam, K., & Ateljevic, I. (Eds.). (2007). *Backpacker tourism: Concept and profile.* Clevedon: Channel View Publications.

Harrison, D., & Schipani, S. (2007). Laos tourism and poverty alleviation: Community-based tourism and the private sector. *Current Issues in Tourism* 10(2–3), 194–230.

Harvey, D. (2005). *A brief history of neoliberalism.* Oxford: Oxford University Press

Henderson, J.C. (2009). The meanings, marketing, and management of heritage tourism in Southeast Asia. In D.J. Timothy & G.P. Nyaupane (Eds.), *Cultural heritage and tourism in the developing world* (pp. 87–106). Abingdon: Routledge.

Henderson, J.C., & Smith, R.A. (2009). The informal tourism economy at beach resorts: A comparison of Cha-Am and Laguna Phuket in Thailand. *Tourism Recreation Research* 34(1), 13–22.

Hickel, J. (2015). Forget 'developing' poor countries, it's time to 'de-develop' rich countries. *The Guardian.* Retrieved from: https://www.theguardian.com/global-developm ent-professionals-network/2015/sep/23/developing-poor-countries-de-develop-rich-cou ntries-sdgs.

Holden, A. (2013). *Tourism, poverty and development.* Abingdon: Routledge.

Holden, A., Sonne, J., & Novelli, M. (2011). Tourism and poverty reduction: An interpretation by the poor of Elmina, Ghana. *Tourism Planning & Development* 8 (3), 317–334,

Hummel, J., van der Dium, R., & Ritsma, N. (2013). Evolution of tourism approach for poverty reduction impact in SNV Asia: Cases from Laos PDR, Bhutan and Vietnam. *Asia Pacific Journal of Tourism Research* 18(4), 369–384.

Jalani, J.O. (2012). Local people's perception on the impacts and importance of ecotourism in Sabang Palawan, Philippines. *Procedia – Social and Behavioral Sciences* 57(9), 247–254.

Kayat, K. (2007). Exploring factors influencing individual participation in community-based tourism: The case study of Kampung Relau homestay program, Malaysia. *Asia Pacific Journal of Tourism Research* 7(2), 19–27.

King, V.T. (2015). Encounters and mobilities: Conceptual issues in tourism studies in Southeast Asia. *SOJOURN: Journal of Social Issues in Southeast Asia* 30(2), 497–527.

Klein, E., & Morreo, C.E. (2019). Introduction. In E. Klein & C.E. Morreo (Eds.), *Postdevelopment in practice: Alternatives, economies, ontologies* (pp. 1–18). Abingdon: Routledge.

Kontogeorgopoulos, N. (2003). Towards a Southeast Asian model of resort-based 'mass ecotourism': Evidence from Phuket, Thailand and Bali, Indonesia. *ASEAN Journal on Hospitality and Tourism* 2, 1–16.

Kontogeorgopoulos, N. (1999). Sustainable tourism or sustainable development? Financial crisis, ecotourism, and the 'Amazing Thailand' campaign. *Current Issues in Tourism* 2(4), 316–332.

Kontogeorgopoulos, N., Churyen, A., & Duangsaeng, V. (2014). Success factors in community-based tourism in Thailand; The role of luck, external support, and local leadership. *Tourism Planning & Development* 11(1), 106–124.

Lansing, P., & De Vries, P. (2007). Sustainable tourism: Ethical alternative or marketing ploy? *Journal of Business Ethics* 72, 77–85.

Lasso, A., & Dahles, H. (2018). Are tourism livelihoods sustainable? Tourism development and economic transformation on Komodo Island, Indonesia. *Asia Pacific Journal of Tourism Research* 23(5), 473–485.

Law, L. (2000). *Sex work in Southeast Asia: The place of desire in a time of AIDS.* London: Routledge.

Lee, O.A. (2010). Coastal resort development in Malaysia: A review of policy use in the pre-construction and post-construction phase. *Ocean & Coastal Management* 53 (8), 439–446.

Ly, T.P., & Bauer, T. (2016). Ecotourism in mainland Southeast Asia: Theory and practice. *Tourism, Leisure and Global Change* 1(1), 61–80.

MacCannell, D. (1976). *The tourist: A new theory of the leisure class.* New York: Schocken.

Mao, N., DeLacy, T., & Grundfield, H. (2014). Agriculture and tourism linkage constraints in Siem Reap – Angkor region of Cambodia. *Tourism Geographies* 16(4), 669–686.

Mathieson, A., & Wall, G. (1982). *Tourism: Economic, physical and social impacts.* London: Longman.

Michaud, J., & Turner, S. (2006). Contending visions of a hill-station in Vietnam. *Annals of Tourism Research* 33(3), 785–808.

Moscardo, G. (2009). Tourism and quality of life: Towards a more critical approach. *Tourism and Hospitality Research* 9(2), 159–170.

Mowforth, M., & Munt, I. (2016). *Tourism and sustainability: Development, globalisation and new tourism in the Third World.* Abingdon: Routledge.

Muzaini, H. (2006). Backpacking Southeast Asia: Strategies of "looking local". *Annals of Tourism Research* 33(1), 144–161.

Novelli, M. (2016). *Tourism and development in Sub-Saharan Africa: Current issues and local realities.* Abingdon: Routledge.

Ong, L.T.J., Storey, D., & Minnery, J. (2011). Beyond the beach: Balancing environmental and socio-cultural sustainability in Boracay, the Philippines. *Tourism Geographies* 13 (4), 549–569.

Parnwell, M. (2008). A political ecology of sustainable tourism in Southeast Asia. In M. Hitchcock, V.T. King & M. Parnwell (Eds.), *Tourism in Southeast Asia: Challenges and New Directions* (pp. 236–253). Copenhagen: NIAS Press.

Picard, M. (1992). *Bali: Tourisme culturel et culture touristique* [*Bali: Cultural tourism and touristic culture*]. Paris: l'Harmattan.

Redcliff, M. (1987). *Sustainable development: Exploring the contradictions.* New York: Routledge.

REST (2003). *Community-based tourism handbook.* Bangkok: REST.

Rostow, W. (1960). *The stages of economic growth: A non-communist manifesto.* Cambridge: Cambridge University Press.

Saarinen, J. (2006). Traditions of sustainability in tourism studies. *Annals of Tourism Research* 33(4), 1121–1140.

Scheyvens, R. (2002). *Tourism for development: Empowering communities.* Harlow: Prentice Hall.

Scheyvens, R. (2000). Promoting women's empowerment through involvement in eco-tourism: Experiences from the Third World. *Journal of Sustainable Tourism* 8(3), 232–249.

Seers, D. (1977). The new meaning of development. *International Development Review* 19(3), 2–7.

Seers, D. (1969). The meaning of development. *International Development Review* 11 (4), 2–6.

Shackley, M. (2006). *Atlas of travel and tourism development.* Oxford: Butterworth-Heinemann.

Sharpley, R. (2000). Tourism and sustainable development: Exploring the theoretical divide. *Journal of Sustainable Tourism* 8(1), 1–19.

Sharpley, R., & McGrath, P. (2017). Tourism in Cambodia: Opportunities and challenges. In K. Brickell & S. Springer (Eds.), *The Handbook of Contemporary Cambodia* (pp. 87–98). Abingdon: Routledge.

Sheldon, P.J., & Daniele, R. (Eds.) (2017). *Social entrepreneurship and tourism: Philosophy and practice.* London: Springer

Sidaway, J.D. (2014). Post-development. In V. Desai & R. Potter (Eds.), *The Companion to development studies* (pp.147–151). Abingdon: Routledge.

Spreitzhofer, G. (2008). Zwischen Khao San und Lonely Planet: Aspekte der post-modernen Backpacking-Identität in Südostasien [In-between Khao San and Lonely Planet: Aspects of the postmodern backpacking-identity in Southeast Asia]. *Austrian Journal of South-East Asian Studies* 1(2), 140–161.

Telfer, D.J., & Sharpley, R. (2014). *Tourism and development in the developing world.* Abingdon: Routledge.

Teo, P., & Huang, S. (1995). Tourism and heritage conservation in Singapore. *Annals of Tourism Research* 22(3), 589–615.

Teo, P., & Leong, S. (2006). A postcolonial analysis of backpacking. *Annals of Tourism Research* 33(1), 109–131.

Thomas, A. (2000). Meaning and views of development. In T. Allen & A. Thomas (Eds.), *Poverty and development into the 21st century* (pp. 23–48). Oxford: Oxford University Press.

Truong, D.V., & Hall, C.M. (2015). Exploring the poverty reduction potential of social marketing in tourism development. *Austrian Journal of South-East Asian Studies* 8(2), 125–142.

Truong, D.V., Hall, C.M., & Garry, T. (2014). Tourism and poverty alleviation: Perceptions and experience of poor people in Sapa, Vietnam. *Journal of Sustainable Tourism* 23(7), 1071–1089.

Trupp, A. (2016). *Migration, micro-business and tourism in Thailand: Highlanders in the city.* Abingdon: Routledge.

Trupp, A. (2015). Agency, social capital, and mixed embeddedness among akha ethnic minority street vendors in Thailand's tourist areas. *SOJOURN: Journal of Social Issues in Southeast Asia* 30(3), 780–818.

Trupp, A. (2011). Exhibiting the 'other' then and now: 'Human zoos' in Southern China and Thailand. *Austrian Journal of South-East Asian Studies* 4(1), 139–149.

Turner, L., & Ash, J. (1975). *The golden hordes: International tourism and the pleasure periphery.* London: Constable

UNDP (1990). *Human Development Report 1990.* New York: Oxford University Press.

Wallerstein, I. (1979). *The capitalist world economy.* Cambridge: Cambridge University Press.

Weaver, D., & Lawton, L. (2010). *Tourism management* (4th ed.). Milton: John Wiley & Sons.

Weaver, D., & Oppermann, M. (2000). *Tourism management.* Wallingford: CABI.

Winter, T. (2010). Heritage tourism: The dawn of a new era? In S. Labadi & C. Long (Eds.), *Heritage and globalisation* (pp. 131–143). Abingdon: Routledge.

Wong, P.P. (1998). Coastal tourism development in Southeast Asia: Relevance and lessons for coastal zone management. *Ocean & Coastal Management* 38(2), 89–109.

World Bank (1974). *Appraisal of the Bali tourism project Indonesia.* Retrieved from: http://wwwwds.worldbank.org/servlet/WDSContentServer/IW3P/IB/2000/04/27/000178830_98101912562466/Rendered/PDF/multi_page.pdf.

Wood, R.E. (1980). International tourism and cultural change in Southeast Asia. *Economic Development and Cultural Change* 28(3), 561–581.

WTTC. (2019). *Travel & tourism economic impact 2019: Southeast Asia.* London: World Travel and Tourism Council.

Yamashita, S. (2009). Southeast Asian tourism from a Japanese perspective. In M. Hitchcock, V. King & M. Parnwell (Eds.), *Tourism in Southeast Asia: Challenges and new directions* (pp. 189–205). Copenhagen: NIAS Press.

Yamashita, S. (2003). *Bali and beyond: Explorations in the anthropology of tourism.* Oxford: Berghahn Books.

3 Researching tourism and development in Southeast Asia

Methodological insights

Claudia Dolezal, Alexander Trupp and Prasit Leepreecha

Introduction

The previous chapters have established the significance of tourism in the region of Southeast Asia, both in its contribution to economy and sustainable development. They also demonstrated the widely researched nature of the field, engaged in both by scholars from the region, and researchers from other parts of the world. Little though has been written specifically on conducting research in the region from a methodological point of view. Amongst very few discussions on research methodology, Mura and Pahlevan Sharif (2015) mapped tourism research in Southeast Asia and showed that quantitative approaches are generally preferred over qualitative methodologies. More extensively, Mura and Khoo-Lattimore (2018) in their edited volume on Asian qualitative research, compiled 16 chapters discussing ontological, epistemological, and methodological assumptions underlying Asian tourism research. The book shows the diversity of 'Asian' qualitative tourism research, reflects on common methodologies, including ethnography and auto-ethnography, and calls for alternative discourses in tourism studies.

This chapter looks specifically into ethnography as a method which has shaped tourism research in the area (Adams, 2019; Andrews, Takamitsu, & Dixon, 2018), particularly on topics such as cultural change (Picard, 2008), commodification (Cohen, 1988), identities (Adams, 2006), moral encounters (Mostafanezhad & Hannam, 2016), and touristic production (Bruner, 2005), as well as power inequalities and access to water (Cole, 2012). The authors of the present chapter draw on their experience doing ethnographic research in Thailand (Dolezal, 2011, 2015; Trupp, 2014, 2017; Leepreecha, 2014, 2016) and Indonesia (Dolezal, 2013) in the context of host perceptions (Trupp, 2014), community-based tourism (CBT) (Dolezal, 2015), gender (Trupp & Sunanta, 2017), micro-entrepreneurship (Trupp, 2017), and power relations (Dolezal, 2011, 2015; Evrard & Leepreecha, 2009a; Leepreecha, 2014; Trupp, 2015).

When researching tourism and development in Southeast Asia, scholars have been facing various challenges. Reflecting on our own personal fieldwork/research experiences while taking into consideration the works of other scholars in the region, many share similar challenges, including access to the field, language or working with interpreters, and power relations in the field. The present chapter debates these challenges and points towards ways to address these by drawing on examples from the authors' fieldwork in foreign (Dolezal, Trupp) or familiar fields (Leepreecha). These examples include discussions on the above-mentioned challenges, with a specific focus on the emic versus etic perspective, also seen as the 'insider-outsider' debate. This juxtaposition of research away versus research at home is particularly useful for the present volume, not just to underline the culturally diverse backgrounds and approaches we take for our research but also to understand the different kinds of challenges we encounter – be it as researchers in familiar or foreign fields. Before reflecting on these personal experiences though, this chapter first of all sets the scene by offering a brief theoretical introduction to those thematic areas mentioned above.

Methodological and fieldwork challenges: Theoretical perspectives

Access to the field / insider vs. outsider perspective

A discussion about access to the field needs to first of all debate the concept of the 'field' itself. In a post-modern sense, the field is related to home, our values and background (Mosse, 2005). However, at the same time, as Marcus (1995, p. 102) argues, research takes place in 'real-world sites of investigation' and hence the field often has clear geographical boundaries that we travel to and depart from again (Dolezal, 2018). Our perception of the field and the access we gain often relates to whether we can be regarded as an insider or outsider in the chosen location or social group. Earlier accounts of anthropological fieldwork made a division into emic and etic perspective, or the insider's and the outsider's view (Geertz, 1973). Since Malinowski's (1984) idea of fieldwork, the anthropologist pursued an emic perspective to become part of the culture under study (Bahadir, 2004) – although more recent anthropological works show that one does not necessarily have to 'go native' to understand another culture (Madden, 2010).

Working with research assistants and interpreters

Southeast Asia is home to a variety of languages and dialects (Goddard, 2005). Even if one conducts research is his/her home country, chances are high that one has to rely on the skills of an interpreter. Although researchers regularly work with interpreters when they cannot speak the local language, they remain largely silent about it (Borchgrevink, 2003). Often, 'the silence regarding interpreter use is linked to the anthropologist's need for establishing authority [in the academic environment, not in the field] and to the position that fieldwork has within the discipline' (Borchgrevink 2003, p. 95). Whereas formerly regarded as invisible, detached and as a medium used to arrive at verbatim translations, there is an increasing acknowledgement that the interpreter brings his/her own assumptions, views and social background to the interview and that these influence the data collection and interpretation (Bahadir, 2004; Shimpuku & Norr, 2012). They are an essential part of the process of knowledge creation (Temple & Young, 2004) and often even act as gatekeepers and cultural brokers. However, working with interpreters or even research assistants can be a challenge in itself, which the case studies below discuss.

Fieldwork relations and reflexivity

Social science research is inherently characterised by power relations. On the one side, power relations between actors are often at the centre of our investigations; on the other side, power relations emerge between researchers and participants and shape our inter-subjectivities in the field (Guillemin & Gillam, 2004). These are important to understand to assist with data analysis purposes and make sense of one's findings, particularly in a time where the researcher's role and personal involvement in the field are openly acknowledged (Denzin & Lincoln, 2000). At the same time, these power relations can also pose challenges in the field, such as ethical concerns and community attachment (Leopold, 2011). The practise of reflexivity is particularly useful to understand how we form part of the world we are studying (Feighery, 2006), how power shapes the interactions in the field (Crapanzano, 1980) and how our own assumptions and positionality impact on these as well as our findings (Mauthner & Doucet, 2003). The case studies below derive directly from the authors' fieldwork and therefore focus on the various challenges while entering and being in the field in Southeast Asia.

Researching empowerment in community-based tourism in Bali (Claudia Dolezal)

In this section I reflect on my experiences doing field work in Bali and researching power relations and empowerment in CBT. In this context I regard myself as a foreign researcher and hence was faced with certain challenges. I discuss the access to the field and the challenges that come not only with entering a new cultural context but also with easing into the early beginnings of the ethnographic process, accompanied by issues of translation, shifting power relations and disempowerment in the field.

Entering the Balinese village: A field of difference and disillusions

Bali (Indonesia) was a new research site for me – I had spent time travelling in the country but was still a 'cultural newbie'. I had prepared beforehand by reading, getting in touch with a local NGO as gatekeeper, having decided which villages to live in as well as what methods to use (interviews and participatory methods). I thought I was prepared and somewhat naively felt I would become part of a community, after all I was researching community-based tourism. However, upon arrival, I had trouble identifying myself with the cultural practices and symbols and – even though I knew that it would take time to familiarise myself – it felt like an unsurmountable task at the time. I was under time and money pressures and the pressure to collect 'data' for my PhD, when residents were not enthusiastic about my research – understandably, as they had other priorities such as agricultural work.

I felt not only disillusioned and a certain loss of identity in a field that was yet more foreign than I had imagined but also a gripping feeling that I could never produce meaning and speak from a position of authority. Who am I to talk about people's lives when I am not even part of it? As the weeks progressed, I felt more and more that I got an insight into people's lives but that 'all I could ever secure were limited perspectives of social spheres' (Dolezal, 2019, p. 104). Having faced the realities of social science research, I had doubts about my own project. To overcome the feeling of difference between my informants, the 'field' and myself, I sought desperately 'to learn more in order to overcome distance' (Hammoudi & Borneman 2009, p. 271), and started 'fishing for facts' (Crapanzano, 2012, p. 551).

The field, for me, however, remained a place I would travel to and depart from again (Amit 2000), a place where I was completing my field*work*. Regarding my research as work, although it is a big passion of mine, impacted the relationships I was forming in the beginning. I therefore not only began to make the foreign familiar (Marcus & Fischer, 1986) by learning more, spending every possible moment with my hosts and participating in the daily local life, but also created personal bonds. One of these was my research interpreters as described below.

Lost in translation? The politics of working with interpreters

Given that I only spoke a few words in Balinese and that the Balinese caste system is characterised by a complexity of different dialects, I relied on the help of three local interpreters to conduct my research, with the first two collaborations being rather challenging. The first interpreter, a journalist, had her own agenda by coming to the village and sharing few translations with me. Luckily, one of the members of the tourism team in the village volunteered to help. The problem in working with him, however, was that he was rarely available and, most importantly, his views on the topic seemed to be biased as he was part of the tourism team, trying to promote tourism. In addition, a more central issue emerged after a few interviews. He was from the highest caste in the village (i.e. *Brahmin*), which (as their body language and responses showed me) made interviewees feel intimidated. Being involved in tourism himself, the interpreter and his role seemed too political. Obviously, interpreters never translate from a neutral standpoint (Temple & Young, 2004). Essentially, the interpreter forms part of knowledge production, given that it is never just the two, the anthropologist and the interlocutor, but the 'third', who mediates between and shapes the interpretive process between strangers (Crapanzano, 1980). Although the interpreter assisted me in the process of conducting interviews and I gained insights into power relations, in this case the interpreter's positionality appeared too large an obstacle.

The third interpreter to help me with interviews was a local tour guide. For the first time, I really had access to my respondents. He could speak the dialects of every caste and was – at least according to my cultural norms of interpersonal relations – respectful towards interviewees at all times and particularly accessible for the lowest caste. We developed a friendship over the weeks, met regularly for interviews and lunches, and had discussions about what people said and what was going on in the villages. He taught me about Balinese culture, customs and the role of the caste system. He was both a teacher and a friend who helped me through times of loneliness by checking daily on how I was doing. In addition to that, he tried to bridge the cultural gap between the interviewee and myself. As time passed by, he became my gatekeeper and friend.

Reflecting back, I realised that what I was collecting were views of village life from several perspectives, but what every experience – be it positive or negative at the time – offered me was another piece of the puzzle, of understanding the greater picture of tourism and power relations in the village. Therefore, in writing up my research findings I tried to 'embrace, incorporate and "translate" the effect of these interactions rather than try to avoid them' (Goodman, 2000, p. 152). I acknowledged this 'triple subjectivity' (Temple & Edwards, 2002, p. 6) by interviewing my interpreter(s) and questioning how their underlying assumptions and worldviews impacted on the data. I started to understand the complex power relations that I was part of, which the section below elaborates further.

Fieldwork relationships and disempowerment in the field

Power was one of the key concepts I was researching as part of my study on empowerment. Given that I was well aware of the criticism of the colonial approach that anthropology often experiences, I strongly tried to level power relations between myself and participants, for example with participatory drawing methods, often seen as a useful tool to enable participants to inform the questions and issues that were most important to them (Aziz, Shams, & Khan, 2011). However, once we engaged in these drawing exercises (e.g. drawing the village) I realised the inappropriateness of these methods – I got the sense that the families participating were merely drawing the maps for me and did not get much benefit from it. At the same time, I became increasingly aware of the impossibility of letting somebody speak in a narrative that is not theirs – after all, the final written work was based on my writing and choices of what and who I would present (England, 1994).

My attempt to enable residents to have more power in producing the data seemed to have failed – while at the same time I realised that residents were extremely powerful. They were the ones that, as Sofield (2003, p. 59) says 'pipe(d) the tune to which the tourists (and myself) dance'. The residents had much more power than me: not only did I find myself in a foreign environment, where I struggled with ambiguity, uncertainty and being dependent on my hosts, but I also felt that my social relationships in the field were dominated by demands related to money. I was regarded as a wealthy white foreigner, a potential investor who could help with tourism promotion. All of this resulted in feelings of unease and disempowerment on my side – the researcher, who, paradoxically, was studying empowerment. I found myself in a limbo of ever-changing power relations and ethical dilemmas. On the one hand I felt guilty for exploiting residents for information to progress my research, and on the other hand, I wanted to give back somehow, but not necessarily in the ways that residents had in mind.

In addition to these ethical dilemmas and the business relationships that seemed to emerge between us, I often felt stereotyped as a culture-less, white, primitive foreigner, which taught me that, to them, I may have just been a tourist like everybody else. However, I noticed that this was not necessarily done for the purposes of criticising Westerners, given that the Balinese 'also make use of this dichotomy [between "us" Balinese versus "them" Westerners] to simultaneously [...] articulate views on Balinese traditions and culture' (Hitchcock & Darma Putra, 2007, p. 91). It seemed like I experienced 'Occidentalism' first-hand, a type of reversed Orientalism, which may constitute a conscious way for the Balinese to clarify that 'the Balinese are open in their socialization with Westerners, but are not easily westernized' (Hitchcock & Darma Putra, 2007, p. 93). Experiencing the local gaze first-hand, I learned that much of the anthropological literature on tourism and development portrayed residents as passive, having little agency and power, which had little relation to reality.

Researching tourism, migration and microbusinesses in Thailand (Alexander Trupp)

In this section, I reflect on my experiences of doing fieldwork across different urban tourist zones in Thailand. In order to reconstruct the evolvement of Akha souvenir businesses over time and space, to explore vendors' opportunities, strategies and challenges as well as their multiple forms of embeddedness, I aimed to use various forms of observation including informal conversations, semi-structured interviews, and personal network analysis. I followed an approach which Marcus (1995, p. 99) terms 'multi-sited ethnography' suggesting to 'follow the people' (i.e. to follow and accompany micro-entrepreneurs along their movements and daily activities) and to 'follow the thing' (to trace the circulation through different contexts of the material object of the study, e.g. souvenirs). My experiences and reflections whilst entering the field and doing fieldwork are shared and discussed below.

The beginnings: delusive confidence

Prior to my planned research in a Thai urban tourist setting, I already carried out fieldwork in Northern Thailand in the context of my master's thesis on ethnic minority tourism in Northern Thailand (Trupp, 2007). My four-month research stay abroad took place in the city of Chiang Mai and two highland ethnic minority villages, one Karen and one Akha village. At the time, I could establish a rapport with some Akha villagers and urban-based Akha in Chiang Mai involved in social movements, NGO work, and the souvenir trade.

In addition, I was already in contact with a research assistant I knew well from previous small projects who agreed to work with me to gain access to the Akha communities and act as a translator during interviews. Even though there are concerns in tourism, human geography and anthropology when it comes to the subjectivity and reflexivity of the researcher, there is a general silence on reflections about or even credit for research assistants and interpreters (Turner, 2010). As my research assistant and translator was of invaluable help, but also influenced my research in many ways, I consider it necessary to shed more light on the person contributing substantial work in the background, who over the last 13 years has not only been my colleague and part of the research, but also my partner. She agreed to use her real name, Kosita Butratana, and provided the following information about herself: Kosita was born in the South of Thailand. Her parents come from the northern province of Phrae, but she partly grew up in the Northeast, went to school in Bangkok, and studied psychology and education at Chiang Mai University. Due to her own migration history, she is able to speak and understand the different regional Thai dialects, but she is a member of the so-called Thai mainstream society, went through the Thai schooling system, and like any other researcher, she brought her own preconceptions and values into the field. During the fieldwork, she tried to learn the Akha language, shared many of her life experiences with research participants, translated my stories and motivation, and was crucial to the process of building rapport. After interviews or observational situations, we regularly sat together and exchanged our views and perceptions of the fieldwork. It is important to work with research assistants who have the methodological skills and, maybe even more importantly, the social skills to encounter research participants with honest interest, respect, and sensibility.

In addition to finding a suitable research assistant, I also successfully applied for a research permit at the National Research Council of Thailand, which is a formal government requirement for foreign researchers. Moreover, my research stay was hosted by Chiang Mai University where I was supervised by Dr. Prasit Leepreecha, a leading expert on ethnic and indigenous studies and development in the region. Endowed with social capital in terms of having good relations to Akha representatives, with institutional capital in the form of an official research permit and a local university affiliation, and with incorporated cultural capital embodied in the years of study at my university, the previous fieldwork experience, and in terms of cooperating with a reliable research assistant, I was confident to start my new fieldwork in an urban setting.

Entering the streets and homes: 'Why do you do this?'

The first days of fieldwork in Bangkok were frustrating. As neither my research assistant nor I had any personal contact to Akha vendors in the capital city Bangkok, we started to approach mobile sellers in Khaosan Road by introducing ourselves and the research idea. The first replies were demotivating as they said that they did not have much to tell us. One vendor answered, 'I need to earn money. That's it.' and walked away. After several attempts, we were able to enter into a longer conversation, also giving us the chance to introduce ourselves in Akha language. Also, my research assistant and I got Akha first names from our Akha friend and NGO leader Miqjur Manqlaeq in Northern Thailand, which indicated our sincere interest. After two weeks, we got the first invitation to visit an Akha vendor in her home (a small room) in Bangkok and carry out the first interview. She was a vendor with much sales experience at different tourist areas throughout Thailand. On this occasion, we also met the roommates (also female Akha vendors) of our interview partner and they too became interested in learning about us and the motivations for this study.

I was frequently asked by Akha vendors why I carried out this study and how I benefited from it. I felt that I should first outline my background and intentions before they shared their experiences. My honest answer was that I was a PhD student who was interested in ethnic minorities, especially Akha, as I knew that they were popular in tourism contexts and that I would like to know more about their businesses and why it expanded from the hill villages to Chiang Mai and even the capital city Bangkok. I also told them that I had gotten a small scholarship from Austria, which covered the costs of my flight and accommodation, and that I (at the time) had no other job. The benefits were knowledge acquisition, maybe some publications, and eventually a PhD that could help me get a better job at a university or elsewhere later on. Next, it was my research assistant's task to introduce herself and to share how she got involved in this project. The research participants told us that some Akha vendors had already had bad experiences with Thai journalists who had spread wrong information about them and they had therefore become more careful about sharing their knowledge and experiences. After building rapport with the first vendors, it became easier to get to know further research participants. On the one hand, our first research participant became a kind of gatekeeper by introducing us to her roommates and other sellers on Khaosan Road, and on the other hand, the Akha seller community started to talk about this 'researching couple'.

Still lost in translation

An obstacle in the context of my field research and a deficiency of this study were my insufficient language skills. I learnt Thai before starting my fieldwork and was able to carry out everyday conversations and informal talks, but, in the context of in-depth interviews, I heavily relied on my research assistant. Yet, my Thai language skills were sufficient to understand the main contents of the interviews, thus keeping at least a certain amount of control and partial autonomy over the interviews and translations. I also attempted to minimise misunderstandings by frequent questioning and discussion of the translations. Moreover, seemingly relevant emic expressions by research participants were not only literally translated, but also recontextualised. However, I had to accept that – even working with a well-trained and sensitive research assistant and translator – details and particular meanings of words got lost in translation. Translators bring their own interpretations and subjectivity to the data (Kruse, Bethmann, Nierman, & Schmieder, 2012) – a challenge this study could not overcome. For most Akha, Thai is their second language, but the younger generation especially is fluent in Thai. For part of the younger urban Chiang Mai-based generation, Thai has become the main language and Akha language skills shrink in importance. Some of the souvenir vendors also have good English language skills, so some of the informal conversations were a mix of Thai and English. Furthermore, I attempted to learn the Akha language, but time was too short and I was just able to learn some basic vocabulary and common colloquial formulations, which was nevertheless highly appreciated by my research participants.

Reflections on power relations and field sites

When a white Austrian male researcher attempts to carry out fieldwork among an ethnic minority group mainly consisting of female souvenir sellers working in the informal sector in a country of the Global South, asymmetric relations between the researcher and the 'researched' are evident. Moreover, research assistants and translators form an important part of the field and the knowledge production process since they influence relationships and differential access to research participants and resources (Turner, 2010). Gender plays an important role in fieldwork processes as it limits access to certain information by how one perceives or is perceived by others (Bernard, 2013). I also felt that doing fieldwork as a couple in this particular research context made it easier to gain access to and trust among a female-occupied research setting. Compared to my previous fieldwork experience in village contexts, I perceived urban-based research to be more difficult and demanding. The village somehow appeared to be a more compact unit, while Akha working activities in urban contexts were often scattered around the city and took place between late evenings and early mornings resulting in the fact that interview or observational times frequently lasted until 03.00 AM. In retrospect, I appreciate much more the time I could spend in the field. My main fieldwork time spanned nine months, providing the opportunities to create trust and build relationships with actors in the field, a luxury which has faded away since gaining full-time employment in academia.

Indigenous methodologies and doing fieldwork (Prasit Leepreecha)

This part deals with indigenous methodologies and doing fieldwork, since I am indigenous myself, more precisely part of the Hmong people. In contemporary Thailand, the term *chon phao phuen muang* refers to indigenous people, a term which has been coined by young leaders of highland ethnic groups who were previously referred to as 'hill tribes' since 2007 (see Leepreecha, 2019; Morton & Baird, 2019). I myself was born and educated in Thailand, through the Thai government's educational institutions, but I have also studied abroad in the United States, where I completed my PhD in social anthropology before returning to Thailand to work at Chiang Mai University. Due to my indigenous and educational background, I speak Hmong, Northern Thai, Central Thai, English and Lao. Below, I elaborate on the ways in which I conceptualise indigenous tourism research and how I proceed in analysing the data in my research. I argue that despite belonging to a group of indigenous people, it is impossible to become an insider when conducting research on tourism. Interestingly, I also regularly face difficulties observing and interviewing non-indigenous stakeholders, making me reliant on other sources of information and help.

Being an indigenous researcher

As a Hmong from Nan province in the Eastern part of Northern Thailand, I had visited and contacted the Hmong in the tourism village of Doi Pui and nearby villages selling their souvenirs in urban Chiang Mai and Bangkok since the 1980s (Evrard & Leepreecha, 2009b). In towns, Hmong mainly gather in crowded places, such as bus stations and markets, always dress up in Hmong and put their souvenirs (silver bracelets, necklets, rings, etc.) in rice-winnowing baskets, sitting on the floor to sell them to Thai and foreign customers. One day I listened to a conversation between Hmong vendors and Thai customers: 'do you make these souvenirs yourselves?' The answer was: 'Yes, we make them ourselves. They are one hundred percent silver'. This is an example of popular conversions between Hmong souvenir sellers and Thai customers I often heard. However, when I personally communicated with the vendors in Hmong, without a non-Hmong customer nearby, I was told that those were factory-made souvenirs and not genuine silver souvenirs. On another occasion, in a Hmong tourism village, I intended to buy a Hmong shirt, but the female Hmong vendor told me 'that's not a good quality shirt. We just made it very simple for selling to tourists. If you really want to buy for dressing, better we do a new and better quality for you'. These incidences reveal at least two key issues in relation to indigenous tourism: being an insider and authenticity. I will focus only on the issue of being insider in the present reflection driven by the main questions: How far I can become an insider while conducting fieldwork on tourism with indigenous people; and what is the nature of the power relations between indigenous people and myself?

Doing fieldwork among indigenous people

Metaphorically, to me, being an insider while carrying out fieldwork on tourism feels like not just standing in the front yard but being allowed to enter the sellers' houses and sit down to have a conversation with informants in Hmong language. In other words, ethnic vendors on tourism have many faces and as an indigenous researcher, you would usually see more of these than a non-indigenous researcher (Berreman, 1962). However, I argue that as a researcher I can never entirely become an insider, neither amongst Hmong nor non-Hmong indigenous people.

My interest in carrying out research on tourism in Hmong villages began in the early 1990s. As a Hmong man, I always spoke Hmong (which is also my mother tongue) with Hmong silverware and flower vendors. Unlike non-Hmong tourists, adult Hmong silverware vendors did not try to persuade me to buy their souvenirs, since they knew that Hmong men would not use it in everyday life, except young people who dress up during Hmong New Year celebrations. Meanwhile, Hmong children who sell dried flowers tended to give me some of their products for free, just like my close relatives who sell vegetables for tourists, since agricultural products are not for sale in traditionally Hmong society but now become one of the main goods villagers sell to tourist. I felt that I had special access to my informants and was experiencing certain privileges as an indigenous researcher. For example, entering a museum zone in a tourist village, a Hmong gatekeeper said to me in Hmong that 'if you are Hmong, we don't collect your money'. They also tell you much more true stories, such as 'we bought these pickled peaches and strawberries from factory in town', while telling tourists that 'we pickled them ourselves'.

However, there are also limits to the access to information I gain, and hence, it is, for example, impossible for me to know how much they buy products for – they will only tell me the selling price. Nevertheless, within only a few days in the village, I learned much about conflicts between local vendors, however, again, nobody wanted to tell me the details. Therefore, we could say, in metaphorical terms, that I had just entered their living room but was not allowed in the kitchen, while Thai and foreign tourists can stay in their front yard. To my observation, whether deeper layers of relationships emerge depends on the length of time one spends in the village. I spent a few days in the village conducting field research, while Thai and foreign tourists just visited the village for a few hours, taking photos and buying souvenirs, then leave. These tourists do not even explore the Hmong and other indigenous people's culture in detail. This also means that, probably, if I were to stay longer – maybe even a year or so – I would build even more trust and potentially 'reach the kitchen'.

Becoming an insider amongst the Hmong community?

Interestingly, on the one hand, informants perceived me as a Hmong just like them, on the other hand though, they still identified me as a visitor or stranger like other tourists. They treated me as a Hmong just like them because I clearly identified myself to them as Hmong and spoke Hmong with them, though my hometown is different from theirs. However, due to my role as a researcher who comes from outside and being in the village for only a few days, they feel reluctant to tell me everything. Importantly, if I talked to Hmong vendors who belong to the Lee clan, the same as mine, they would be more open to sharing with me some in-depth information, compared with those who belong to other clans.

In addition to the Hmong, there are other highland ethnic groups involved with ethnic tourism in Northern Thailand. Those include Karen, Mien, Lisu, Lahu, Akha, Lua, Mlabri, Kayan, and more (Leepreecha, 2019). Despite being indigenous just like them, I am of course not from the same ethnic background and hence learned that it is difficult to become an insider while conducting research with other indigenous people in Thailand. One issue is that I don't speak their ethnic languages – I use northern Thai dialect without a translator but that way I don't identify as insider. Nevertheless, once I identified myself as Hmong, one of the highland indigenous people brought me closer to the local residents – compared with other Thais or foreign tourists, who do not have the same access. However, there is still a significant gap between me and them. For example, vendors don't tell me which items of their souvenir or handicraft are genuine or not, since I am not familiar with their products. Unlike the Hmong, those non-Hmong ethnic vendors never give me any free items they sell for tourists. Nevertheless, they provided me with quite some in-depth knowledge on their tourism-related business.

Overall, there are many complex layers in Hmong society, which makes being a true insider a difficult task. It shows that being part of the same ethnic group will not automatically make me an insider and that it takes time to establish trust and rapport. However, being part of an indigenous group will offer you a more privileged position when researching indigenous people – even if not from the same clan. Nevertheless, doing research 'at home', particularly as a globalised Thai man, has been somewhat romanticised as giving a more truthful account of reality, which the above reflection attempted to rectify.

Conclusions

This chapter has offered a discussion of the fieldwork challenges that arise when using ethnographic methods in Southeast Asia, focusing specifically on issues relating to the insider-outsider debate, power relations, access to the field, and language. What emerged from the above is the complex nature of these issues – with access to the field depending not only on cultural background but also on gender, gatekeepers and pre-existing field relationships, as well as time spent in the field. The three cases presented here were inherently different – starting with the foreign researcher relying on local help, followed by the foreign researcher with a good level of local knowledge and equipped with the help of a local gatekeeper/partner and finishing off the discussion with the indigenous researcher whose entrance into the field seems smoother but was nevertheless challenging.

In particular, the discussion on being an indigenous researcher in indigenous Thai villages has shown that being indigenous does not automatically translate into better access in the field. Weiner-Levy and Queder (2012, p. 1163) remind us that '[a]t times, belonging to the same culture or people and the consequent expectations of similarity might actually accentuate differences in status and lifestyle between researcher and participants' and that positionalities often shift and fluctuate, depending on how one is perceived by their informants (Ergun & Erdemir, 2010; Weiner-Levy & Queder, 2012). What emerged was that, oftentimes, what is really needed to build rapport with informants, both for the cultural outsider but also the insider, is time. Increasingly researchers are facing the pressures by academic institutions to deliver results and 'impact' quickly, which often results in long fieldwork periods being difficult to pursue. At the same time, though, we need to remind ourselves that although 'short fieldwork periods in foreign fields can make deep relationships difficult to forge [...], [t]his does not mean [...] that our research will be any less valid' (Dolezal, 2018, p. 109) – neither does being an outsider, which this chapter has demonstrated. The support that often comes from cultural brokers and interpreters is invaluable in gaining access to the field and data collection, nevertheless, these have not been sufficiently acknowledged in the past. Interpreters have somewhat remained behind the curtains, acting mainly in the background. This chapter therefore asks for a more open and honest inclusion of the support we receive, particularly as foreign researchers who are not fluent in the local language.

At the same time, the above reflections by three different academics with very different levels of access to the field and time spent in the field, have reminded us of the relevance of cultural difference, which, despite the researcher's empathy and cultural understanding, impacts on the research. Southeast Asia in particular is a highly complex region in terms of cultural variances, ethnic minorities and indigenous populations, one cannot make prior assumptions about how fieldwork relationships are going to work out. It is the experiences of *being* in the field and our ability to reflect on these that enable us to produce richer accounts of fieldwork. The discussion above thus sets out to remind us of the complexities of power relations in the field and that 'there is neither a comfortable insider nor a comfortable outsider position' (Ergun & Erdemir, 2010, p. 34). However, there is much that the researcher can do in terms of showing an awareness and reflecting on these. It is the researcher's responsibility therefore to analyse these complex power relations, to understand the moments of difference and discomfort in one's research and, in doing so, to make ethnographic research in Southeast Asia a yet more rigorous practice.

References

Adams, K. (2019). *Indonesia: History, heritage, culture.* Ann Arbor: Association for Asian Studies.

Adams, K. (2006). *Art as politics: Re-crafting identities, tourism, and power in Tana Toraja, Indonesia.* Honolulu: University of Hawaii Press.

Amit, V. (2000). Introduction: Constructing the field. In V. Amit (Ed.), *Constructing the field: Ethnographic fieldwork in the contemporary world* (pp. 1–18). London: Routledge.

Andrews, H., Takamitsu, J., & Dixon, L. (Eds). (2018) *Tourism ethnographies: Ethics, methods, application and reflexivity.* Abingdon: Routledge.

Aziz, A., Shams, M., & Khan, K.S. (2011). Participatory action research as the approach for women's empowerment. *Action Research* 9(3), 303–323.

Bahadir, S. (2004). Moving in-between: The interpreter as ethnographer and the inter-preting-researcher as anthropologist. *Meta: Translators' Journal* 49(4), 805–821.

Berreman, G.D. (1962). *Behind many masks: Ethnography and impression management in a Himalayan Village.* Ithaca: The Society for Applied Anthropology.

Bernard, H.R. (2013). *Social research methods: Qualitative and quantitative approaches.* Los Angeles: SAGE Publications.

Borchgrevink, A. (2003). Silencing language: Of anthropologists and interpreters. *Ethnography* 4(1), 95–121.

Bruner, E.M. (2005). *Culture on tour: Ethnographies of travel.* Chicago: Chicago University Press.

Cohen, E. (1988). Authenticity and commoditization in tourism. *Annals of Tourism Research* 15(3), 371–386

Cole, S. (2012). A political ecology of water equity and tourism: A case study from Bali. *Annals of Tourism Research* 39(2), 1221–1241.

Crapanzano, V. (2012). "At the heart of the discipline": Critical reflections on fieldwork. In A.C.G.M. Robben & J.A. Sluka, (Eds.), *Ethnographic fieldwork: An anthropological reader*, 2nd edition (pp. 547–562). Oxford: John Wiley & Sons.

Crapanzano, V. (1980). *Tuhami: Portrait of a Moroccan.* Chicago: University of Chicago Press.

Denzin, N.K., & Lincoln, Y.S. (2000). Introduction: The discipline and practice of qualitative research. In N.K. Denzin & Y.S. Lincoln (Eds.), *Handbook of qualitative research*, 2nd edition (pp. 1–28). London: SAGE.

Dolezal, C. (2018). Being in the field in Bali: A reflection on fieldwork challenges in community-based tourism research. In H. Andrews, J. Takamitsu & L. Dixon (Eds), *Tourism ethnographies: Ethics, methods, application and reflexivity* (pp. 97–111). Abingdon: Routledge.

Dolezal, C. (2015). The tourism encounter in community-based tourism in Northern Thailand: Empty meeting ground or space for change? *Austrian Journal of South-East Asian Studies* 8(2), 165–186.

Dolezal, C. (2013). Community-based tourism in Bali: On the road towards empowerment? An interview with Djinaldi Gosana. *Austrian Journal of South-East Asian Studies* 6(2), 366–373.

Dolezal, C. (2011). Community-based tourism in Thailand: (Dis-)illusions of authenticity and the necessity for dynamic concepts of culture and power. *Austrian Journal of South-East Asian Studies* 4(1), 129–138.

England, H.V.L. (1994). Getting personal: Reflexivity, positionality, and feminist research. *The Professional Geographer* 46(1), 80–89.

Ergun, A., & Erdemir, A. (2010). Negotiating insider and outsider identities in the field: "Insider" in a foreign land; "outsider" in one's own land. *Field Methods* 22(1), 16–38.

Evrard, O., & Leepreecha, P. (2009a). Staging the nation, exploring the margins: Tourism and its political implications in northern Thailand. In T. Winter, P. Teo & T. Chang (Eds.), *Asia on tour: Exploring the rise of Asian tourism* (pp. 239–252). Abingdon: Routledge.

Evrard, O., & Leepreecha, P. (2009b). Monks, monarchs and mountain folks. *Critique of Anthropology* 29(3), 300–323.

Feighery, W. (2006). Reflexivity and tourism research: Telling an(other) story. *Current Issues in Tourism* 9(3), 269–282.

Geertz, C. (1973). *The interpretation of cultures*. New York: Basic Books.

Goddard, C. (2005). *The languages of East and Southeast Asia: An introduction*. Oxford: Oxford University Press.

Goodman, R. (2000). Fieldwork and reflexivity: Thoughts from the anthropology of Japan. In P. Dresch, W. James & D. Parkin (Eds.), *Anthropologists in a wider world* (pp. 151–203). Oxford: Berghahn Books.

Guillemin, M., & Gillam, L. (2004). Ethics, reflexivity, and "ethically important moments" in research. *Qualitative Inquiry* 10(2), 261–280.

Hammoudi, A., & Borneman, J. (2009). Afterthoughts: The experience and agony of fieldwork. In J. Borneman (Ed.), *Being there: The fieldwork encounter and the making of truth* (pp. 259–272). Berkeley: University of California Press.

Hitchcock, M., & Darma Putra, I. N. (2007). *Tourism, development and terrorism in Bali*. Bodmin: MPG Books.

Kruse, J., Bethmann, S., Nierman, D., & Schmieder, C. (Eds.). (2012). *Qualitative Interviewforschung in und mit fremden Sprachen: Eine Einführung in Theorie und Praxis*. Weinheim; Basel: Beltz Juwena.

Leepreecha, P. (2019). Becoming indigenous peoples in Thailand. *Journal of Southeast Asian Studies* 50(1), 32–50.

Leepreecha, P. (2016). Commoditizing His Majesty's footprints: Tourism in highland ethnic communities in Northern Thailand. In P. Porananond & King, V. (Eds.), *Tourism and monarchy in Southeast Asia*, (pp. 69–88). Newcastle upon Tyne: Cambridge Scholars Publishing.

Leepreecha, P. (2014). Tourism in mountainous communities: The politics of ethnic tourism in Northern Thailand. In K. Husa, A. Trupp & H. Wohlschlägl (Eds.), *Southeast Asia mobility transition: Issues and trends in migration and tourism* (pp. 329–345). Vienna: Department of Geography and Regional Research, University of Vienna.

Leopold, T. (2011). Reflexivity and ethnography in community tourism research. In C. M. Hall (Ed.). *Fieldwork in tourism: Methods, issues and reflections* (pp. 87–98). Abingdon: Routledge.

Madden, R. (2010). *Being ethnographic: A guide to the theory and practice of ethnography*. London: SAGE.

Malinowski, B. (1984). *Argonauts of the Western Pacific*. Prospect Heights: Waveland Press.

Marcus, G.E. (1995). Ethnography in/of the world system: The emergence of multi-sited ethnography. *Annual Review of Anthropology* 24, 95–117.

Marcus, G.E., & Fischer, M.M.J. (1986). *Anthropology as cultural critique: An experimental moment in the human sciences*. Chicago: University of Chicago Press.

Mauthner, N.S., & Doucet, A. (2003). Reflexive accounts and accounts of reflexivity in qualitative data analysis. *Sociology* 37(3), 413–431.

Morton, M., & Baird, I. (2019). From hill tribes to indigenous peoples: The localisation of a global movement in Thailand. *Journal of Southeast Asian Studies* 20(1), 7–31.

Mosse, D. (2005). *Cultivating development: An ethnography of aid policy and practice.* London: Pluto Press.

Mostafanezhad, M., & Hannam, K. (Eds.) (2016). *Moral encounters in tourism.* Abingdon: Routledge.

Mura, P., & Khoo-Lattimore, C. (2018). *Asian qualitative research in tourism: Ontologies, epistemologies, methodologies, and methods.* Singapore: Springer.

Mura, P., & Pahlevan Sharif, S. (2015). The crisis of the 'crisis of representation': Mapping qualitative tourism research in Southeast Asia. *Current Issues in Tourism* 18(9), 828–844.

Picard, M. (2008). Balinese identity as tourist attraction: From 'cultural tourism' (pariwisata budaya) to 'Bali erect' (ajeg Bali). *Tourist Studies* 8(2), 155–173.

Shimpuku, Y., & Norr, K.F. (2012). Working with interpreters in cross-cultural qualitative research in the context of a developing country: Systematic literature review. *Journal of Advanced Nursing* 68(8), 1692–1706.

Sofield, T.H.B. (2003). *Empowerment for sustainable tourism development.* Oxford: Elsevier.

Temple, B., & Edwards, R. (2002). Interpreters/translators and cross-language research: Reflexivity and border crossings. *International Journal of Qualitative Methods* 1(2).

Temple, B., & Young, A. (2004). Qualitative research and translation dilemmas. *Qualitative Research* 4(2), 161–178.

Trupp, A. (2017). *Migration, micro-business and tourism in Thailand: Highlanders in the city.* Abingdon: Routledge.

Trupp, A. (2015). Agency, social capital, and mixed embeddedness among Akha ethnic minority street vendors in Thailand's tourist areas. *SOJOURN: Journal of Social Issues in Southeast Asia* 30(3), 779–817.

Trupp, A. (2014). Host perspectives on ethnic minority tourism in Northern Thailand. *Journal of Tourism Consumption and Practice* 6(1), 52–80.

Trupp, A. (2007). Ethnotourismus in Nordthailand: Perspektiven der Akha und Karen, dargestellt am Beispiel zweier touristisch unterschiedlich entwickelter Hilltribedörfer. *Geographischer Jahresbericht Aus Österreich* 62, 185–213.

Trupp, A., & Sunanta, S. (2017). Gendered practices in urban ethnic tourism in Thailand. *Annals of Tourism Research* 64, 76–86.

Turner, S. (2010). Research Note: The silenced assistant. Reflections of invisible interpreters and research assistants. *Asia Pacific Viewpoint* 51(2), 206–219.

Weiner-Levy, N., & Queder, S.A.R. (2012). Researching my people, researching the "other": Field experiences of two researchers along shifting positionalities. *Qual Quant* 46, 1151–1166.

Part II

Tourism and development in protected areas

4 Ecotourism and sustainable development in Vietnam's protected areas

Pham Hong Long and Huong T. Bui

Introduction

The Vietnamese government has declared ecotourism to be one of the country's key tourism products for generating an indirect source of income for local communities, and to contribute to environmental education (Buckley, 1999), and women's empowerment (Tran & Walter, 2014). The Vietnam Forestry Development Strategy 2006–2020 (Prime Minister's Office, 2007, p. 25) even states: 'Forestry development planning should be made available to the public, and to pilot and scale up the tendering and leasing special use forests (SUFs) for ecotourism and recreation purposes'. Introduced in 1986, the 'open-door' (*doimoi*) policy encouraged a shift from a socialist-oriented economy to a market-driven economy. The *doimoi* policy calls for the decentralization of the Vietnamese park system with new policies encouraging the National Park management board to seek out alternative financial solutions to reduce its dependence on the state budget (Ly & Xiao, 2016). Within this context, the utilization of forest resources for ecotourism development has been justified as Vietnam has rich resources for development (USAID, 2013):

- 33 national parks;
- 57 nature reserves;
- 12 species/habitat conservation areas;
- 53 landscape protection areas;
- 9 experimental and scientific research areas.

Ecotourism development is a relatively new economic activity in protected areas in Vietnam, which has the potential to generate additional funds for forest redevelopment and conservation of biodiversity, as well as providing a new source of income for locals. Revenue from ecotourism activities is considered a more innovative method for self-financing aimed at a reduction of dependence on the state budget. Among a broad range of innovative financing for Protected Areas (PAs), Payments for Forest Environmental Services (PFES) emerges as a potential alternative source of funding. Vietnam is the first country in Southeast Asia to implement and legalize PFES. However, the implementation of PEFS pilot projects in Vietnam does not follow predicted orthodox 'neoliberalization of nature' (McElwee, 2012, p. 412) approaches in their use of market instruments as a strong role of the state in forest management continues to dominate; therefore, PEFS is unlikely to tackle several of the key underlying causes for deforestation.

Ecotourism is among the economic activities that utilize natural resources, forests in particular, and is subject to PFES. In addition to PFES, ecotourism also generates revenue from regular entrance tickets and other economic activities such as leasing land, sites, and operations of ecotourism services. Until recently, there has not been any research discussing ecotourism or PFES in relation financing PAs, therefore, the current study focuses on analysing the extent to which ecotourism contributes to the sustainable financing of PAs. Through reviewing industry reports and utilizing secondary data collected from various government organizations, the authors compare and contrast the economic outcomes of the three options of PFES, revenue from entrance tickets, and income from ecotourism services. The authors further outline the relevant legal and institutional frameworks, policies, and implementations of the financing of protected areas.

Financing protected areas (PAs)

Funding for PAs comes from three main sources: state budget, non-state funds and international donors, and revenue from tourism services. First, state budget funds (channelled through central and local levels of government), account for 34% of total PAs funding, including 'regular capital budgets' allocated for investment projects prepared under the 10-year master plans that are developed for PAs. Capital investment projects in PAs may also be funded under irregular investment on special projects, national target programs, and loans for revenue-generating investments. The most significant national target program for PAs is the Five Million Hectare Reforestation Program (5MHRP), one of the first nationwide attempts to generate direct payments to local communities for undertaking forest protection activities, via forest protection contracts, generating 22% of budget funds for target PAs (Emerton, Pham, & Ha, 2011).

Second, 34% of funding for PAs comes from special funds which remain outside of regular state budget planning processes, from international donors, and from other domestic sources, such as the Vietnam Conservation Fund (VCF), the Vietnam Environment Protection Fund (VEPF), the Trust Fund for Forests (TFF), and the Forest Protection and Development Fund (FPDF). Additional public funding is also available for scientific research through application to the relevant government departments' funding windows (Emerton, Pham, & Ha, 2011). Third, some PAs earn self-generated income, accounting for about 1% of funding, particularly from tourism. Decree 117 allows PA management boards to arrange tourism activities, to lease out land for others to conduct tourism, and to form joint ventures or associations with the private sector in order to implement tourism businesses. It is important to remember that Vietnam is a 'socialist-oriented market economy' (Arndt, Garcia, Tarp, & Thurlow, 2012, p. 744), which retains a high degree of state intervention and control.

Analysing the structure of PA financing, researchers conclude that central and provincial budgets were crucial funding sources to cover the costs of PA management and conservation (Le, Markowski, & Bartos, 2018). Significant differences were found between the two groups of national parks with respect to central and provincial budgets, as expenditure of the state budget for national parks managed by the Ministry of Agriculture and Rural Development (MARD) was higher than for the provincially managed national parks. This is partly because provincial national parks have generally had less access to funds than those managed by MARD (Emerton, Pham, & Ha, 2011).

The volume of funding allocated by the government to Vietnam's PAs has remained relatively stable in recent years, accounting for an average of 0.13% of GDP, 0.5% of total public budget allocation, or between USD 3.0–3.5 million per year. When considered on a regional area basis, the financial status of Vietnam's PAs compares well to other parts of Asia and the world (Emerton, Bishop, & Thomas, 2006). According to one recent analysis, annual government spending on PAs averages just under USD 2,000/km^2 in developed countries, USD 150/km^2 in developing countries in general, and USD 500/km^2 in South and Southeast Asia (including developing Southeast Asian countries). At more than USD 1,200/km^2, Vietnam's state budget allocations for PAs are significantly greater than expenditures in other parts of Asia and are comparable to public budget allocations for PA management in Europe and North America (Berghöfer et al., 2017). Given this impressive and stable level of public support, one might question whether and why funding is in fact a problem for Vietnam's national PA network. Emerton, Pham, and Ha (2011) found that Vietnam's PAs face major financial problems, which in turn translate into serious management constraints. First, the bulk of annual budgets are for capital expenditures and focused on infrastructure with little funding available for routine maintenance or conservation activities. Second, public sector budgeting procedures are subject to long delays and frequent readjustments; therefore, it is hard for PA managers to plan or implement a coherent set of conservation activities. Third, annual budget allocations are tied closely to the investment plan which is prepared when a PA is first established. This makes it difficult to build in flexibility or responsiveness to changing management needs and conservation priorities. Fourth, Vietnam's PAs rely almost entirely on centralized public funding. There are only limited opportunities to generate or retain surplus income. This translates into an extremely narrow financial base, and little incentive to generate funds at the individual PAs level (Emerton, Pham, & Ha, 2011).

Ecotourism and revenue generation for PAs

Since the late 1990s, the emphasis of national forest policy has shifted from production to protection, including the management of forests for conservation, livelihoods, and economic development. The government's open-door policy has encouraged the participation of foreign NGOs in Vietnam's natural areas and has allowed the growth of ecotourism in national parks and protected areas (Suntikul, Butler, & Airey, 2010). Tourism is not only an important source of revenue for some PAs, but it also acts as a driver for economic development more generally, supporting a variety of local and national businesses, such as restaurants, hotels, transport, and the production of souvenirs.

Table 4.1 shows major sources of revenue for PAs in 2015. The central government contributes up to 78.07% of revenue for national parks including investment for infrastructure (52.48%), subcontract for forest protection (19.33%), and funds for community development (6.26%), whereas revenue from payments for environmental services account for 18.50%. Ecotourism services contribute only 3.43% and entrance fees account for a small fraction of less than 1%. Three ways in which ecotourism contributes to PA funding are entrance fees, ecotourism services, lease and joint ventures, and PFES. Estimated revenue for PFES by tourism firms is about 1% of the total PFES revenue. In general, revenue from tourism represents approximately 4% of total funding for PAs.

Table 4.1 Revenue of national parks in 2015

No	Source of revenue	Number of national parks	Revenue (in thousand VND*)	
			Revenue	Percentage
1	Entrance fee	4/33	1,684,200	0.96%
2	Ecotourism services	6/33	4,008,615	2.30%
3	Lease for ecotourism development	3/33	300,000	0.17%
4	Joint venture for ecotourism development	0	0	0
5	Payments for environmental services	13/33	32,392,871	18.50%
6	Investment for infrastructure	22/33	91,873,335	52.48%
7	Subcontract for forest protection (QĐ 24)	19/33	33,832,927	19.33%
8	Funds for community development	16/33	10,960,000	6.26%
9	Total		175,051,948	100%

Source: Division of Nature Conservation – General Department of Forestry, Document Number 1089/TCLN-BTTN dated12/7/2016 – adapted from Ngo & Pham, 2016
* 1 US$ = 22,000 VND

Payments for Forest Environmental Services through tourism

Payments for Environmental Services (PES) is defined as 'a voluntary, conditional transaction with at least one seller, one buyer, and a well-defined environmental service' (Wunder, 2005, p. 1). Although PES was originally defined as a voluntary transaction, such transactions often require states, donors, and civil society to create new markets and associated institutions (Vatn, 2010). The primary functions of PES are to 'translate external, non-market values of the environment into real financial incentives for local actors to provide such services' (Engel, Pagiola & Wunder, 2008, p. 663).

Based on the principle of PES, the government established its own version with a pilot policy framework for Payment for Forest Environmental Services (PFES Decision 380/QD-Ttg) (The Prime Minister of the Government, 2008). This was the first national policy to set out basic definitions for 'environmental service providers' and those who benefit from forest-based ecosystem services – the 'service users'. Two provinces with different forest ecosystems were selected for the pilot phase – Lam Dong in the Central Highlands and Son La in the north. The results from the pilot projects in Lam Dong and Son La were used to scale up PES models to 14 forested provinces (Table 4.2). On this basis, the government prepared a proposal for a national decree on PFES (Decree 99/2010/ND-CP) (The Government, 2010) to be adopted countrywide. The decree was passed in 2010. Forest environmental services stipulated under the PFES scheme are: (1) soil protection and erosion control; (2) water regulation and supply; and (3) biodiversity conservation and natural landscape beauty. PFES users are: (1) hydropower generators pay VND 20,000/kwh, which contributes 97.04% of the total PFES; (2) clean water suppliers pay VND 40,000/m^3, accounting for 2.37% of the total PFES; and (3) tourism service providers contribute 1%–2% of revenue, which accounted for less than 0.23% of PFES in 2016. The total revenue of PFES in 2016 was VND 6,510.6 billion, of which 73.2% was collected for the national budget and 26.8% was retained for the provincial budget (Pham, 2018). The payments made by tourism businesses such as tour operators, restaurants, hotels, and souvenir vendors are intended to financially support the forest protection activities that contribute to conservation of biodiversity and natural landscape beauty. Forest owners or actors contracted by the forest owners, such as organizations, households or village communities, are entitled to receive payments for ecosystem services (Decree 99/2010, Article 8.) (The Government, 2010). Currently, the implementation of Decree 99 focuses heavily on hydropower plants and water companies as payers for PFES. Only a pilot project in Lam Dong Province includes PFES from tourism. In that project 14 tourism businesses contribute 1% of their revenue to the provincial forest protection and development fund.

However, implementation of PFES for tourism faces various challenges concerning identification of payers, actors, the payment mechanism, and levels of policy awareness, as demonstrated in a study by GIZ (2012). First, tourism

Table 4.2 Revenue from PFES at 14 national parks

TT	National parks	Province	Area benefits from PFES	Revenue from PFES in 2015 (in thousand VND)	Revenue from PFES in 2016 (in thousand VND)
1	Bi Doup - Núi Bà	Lâm Đồng	57,720.59	22,487,976.50	28,088,000
2	Bù Gia Mập	Bình Phước	24,700	10,127,000	12,350,000
3	Chư Yang Sin	Đắk Lắk	58,970.50	17,691,150	9,546,992.10
4	Hoàng Liên	Lào Cai	18,658.80	6,101,427.60	6,150,000
5	Núi Chúa	Ninh Thuận	4,469	1,520,747.95	1,129,259.95
8	Bạch Mã	Thừa Thiên Huế	14,310.15	992,584.81	976,150.27
9	Bến En	Thanh Hóa	9,932	20,905.89	24,405
10	Cát Tiên	Đồng Nai	30,311	16,465,264.26	17,848,182.17
11	Chư Mom Rây	Kon Tum	9,503	3,780,991.95	4,119,842.66
12	Phước Bình	Ninh Thuận	15,854	95,869.41	102,329.56
13	Ba Bể	Bắc Kạn	7812.64	1,328,148.80	547,414.70
14	Kon Ka Kinh	Gia Lai	39,335.50	8,219,681	6,808,096
Total			291,577.33	88,831,748.17	87,690,672.41

Source: Fund for Forest Protected and Development, 2015 – adapted from Ngo & Pham, 2016

stakeholders are diverse in terms of business location, size, and product. Second, actors entitled to receive PFES are forest owners and actors contracted by forest owners, who might be organizations, households or villages (Decree 99/2010, Article 8) (The Government, 2010). The PA management board is considered the forest owner and it is therefore both a provider and recipient of PFES. As local communities and individuals only receive benefits under a PFES scheme if the PA management board has given them a contract for park protection services the payment can fall short of contributing to the objective of poverty alleviation in cases where no protection contracts are in place. Third, there are misinterpretations of the legal regulations concerning the mechanism of payments. The direct payment mechanism for PFES is currently applied without agreeing with the payers on the payment level. Fourth, in order to implement a PFES scheme, the stakeholders involved need to be informed about the concept and the mechanism. The lack of clear implementation guidelines for PFES for landscape beauty and biodiversity conservation makes it difficult to raise awareness and understanding (GIZ, 2012). Having faced numerous challenges in interpretation and implementation, PFES revenue from tourism contributes only 0.2% to the total revenue of PFES. Ultimately, the question for administrators and policy makers is how to increase the effectiveness of governance of PFES with respect to ecotourism in PAs.

Entrance tickets into protected areas and national parks

As shown in Table 4.1, revenue from entrance fees is limited, accounting for just 0.96% of the total revenue for national parks. The entrance fee system of the national parks reveals two issues in relation to the calculation and management of the fee. First, the fee system is based on a fixed price and is not contingent on the resources and conditions of national parks. Entrance fees for national parks have remained unchanged for more than 18 years, since the promulgation of the Decree on Fees and Payments in 2001, despite variation in market demand and product quality. In 2016, the entrance fees were allowed to change by Ministry of Finance (MOF). In detail, the price for adults is VND 60,000; the price for students and pupils is VND 20,000; and the price for children is VND 10,000; and there is a discount of 50% for persons with disabilities and for seniors. This pricing applies to all national parks managed by MARD. In reality, visitor arrivals to national parks vary greatly owing to the competitive advantage of the national parks based on biological conditions, location, accessibility, landscape, infrastructure, and product quality. For example, revenue from entrance fees is higher for Ba Vi National Park, simply because of a higher volume of visitors who can easily access the park from the capital city of Hanoi. A similar observation can be made for Cat Tien National Park, located in the South, not too far from Ho Chi Minh City. Cuc Phuong National Park, also relatively close to Hanoi, shows a constant income from entrance fees of around VND 5.5 billion (Table 4.3). These three national parks with high revenue from tourism share similar characteristics: The locations are closer to large cities and they are therefore easy to access; good infrastructure is in place including such elements as road condition, accommodation, establishment of visitor centres, and qualified human resources; and they have well-established images and brands via advertisement and promotion. Therefore, these national parks have competitive advantages over other parks. Until 2016, entrance tickets to national parks had been classified as fees. Park administrators retain 80% of the revenue from fees paid to cover expenses raised from regulation and administration of the fee-paying system, while 20% of the revenue is to be collected for the national budget. The new Law on Fees and Circulars, promulgated in 2017, has triggered a dramatic change from the fixed fee-paying system to a market-based price. However, until the time of this research, no significant change has been made to the entrance fee system.

Second, problems arise from organizations involved in managing ecotourism activities in national parks. Ecotourism is a leisure activity, therefore revenue and investment for ecotourism should be under the direction of the Ministry of Culture, Tourism and Sport, which is different from the main provider of state funding to national parks – MARD. Consequently, the entrance fee falls under the mandate of the Ministry of Culture, Tourism and Sport, while national park management and investment are the responsibilities of MARD. Therefore, ecotourism development in national parks and related fee-payment activities have not yet received enough attention from park rangers and mandated

Table 4.3 Revenue from entrance fees of six national parks, 2013–2017 (in thousands VND)

No	National park	2013	2014	2015	2016	2017	Expected 2018
1	Ba Vì	4,934,220	5,247,680	7,559,880	13,009,740	19,593,949	19,050,000
2	Tam Đào	0	204,680	348,340	274,741	143,180	0
3	Cúc Phương	2,624,000	2,176,000	2,574,000	3,393,080	5,561,000	4,000,000
4	Bạch Mã	369,117	580,050	552,050	620,850	860,650	550,000
5	Yok Don	0	0	0	36,900	29,520	0
6	Cát Tiên	652,340	802,040	917,200	1,135,600	1,556,160	1,600,000
	Total	8,579,677	9,010,450	11,951,470	18,470,911	27,744,459	25,200,000

Source: General Administration of Forestry – adapted from Pham, 2018

organizations. Responsibility for ecotourism activities is unclearly regulated owing to the overlapping mandates of the two ministries.

From the viewpoint of a market-based fee payment system, the resources for ecotourism in national parks are undervalued. This is reflected in studies of visitors' willingness to pay, showing that 88.5% of visitors to national parks were willing to pay a higher fee for entering national parks and 74% of visitors at travel agents showed their willingness to do so (Ngo & Pham, 2016). The average level of the fee that tourists were willing to pay was 2.5 times higher than the current prices for entrance. In addition, interviews with park rangers also indicate the possibility of increasing entrance fees. For Cuc Phuong National Park, tourists' willingness to pay for entrance fee is about VND 50,000. A higher fee was confirmed among rangers of Cat Tien National Park with visitors' willingness to pay VND 100,000 per visitor. The rangers suggested a two-price system that would apply to foreign and domestic visitors, respectively. The study of visitors' willingness to pay indicates that prices for entrance tickets should be decentralized and that national parks might have the authority to control and change the price for tickets based on seasons and types of visitor groups (Ngo & Pham, 2016).

Ecotourism services

Ecotourism might be viewed as a strategic alliance between tourism and the environment (Buckley, 2004). In Vietnam, ecotourism not only generates additional funds for conservation but also shapes people's attitudes towards the environment and natural resources (Emerton, Bishop, & Thomas, 2006). Despite a general fall in the proportion of state budgets allocated to PAs, revenues from tourism show an increasing trend in national parks (Eagle & Hillel, 2008), however, PAs only capture little of the economic benefit generated by tourism (Emerton, Bishop, & Thomas, 2006). The contribution of ecotourism to the funding of PAs is rather limited owing to the fact that park administrators cannot capture more revenue from tourists beyond entrance fees, owing to issues in the legal and institutional framework in relation to ecotourism in national parks.

In regard to the legal framework for ecotourism development in protect areas, Article 16 of Decision 08/2001/QD-TTG (The Prime Minister of the Government, 2001) states that protected area management boards can organize, lease out or contract the provision of ecotourism services and facilities to organizations, households, and individuals in compliance with existing financial management regulations and subject to a majority of earnings being reinvested in managing, protecting, and developing the protected area (ICEM, 2003). In addition, Decision 104/2007/QD-BNN (The Ministry of Agriculture and Rural Development, 2007) stipulates that management of ecotourism activities in national parks and on nature reserves includes three forms of businesses: (1) self-organization of ecotourism business by the management board of the parks; (2) private sector investment in ecotourism in national parks; and (3) public-private partnerships, i.e. joint ventures for ecotourism initiatives (Pham, 2016). In six national parks under the direct management of MARD, revenue from self-managed ecotourism services is around VND 4 billion, which contributes 2.3% of total park revenue (see Table 4.1). Leasing land and equipment was implemented in three national parks, which generated limited income. Joint ventures only exist on paper and have not yet been established in any of the national parks (Pham, 2016). Similar to the mechanism of income generation through entrance tickets, ecotourism services have yet to be successful in attracting different economic sectors' participation. A recent study reveals a significant difference between MARD-managed and provincially managed national parks with respect to revenues from forest environmental services, with the former reporting higher revenues from PFES than the latter (Le, Markowski, & Bartos, 2018). However, no statistically significant difference was found between the two groups with respect to revenues from tourism activities.

Slowness in adaptation to market demand in national parks can be explained from a park management perspective. The Vietnamese national park management lacks experience in managing tourism in the park, especially after the decentralization of power to lower levels of government (Suntikul, Butler, & Airey, 2010). Despite the Ministry of Agriculture and Rural Development and/ or Provincial People's Committee taking on the responsibility for the management of national parks directly, they do not participate in the daily operational management of the parks. This task is delegated to the national park management board, a state-owned organization, which has the functions and tasks of forest owners and the state-assured conditions for managing, protecting, and developing the PAs. This unit conducts and manages tourism business in parks via a sub-unit – the Tourism Management Unit. In some popular tourist sites, such as Phong Nha-Ke Bang, major stakeholders make decisions on the management effectiveness of park tourism/recreation businesses including the national park management board, the Tourism Management Unit, and a private company (Ly & Xiao, 2016). However, this co-management model might not be applicable to all national parks, particularly the provincially managed parks.

Even though a number of national parks and nature reserves have ecotourism development plans (e.g. Con Dao, Phong Nha-Ke Bang, Bidoup-Nui Ba, Yok Don, Cuc Phuong, Cat Tien, and Ba Vi), these plans cannot be fully implemented due to shortages of human resources, such as technical staff on ecotourism, to meet the requirements of operating professional tourism activities. In addition, there are no quality standards in terms of infrastructure, technical facilities, and services for tourism in order to be able to meet the standard requirements of ecotourists. Shortages of investment in information and promotion result in a lack of unified and synchronous information systems linking all national parks and nature reserves to tourist centres. International travel companies have limited access to information on the ecotourism potential of national parks and nature reserves for large numbers of tourists, both domestic and international.

Protected areas face limitations and challenges from both the supply and the demand side. Visitors to national parks and nature reserves in Vietnam are unevenly distributed between and within the parks; they are mostly domestic (Buckley, 2004), including students on school outings who travel to national parks in Vietnam either on day trips or trips that last two days and one night, concentrating in areas with good infrastructure and easy access (Pham, 2016). Despite having great potential for more diversified activities, areas with greater biodiversity or unique scenery are unable to attract visitors to stay longer in the national parks. To fulfil the financial quotas required by the central government, national parks need to generate income from selling tickets in order to maintain their current management teams. In this case, economic benefits seem to overshadow ecological considerations with issues related to carrying capacity likely to be neglected (Ly & Nguyen, 2017).

Discussion and conclusion

Our research analysed the economic contribution of ecotourism to the finances of PAs in Vietnam. The development of 'innovative' financing mechanisms from ecotourism, such as PFES, in addition to 'traditional' forms of financing, for example, entrance fees and ecotourism services, is expected to increase funding for PAs in biodiversity conservation and generate financial and economic incentives for local communities (USAID, 2013). Having compared revenues from three options for financing PAs from ecotourism, dissonance exists in the design and implementation of all three options of PFES, entrance fees, and ecotourism services. First, although all three forms of ecotourism-driven financing are designed as market-based options, the government defines the payment framework, regulates the payment mechanisms, decides on the types of services, identifies the buyers and sellers, and ensures that the 'transaction' or the payment occurs. This top-down, centrally planned approach to PFES, in particular, is in sharp contrast with the neoliberal approaches in their use of market instruments (McElwee, 2012). The dissonance in Vietnam's PFES program design and implementation is driven primarily by the Vietnamese government to justify its goals of increasing revenue as a means of financing forest protection, thus enabling the state to sustain and expand its role and importance in natural resource management (To et al., 2012).

While ecotourism may have served as a mechanism to reduce state budget burdens in the forestry sector, its contribution to forest protection might be limited owing to issues of forest governance. This is because state structures in developing countries often have weak resource governance, high transaction costs, and information problems. Governance of entrance fees and ecotourism services functions on the principles of a centrally planned economy, where fees are fixed for all national parks and the management unit for ecotourism is a state-owned organization. Private sector participation in ecotourism management in national parks is limited, as discussed by Suntikul et al., (2010). Similar to PFES, entrance fees are strictly controlled by government and 20% of the revenue from this source is to be collected for the state budget. The fixed price system disregards visitors' willingness to pay more, thus leading to inefficient and insufficient generation of funds.

Ecotourism in Vietnam aims at maximizing economic benefits driven by large-scale tourism at the expense of environmental and social sustainability (Ngo & Pham, 2016), which stands in contrast to the conventional understanding of ecotourism as being alternative, and small-scale, with an emphasis on environmental protection (Duffy, 2013). Low prices for entrance tickets makes ecotourism in this context affordable for various social groups, as well as to those with social disadvantages such as students and seniors, thus fulfilling the social objectives of making natural sites accessible to all social classes. However, the low-price entrance policy conflicts with the goal of maximizing revenue in order to ensure economic sustainability. Therefore, in order to reach the target revenue planned by government, national parks have only got one option: to allow unrestricted numbers of visitors in, without consideration for carrying capacity (Ly & Nguyen, 2017). In addition, a lack of high-quality tourism services and relevant interpretation, above all in more international languages, are major reasons for the failure to attract international visitors to national parks in Vietnam.

Having analysed the economic contribution of ecotourism to sustainable financing of PAs in Vietnam, the authors of this study conclude that the economic outcome of ecotourism does not match its potential. Limitations such as an inadequate legal and institutional framework for resource management impede the development of alternative mechanisms for financing PAs, which reflects a transitional period from a centrally planned economy to a market-based economy (Suhardiman et al., 2013). The development of ecotourism in national parks in Vietnam requires radical changes in management structure. More importantly, awareness of ecotourism as a tool for biodiversity protection should be promoted as a replacement for the conventional and current view of ecotourism as an economic tool. If not, promoting ecotourism services will simply impose more stressors on current PAs in Vietnam without fulfilling the objective of having ecotourism bring innovative sources of financing for PAs.

References

Arndt, C., Garcia, A., Tarp, F., & Thurlow, J. (2012). Poverty reduction and economic structure: Comparative path analysis for Mozambique and Vietnam. *Review of Income and Wealth* 58(4), 742–763.

Berghöfer, A., Emerton, L., Moreno Diaz, A., Rode, J., Schröter-Schlaack, C., Wittmer, H., & van Zyl, H. (2017). *Sustainable financing for biodiversity conservation – a review of experiences in German development cooperation*. Study commissioned by GIZ and KfW. Leipzig, Germany.

Buckley, R. (2004). Ecotourism planning and destination management in Vietnam. In D. Diamantis (Ed.) *Ecotourism: Management and assessment* (pp. 313–322). London: Thompson.

Buckley, R. (1999) Planning for a national ecotourism strategy in Vietnam. Workshop on development of a national ecotourism strategy for Vietnam. Hanoi: Vietnam

Duffy, R. (2013). *A trip too far: Ecotourism, politics and exploitation*. Abingdon: Routledge.

Eagles, P., & Hillel, O. (2008). Improving protected area finance through tourism. Paper presented in Second meeting of the ad hoc open-ended working Group on Protected Areas (WGPA-2), Rome, Italy.

Emerton, L., Bishop, J., & Thomas, L. (2006). *Sustainable financing of protected areas: A global review of challenges and options*. Gland; Cambridge: IUCN.

Emerton, L., Pham, X.P., & Ha, T.M. (2011). *PA Financing mechanism in Vietnam: Lessons learned and future direction*. Hanoi: GIZ

Engel, S., Pagiola, S., & Wunder, S. (2008). Designing payments for environmental services in theory and practice: An overview of the issues. *Ecological economics* 65(4), 663–674.

GIZ (2012). *A policy brief for payment for environmental services in tourism*. Hanoi: GIZ.

ICEM (2003). *Vietnam national report on protected areas and development. Review of protected areas and development in the Lower Mekong River Region*. Indooroopilly: ICEM.

Le, A.T., Markowski, J., & Bartos, M. (2018). The comparative analyses of selected aspects of conservation and management of Vietnam's national parks. *Nature Conservation* 25, 1–30.

Ly, T.P., & Nguyen, T.H.H. (2017). Application of carrying capacity management in Vietnamese national parks. *Asia Pacific Journal of Tourism Research* 22(10), 1005–1020.

Ly, T.P., & Xiao, H. (2016). An innovative model of park governance: Evidence from Vietnam. *Journal of Ecotourism* 15(2), 99–121.

McElwee, P.D. (2012). Payments for environmental services as neoliberal market-based forest conservation in Vietnam: Panacea or problem? *Geoforum* 43(3), 412–426.

Ngo, A.T., & Pham, H.L. (2016). *Research on financial mechanism for entrance ticket and pays for forest environmental services in national parks and special use forest* (unpublished report). Hanoi: General Administration of Forestry and GIZ.

Pham, L.H. (2018). Payments for forest environmental services in Vietnam: Situation and solution. *Tạp chí Khoa học và Công nghệ Lâm nghiệp số* 1/2018, pp. 198–202.

Pham, L.H. (2016). Sustainable ecotourism development in protected areas and national parks in Vietnam. *International Conference: Sustainable Tourism Development: The Role of Government, Business and Educational Institution* (pp. 117–132). Hanoi: National Economic University Press.

Prime Minister's Office (2007). *Strategy for forest development 2006–2020*. Hanoi: Vietnam.

Suhardiman, D., Wichelns, D., Lestrelin, G., & Hoanh, C.T. (2013). Payments for ecosystem services in Vietnam: Market-based incentives or state control of resources? *Ecosystem Services* 5, 94–101.

Suntikul, W., Butler, R., & Airey, D. (2010). Implications of political change on national park operations: Doi Moi and tourism to Vietnam's national parks. *Journal of Ecotourism* 9(3), 201–218.

The Government (2010). Decree 99/2010/ND-CP on the policy on payment for forest environmental services (dated Sep. 24, 2010). Retrieved from: https://vanbanphaplua t.co/decree-147-2016-nd-cp-amending-99-2010-nd-cp-policy-payment-of-forest-envir onment-service-charge.

The Ministry of Agriculture and Rural Development (2007). Decision 104/2007/QD-BNN promulgating the regulation on management of ecotourism activities in national parks and nature reserves. Retrieved from: https://thuvienphapluat.vn/van-ban/Thuong-mai/Quyet-dinh-104-2007-QD-BNN-quy-che-quan-ly-hoat-dong-du-lich-sinh-thai-vuon-quoc-gia-khu-bao-ton-thien-nhien-61422.aspx.

The Prime Minister of the Government (2008). Decision 380/QD-TTg on the pilot policy on forest environment service charge payment (dated Apr. 10, 2008). Retrieved from: https://vanbanphapluat.co/quyet-dinh-380-qd-ttg-chinh-sach-thi-diem-chi-tra-dich-vu-moi-truong-rung.

The Prime Minister of the Government (2001). Decision 08/2001/QD-TTG on the regulation on management of special-use forest, protection forests and production forest (dated Dec. 27, 2007). Retrieved from: https://vanbanphapluat.co/08-2001-qd-ttg.

To, P.X., Dressler, W.H., Mahanty, S., Pham, T.T., & Zingerli, C. (2012). The prospects for payment for ecosystem services (PES) in Vietnam: A look at three payment schemes. *Human Ecology* 40(2), 237–249.

Tran, L., & Walter, P. (2014). Ecotourism, gender and development in northern Vietnam. *Annals of Tourism Research* 44, 116–130.

USAID. (2013). *Vietnam tropical forest and biodiversity assessment: US Foreign Assistance Act, Section 118–119- Report*. Aug. 2013.

Vatn, A. (2010). An institutional analysis of payments for environmental services. *Ecological Economics* 60, 1245–1252.

Wunder, S. (2005). Payments for environmental services: Some nuts and bolts. CIFOR Occasional Paper No. 42. Bogor: Center for International Forestry Research.

5 Searching for sustainable tourism in Malaysia

Can Langkawi Geopark rangers offer improved stewardship?

Thomas E. Jones and Natalia B.M.T. Syura

Introduction

This chapter investigates sustainable tourism in Malaysia via a case study of stewardship in Malaysia's Langkawi archipelago. Few destinations better epitomize the meteoric rise of tourism in Southeast Asia, or the challenges that coastal resorts face in coping with unprecedented visitation. Ineffective management has led to a wide-ranging lack of environmental sustainability, or even the abrupt closure of specific island destinations such as Boracay (the Philippines) and Maya Bay on Ko Phi Phi Leh (Thailand). Yet the growth in international tourism has continued to surpass that of trade, so that by 2017 the sector accounted for 7% of global exports in goods and services (UNWTO, 2017). Much of that growth has occurred in the Asia-Pacific region, which experienced the largest increase in international arrivals in 2016, including regional growth of 5% in tourism expenditure to account for 30% of global receipts. Of the 308 million Asia-Pacific tourist arrivals in 2016, a 9% increase was recorded in Southeast Asia, a region rich in islands and coastline attractions (ibid, p. 7). Concurrent with the expansion of international tourism, there has been a steady increase in visitation to natural destinations such as nature reserves and national parks (Boo, 1999; Tisdell & Wilson, 2012). The combined increase in visitor demand and destination vulnerability means that better stewardship is needed to mitigate the environmental impact in search of the oftentimes elusive goal of 'sustainable tourism'.

Malaysia is a tourism trailblazer in Southeast Asia, with a Tourism Development Plan that dates back to 1975 and a series of successful national strategies such as the 'Malaysia, Truly Asia' brand (Bouchon, 2014). The early establishment of dedicated governmental agencies and funding for tourism saw Malaysia join the top 10 most-visited countries in the world by 2012 with 25 million international arrivals and US$25 billion tourism receipts (Figure 5.1). This chapter contextualizes this growth path via the case study of Langkawi, a tropical archipelago near the Thai border whose fortunes were reversed by the establishment of the Langkawi Development Authority (LADA) and extensive infrastructure investment. Over three decades, Langkawi transformed from a sleepy group of fishing islands to hosting over 3.5 million tourist arrivals per

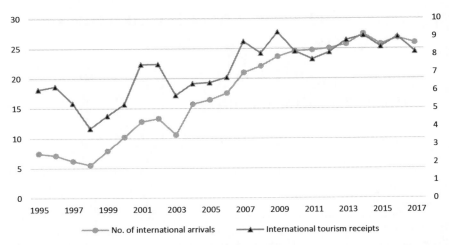

Figure 5.1 Number of Malaysia's international arrivals (millions) and international
tourism receipts (US$ billions) 1995–2017
Source: UNWTO, 2017

annum. Yet, tourism's rise has come with growing recognition of negative socioeconomic and especially environmental impacts (Lee, 2013). Various counter-
strategies have sought to realign the islands' rapid development along a more
sustainable trajectory, typified by Langkawi's inscription as the first geopark in
Southeast Asia in 2007. Although UNESCO has no direct mandate over inscribed territories, the geopark listing process coincides with a broad range of sustainability indicators and objectives (Farsani, Coelho, & Costa, 2012). In response
to specific comments made by geopark inspectors, an inaugural ranger unit was
established within LADA's Geopark Division in 2012 to bolster on-site stewardship. The new system offers insights into attempts to use the geopark as a tool for
improved visitor management, but despite the crucial role for field stewards, few
prior studies have investigated the role of rangers as mediators (Usui , Sheeran, Li,
Sun, Wang, Pritchard, DuVall-Lash, & Wagner, 2014). The principal aim of this
chapter is to investigate Langkawi Geopark rangers' stewardship as a proxy for
efforts to make tourism more sustainable on the islands. Having reflected on
trends in tourism development, primary data is utilized from two interviews conducted on 28th November 2012 with LADA and the Malaysian Nature Society.
These were triangulated with monthly ranger reports from January 2013 to July
2013 to identify obstacles and opportunities for sustainable tourism in Langkawi.

The search for sustainable tourism

There is a lack of empirical studies surrounding the parameters of sustainable
tourism and its relationship with sustainable development – a normative set

of planning ethics that hark back to the Brundtland Report (WCED, 1987). Despite suffering from a 'lack of operational clarity' (Weaver, 2012, p. 1030), it was a similar intergenerational definition (i.e. equity for people now and in the future) that underpinned the conceptual basis of the UN's Sustainable Development Goals (SDGs), introduced in 2015 to extend the Millennium Development Goals. Like sustainable tourism, the SDGs call for collective action and systemic change (Bramwell, Higham, Lane, & Miller, 2017). However, both concepts also stand accused of 'greenwashing' or the ineffective implementation that occurs when unsubstantiated or misleading claims are made about the sustainability of a product, service, or practice (Lee, 2013).

Greenwashing's prevalence derives from the fact that sustainable tourism – like the SDGs' ideology – has ballooned into a set of all-encompassing indicators in the quest for a comprehensive 'triple-bottom line' approach that tackles economic, environmental, and socio-cultural impacts holistically. Weaver (2012) actively employs this triple framework, together with a cost-benefit rationale, as the basis for a revised definition which recognizes the steady, exponential rise of the global travel industry in recent decades. His discussion hinges on the feasibility of making mass tourism more sustainable, and to that end, Weaver pragmatically juxtaposes the concept's widespread acceptance within the concurrent neoliberal economic growth paradigm to propose new models of sustainable mass tourism (SMT).

Although SMT captures the aspirational convergence of mass tourism with sustainability, many researchers refute its inherent feasibility. Peeters (2012) claims that tourism inevitably reverts to unsustainable paths, noting that the remote location of exotic destinations such as Antarctica and the Galapagos inadvertently attracts disproportionately large carbon footprints. This recalls a fundamental criticism even of promising concepts such as ecotourism that the involvement of specific travel segments, such as long-haul travel to Global South destinations, or travel modes, such as cruise ships, score low for sustainability in terms of greenhouse gas emissions (Eijgelaar, Thaper, & Peeters, 2010). Beyond the lack of conceptual consensus, Weaver's (2012) SMT-revised version of Butler's life cycle model was drawn from a purposive sample that leaves considerable room for empirical evidence. Systematically testing proposed paths of 'organic', 'incremental' and 'induced' development – and how they converge toward SMT – thus requires practical applications via case studies that can holistically explore the evolution of a destination and examine the site-specific suitability of 'weaker' or 'stronger' scales of sustainability (Hunter, 1997). This leads to the question of whether rangers can inspire improved stewardship to mitigate mass tourism's environmental impacts. The next section tackles that gap in the literature via an empirical analysis of the drive to make tourism more sustainable in Malaysia's Langkawi archipelago.

Tourism trends in Malaysia and Langkawi

By 2018, the Malaysian economy ranked third largest in Southeast Asia after the city-states of Singapore and Brunei with tourism among the key economic drivers (IMF, 2018). Overseas arrivals increased from 10.2 million in 2000 to 16.4 million in 2005, following the launch in 1999 of a global branding campaign entitled 'Malaysia, Truly Asia'. Tourism became Malaysia's third largest source of income from foreign exchange, accounting for 7% of GDP. Growth remained robust throughout the 2000s apart from a decline in 2003 due to the SARS virus outbreak. The number of arrivals and tourist receipts in 2000 were 10.2 million and US$4.6 billion, respectively, but by 2014 records showed 27.4 million arrivals and US$27.8 billion in receipts, an annual growth rate of 9% and 15%, respectively (Habibi & Ahmadzadeh, 2015). In 2012, Malaysia already ranked within the 10 most visited countries in the world with 25 million international tourist arrivals and US$25 billion tourism receipts accounting for over 8% of total exports (Figure 5.1).

Today, tourism remains a pillar of Malaysia's long-standing policy objective to reach 'developed nation' status by 2020 (Henderson, 2008). However, since 2011 the growth in international arrivals has stagnated, raising questions over the sector's long-term economic sustainability. Meanwhile tourism's environmental cost has also become clearer, especially when islands' or coastal resorts' combination of sandy beaches and coral reefs have suddenly been made more accessible to large numbers of tourists. Infrastructure mega-projects coupled with 'unplanned and spontaneous development' (Wong, 1998, p. 91) invite impacts including deforestation, strip-ribbon development, wetland reclamation or conversion into open sewers, water pollution and inadequate waste-water treatment, damage to coral reefs and beaches due to boat haulage, coastal pollution, illegal dumping of solid waste and littering (Wong, 1998). On Langkawi, Lee (2013) noted three specific negative socio-environmental impacts related to the rapid rise in visitors:

   (i) Kilim Karst Geoforest faces increasing numbers of motorized tour boats resulting in air, water and noise pollution, and damage to the mangroves caused by the boats' wash;
  (ii) the Bat Cave faces (un)intentional damage to stalagmites, limestone removed as souvenirs, noise and flash photography that disturbs the bats; and
 (iii) the feeding of Macaque monkeys encourages habituation and dependence.

The human-wildlife conflict is symbolic of wider issues as Macaques learn to snatch visitors' plastic bags in search of food and drink, resulting in more aggressive behaviour from monkeys and landscape degradation due to littering. Yet some research suggests that such issues could be mediated by an on-site presence of park rangers (Usui et al., 2014), as will now be examined through the case study of improved stewardship at the Langkawi Geopark.

Langkawi case study

The Federation of Malaysia comprises two states on the eastern island of Borneo and 11 on the peninsula. Langkawi is a cluster of islands situated in the Straits of Malacca, 51km west of the mainland. Its location at the north of the peninsula near the Thai border underpins its image as the 'jewel of Kedah' state. The archipelago has a tropical climate with an average daytime temperature of 32 degrees Celsius, and despite a rainy season during August and September, it attracts visitors all year round. The combined islands' land mass is 47,848 hectares, while the main island covers 32,000 hectares that span about 25km from north to south and slightly more from east to west.

Only four of the archipelagos are inhabited – the main island (Pulau Langkawi), Tuba, Rebak, and Dayang Bunting. The national census recorded a population of 73,091 in 2001, but the number of residents had increased to 86,125 by 2005, and to 99,841 in 2010 (Figure 5.2). Of that population, 90% are Malays and the other ethnic groups consist mainly of Chinese, Indians and Thais. The highest population density is in Kuah Town, followed by Padang Mat Sirat and Padang Lalang. The rest of the population is distributed in smaller villages with fewer than 200 households (Mohammed et al., 2010). Prior to tourism development, Langkawi islands had an agro-based economy of paddy and rubber cultivation and fisheries, ranking amongst the region's least developed districts (Din, 1990, cited in Omar, Othman, & Mohamed, 2014).

From an isolated economic backwater, Langkawi's socioeconomic fortunes have been reversed by a series of infrastructure mega-projects including the construction of a cargo jetty (1982), an international airport (1985), and a ferry terminal (1988) (Omar et al., 2014). Selected as a 'regional champion' for tourism development, Langkawi's jurisdictional status as a district in the state of Kedah helped open a direct line to federal public works projects thanks to Mahathir bin Mohamad. Elected for the Langkawi constituency, he served as Prime Minister of Malaysia from 1981 until his retirement in 2003 (and returned to office in 2018), becoming the world's longest-serving elected leader. Under his leadership, Langkawi was declared a 'duty-free island' in 1987 luring large numbers of domestic shoppers. The establishment of LADA in 1990 under the Ministry of Finance channelled further federal development aid to the archipelago, transforming Langkawi into one of Malaysia's most popular destinations (LADA, 2011). The number of annual visitors by air and sea subsequently increased to over 3.5 million in 2013, outnumbering the population of permanent residents on the archipelago (Figure 5.2) by a ratio of 35:1.

In 2018, 86% of the 3.6 million visitors were domestic, with almost 2 million (55%) arriving by sea. In terms of the market breakdown, Langkawi echoes national-level tourism trends, wherein most international visitors to Malaysia originate from within Asia, especially neighbouring Singapore, with an increase in visitors from the Middle East (Henderson, 2008). The dominant domestic market relishes Langkawi's image as a duty-free haven, hence

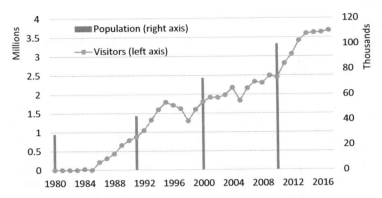

Figure 5.2 Registered resident population and number of visitors to Langkawi 1980–2017

Source: Registered resident population – adapted from Omar, Othman, & Mohamad, 2014, and number of visitors of Langkawi – adapted from Langkawi Development Authority (LADA), 2018

Malaysian tourists rush to shop for chocolates, cosmetics, liquor and tobacco. Popular activities likewise tend to cater for more sedentary lifestyles, with attractions such as aquariums, wildlife parks, golf courses and a cable car, although generic 'mass tourism' has diversified into niches such as yachting and endurance sports, including 'iron man' and triathlon events. Evidence of the economic impact is clear both at the archipelago level, where tourism accounts for 30% of direct employment, and the state level, with Kedah ranking high among the number of overnight hotel stays (Omar et al., 2014).

Beyond infrastructure development, the increase in visitors to Langkawi was driven by a range of marketing campaigns such as the national 'Visit Malaysia' years (1990; 1994; 2007; 2014). The archipelago was also promoted vigorously as a 'duty-free island' (1987) and a 'Tourism City' (2001). These were gradually phased out in favour of 'greener' alternatives such as 'Langkawi Geopark' (2007) and 'Naturally Langkawi' (2012), which remain the contemporary banners of choice. As the shift in brand rhetoric suggests, the search for sustainability has become an increasing priority, culminating in Langkawi's listing as a geopark in 2007.

Global Geoparks Network: A platform for sustainable tourism?

Geoparks were first established in Europe in the 1990s, but by 2018 the list had grown globally to incorporate 127 geoparks in 35 countries. The network was ratified as a UNESCO programme in 2015 in recognition of its rapid spread across Europe and Northeast Asia, notably China and Japan. Earlier, stricter definitions of 'geological tourism' (Hose, 1995) were broadened to include diverse 'geotourism' activities themed around an appreciation of earth sciences achieved through visits to geological features, use of geo-trails and view-points, guided tours, geo-activities, and visitor centres (Newsome & Dowling, 2010). Importantly for this chapter, the listed status as a geopark thus denotes many of the core aspirations of sustainable tourism such as conservation of geological, ecological, archaeological, and cultural heritage sites together with visitor management, and the creation of job opportunities and additional revenue streams for local communities (Farsani, Coelho, & Costa, 2012).

Going green? Langkawi Geopark

Tourism has become one of the major drivers of socioeconomic and cultural change in Southeast Asia, and few destinations epitomize the transformation better than Langkawi, with 3.6 million annual visitors and a 23-fold increase in the built-up area in recent decades. Fragile island environments are especially susceptible to tourism impacts, and one body of research has sought mitigation via restricting visitor activities or limiting numbers (Manning, Valliere, Wang, & Jacobi, 1999). However, the history of state-sponsored development of regional champion destinations like Langkawi effectively negates the feasibility of implementing strict limits on visitor numbers.

Instead, Langkawi was listed in 2007 as Southeast Asia's inaugural geopark, Malaysia's first – and to date still the only – representative on UNESCO's list. Although the geopark area covers the entire archipelago, the focus is on three geoforests that showcase the three dominant rock formations of sandstone (Machinchang Cambrian), limestone karst (Kilim Karst), and marble (Dayang Bunting), together with 97 sites of special geological interest. Langkawi's coastal areas comprise flat, alluvial plains punctuated with limestone karst, one of the three distinct rock formations that support a unique mangrove ecosystem, typified by the Kilim Geoforest that formed some 450–390 million years ago. Diverse flora and fauna include more than 500 species of butterflies and 226 species of birds, with three endemics such as the Brown Winged Kingfisher. Langkawi is also home to some 80 mammals, including iconic species such as the dusky leaf monkey, flying lemurs, and slow loris. The Machinchang rock formation has been dated to approximately 550 million years ago, making it one of Malaysia's oldest tropical forests (Mohammed et al, 2010).

However, due to the speed and scale of the aforementioned tourism development, various environmental impacts have emerged, such as air and water pollution along with deforestation. Omar et al. (2014) report an increase in residential and urban built-up areas on Langkawi from 133 hectares in 1974 to 3,137 hectares in 2005, a 23-fold increase. Rapid unplanned development and land clearing has fragmented the island's forests, threatening biodiversity. Meanwhile land reclamation, water pollution, and soil erosion have occurred along coastline plots developed for beachside accommodation. Unsustainable tourism practices are commonplace, exemplified by boat and jet ski tours that speed through the mangroves, or visitors feeding the eagles in order to secure a better photograph (Lee, 2013).

In response to a geopark evaluation report, a new ranger unit was established within LADA's Geopark Division in 2012 to rein in unsustainable tourism. Effective visitor management is vital both for conservation and to maintain basic facilities – two important roles of rangers. As field stewards, they fulfil a variety of tasks, deterring inappropriate behaviour and enforcing the law where required (Newsome, Moore, & Dowling, 2013). Rangers are not limited to conservation but cover roles ranging from police, fire fighting, search and rescue, education, and interpretation of natural and cultural heritage. Some rangers have specific skills such as protecting tourists from aggressive wildlife, for example 'prohibiting tourists from feeding monkeys, resulting in a reduction of tourist-macaque conflict' (Usui et al., 2014, p. 548). Despite their potential, the fledgling system of rangers at Langkawi has yet to be evaluated for on-site stewardship. The next section investigates the set-up of this new system to ascertain whether it can mitigate some of the negative impacts of mass tourism.

Langkawi Geopark rangers

A Ranger unit was established within LADA's Geopark Division in 2012 with the inaugural batch comprised mostly of high school graduates with an age range of 19–27 years. Interviews with management suggested little prior specialization in ranger-related majors such as conservation biology. Most were 'freshmen' hired without previous experience in parks or visitor management, although on-the-job training was accompanied by bi-annual training workshops conducted at national parks across Malaysia. The recruitment process favoured younger rangers due to their enthusiasm and perceived ability to acquire new skills. Nonetheless, the park/farm assistant monthly salary grade G17 is equivalent to US$470, increasing to US$670 with overtime, comparatively higher than for other high school leavers without a tertiary degree (Syura, 2013). Focusing on the three geoforest sites, ranger records revealed that daily duties revolve around monitoring and patrolling, helping tourists in case of a search and rescue or other emergency, for example administering first aid for monkey bites.

Monthly reports were compiled from a six-month logbook sample of rangers' reports on damage, accidents and incidents, minor maintenance, and conservation activities (Table 5.1). The reports also include the weekly number of tourist arrivals and a summary of ranger responses. Results show that damage reports appear most frequently among the monthly log. For example, a total of 22 damage reports were recorded at the Dayang Bunting Geoforest (January–July 2013) mostly relating to rotten signboards, or damage due to wildlife, especially monkeys. Machinchang Geoforest had 18 reports, mostly related to dysfunctional toilets and fallen trees that damaged the roofs of a prayer room and rest house. Kilim Karst Geoforest had 14 damage reports related to rusty stairs climbing up from the jetty to the bat cave. The second most frequent category was minor maintenance reports,

Table 5.1 Telaga Tujuh Waterfalls (Machinchang Geoforest) ranger report Q1 & Q2 2013

	January	February	March	April	May	June	July	Total
Damage report	5	3	1	3	1	3	2	18
Emergency/accident report	1	0	0	0	0	0	0	1
Minor maintenance report	3	1	1	0	0	1	0	6
Conservation report	0	0	0	0	0	0	0	0
Tourist arrivals per month	5,500	2,113	8,562	7,542	7,764	7,542	N/A	39,023
Number of photos	18	5	10	7	2	9	11	62

Source: Rangers' report adapted by authors from LADA logbook

especially at Machinchang (n=6). Kilim Karst (n=5) referred to mangrove clean-up area activities, while Dayang Bunting (n=2) reported the removal of fallen trees and trail clean-up. There were comparatively few entries in the conservation or emergency/accident categories, although one report mentioned the theft of visitors' luggage near Telaga Tujuh Waterfalls in Machinchang. The reports also included photos taken by rangers as visual evidence of unsustainable behaviour such as jet ski tours of the mangroves (Figure 5.3), although no mention was made of efforts to intervene or administer a warning to rule-breakers.

Can geopark rangers offer improved stewardship?

The review of the new rangers system has highlighted three categories of potential obstacles, related to i) human resources and job conditions; ii) ranger activities; and iii) inter-organizational collaboration. These three issues will now be addressed in turn.

First, as described above, the inaugural crop of rangers are mostly high school graduates without specific qualifications or nature park experience (Syura, 2013). The financial constraints that prevent hiring additional rangers, or more experienced ones, are not unique to Malaysia (Usui et al., 2014). However, specific human resource restraints revealed by interviewees include a lack of incentives or long-term career prospects, as rangers are employed under short-term contracts that are renewed at the end of each year dependent on a performance evaluation. This undermines their motivation and organizational capacity to fulfil the three core objectives of patrolling,

Figure 5.3 Jet ski tours of the mangroves at Kilim Karst Geoforest
Source: Authors' photo

maintenance and conservation that comprise the next set of potential obstacles. Based on analysis of the monthly logbooks, the bulk of the rangers' fieldwork comprises patrolling and reporting the observations with little evidence of pro-active conservation. Unlike the geopark evaluation dossier, rangers' logbooks display little evidence of programmes to raise the awareness of tourists, school children or local residents. Clear incentives could inspire behavioural change, as for example, at Chumbe Island Coral Park. In Zanzibar local fishermen have been re-trained as rangers to provide environmental education for local schools (Dodds, 2012). The lack of a Langkawi equivalent is partly due to reporting problems or to different definitions of 'conservation', because there is evidence on the website that such programmes do exist. The third core objective of the new system was defined as maintenance. Evidence from the monthly reports shows the urgent need for maintenance of damaged pontoons, toilets, rooftops and signs due to a combination of visitor use and climatic conditions leading to fallen trees, amongst other issues. However, despite frequent reports of damaged infrastructure, there is not always evidence of responses taken by the Geopark Division.

The lack of concrete action hints at a third issue – inter-organizational colla-boration. Although the new rangers are employed by LADA, they also conduct vital on-site monitoring as 'the eyes and ears' for other state agencies. However, despite the rangers' regular patrols, effective responses by other relevant agencies such as the Forestry Office or police were largely conspicuous in their absence in the reports. This could reflect a time-lag between reporting and action, or it could suggest a lack of communication between the rangers and the LADA office staff, or with other government agencies. Such inter-organizational colla-boration is essential because unlike at national parks such as Royal Belum, for example, the Langkawi rangers lack any special legal jurisdiction such as the authority to carry weapons to deter poachers or other lawbreakers (Syura, 2013). Poaching remains an issue in Malaysia's protected areas as demonstrated by a 2009 article in The Star reporting that rangers in the Belum-Temengor Forest arrested 10 poachers and removed 102 snares (Foong, 2009, cited in Syura, 2013). To implement meaningful conservation policies, partnerships among various government and NGO actors must therefore be facilitated. The new rangers could encourage the collaboration needed to 'enforce related legisla-tion' across diverse actors. For example, within central government agencies alone the list includes *Jabatan Perhilitan* (Department of Wildlife & National Parks); *Jabatan Perhutanan* (Forestry Department); *Jabatan Pengairan dan Saliran* (Department of Irrigation and Drainage) and *Jabatan Laut* (Marine Department) (Syura, 2013).

From 'greenwashing' to sustainable tourism?

Training programmes and workshops are one option to tackle obstacles rela-ted to the first issue – ranger personnel and job conditions. By offering opportunities to gain better qualifications, this could improve career pro-spects, raise self-esteem, and teach new skills that enable more efficient park management. Bi-annual workshops are currently conducted and could be combined with annual performance evaluations to enhance motivation and performance. The second obstacle concerns organizational capacity. Although the rangers' original objectives were patrols, conservation and maintenance, the monthly reports reveal that the current crop are mostly patrolling, i.e. reporting damage or recommending responses instead of implementing follow-up in line with the latter two missions. Conservation is especially underreported, since interview results suggest that rangers already contribute to environmental education programmes run by the LADA Geopark Division, but such activities should be picked up in the monthly report to encourage formal recognition of their importance. Conservation is a vital part of a ranger's job description and methods of raising public awareness of environmental issues should be more actively pursued. Ideally, rangers could become involved in the provision of geopark themed activities such as mangrove conservation tours, canopy walks, or bird watching. More adventurous visitor segments could select mangrove safaris, rock climbing, geological exploration, or cycle tours. However, visitor education is also paramount in reducing their impact, hence targeted communication programmes should be integrated with tourism programmes.

Current responses seem to be typified by an incident involving macaque monkeys in Dayang Bunting. After the ranger radioed in a call for assistance, the Forestry and Wildlife Department promptly set up a trap to relocate and reduce the number of monkeys disturbing the tourists (Syura, 2013). With better training, more appropriate mediation of visitor-wildlife interactions could be achieved, as in other wildlife tourism hotspots where rangers physically and/or vocally direct tourist-macaque interactions, using warning sounds or gestures to ward off unruly macaques (Usui et al., 2014). However, content analysis of the Langkawi reports revealed scant evidence of rangers having resolved the other two issues mentioned by Lee (2013), i.e. mangrove jet ski tours and eagle-feeding. In fact, a separate paper recently confirmed that wakes from boats and jet skis continue to erode the mangroves, while LADA were rebuked by guides and rangers omitted altogether (Thompson, Gillen, & Friess, 2018). Hence the spectre of greenwashing continues to loom large on the archipelago, questioning the environmental friendliness of tourism, especially as the UNESCO team of inspectors considered a yellow card verdict prior to the 2015 renewal of Langkawi's Global Geopark status (Tyler, 2014).

The third obstacle relates to inter-agency collaboration, with improved communication between agencies to safeguard the rangers' role as effective facilitators. As mentioned above, clear reporting from rangers can form the basis of a prioritized response. Better communication channels also improve relationships between government agencies and thereby help streamline the provision of visitor services. The ranger's role should also be extended to include not only government agencies, but also collaboration with non-government organizations and local communities. This will require a broadening and strengthening of budget allocation, with plans to add up to 20 rangers for core monitoring and conservation tasks, bolstered by additional part-time workers during peak seasons (Syura, 2013). One option is to use tourism as a direct financing tool, collecting entrance fees at key geosites to support conservation and maintenance of basic infrastructure. In the longer term, this could be scaled up across the archipelago, with a 'conservation levy' or 'green tax' on all tourists entering Langkawi as in the Galapagos or the Balearic Islands (Aguiló, Riera, & Rosselló, 2005). In this way, more robust cost-recovery mechanisms could help offset the overall stagnation of international arrivals with a shift in policy towards smaller numbers of tourists willing to pay more for conservation.

Conclusion

Rapid growth in Southeast Asia's tourism sector, combined with the vulnerability of destinations such as island or coastal protected areas, have amplified the need to make mass tourism more sustainable by aligning conservation and development goals. This chapter has investigated tourism's rise on Malaysia's Langkawi archipelago, where it has become the core economic sector. Along with investment in infrastructure and accommodation facilities, Langkawi acquired 'duty-free' status in 1987, and following the establishment of LADA in 1990 to fast-track regional development, the number of annual visitors exceeded 3.5 million. This increase was nurtured by marketing campaigns that gradually acquired a 'greener' image culminating in Langkawi's listing as the first geopark in Southeast Asia in 2007. The cultivation of Pulau Langkawi's myths and marketing is nothing new (Ling, 2006). However, the shift in slogans, combined with Langkawi's inscription as the first geopark in Southeast Asia, symbolized efforts to realign the islands' rapid development along more sustainable trajectories.

In practical terms, an inaugural ranger unit established within LADA's Geopark Division in 2012 offered an opportunity for targeted intervention to mitigate the negative impact of tourism. However, based on rangers' monthly reports, evidence remains unconvincing of stewardship strategies to tackle the visitor management issues raised by Lee (2013) such as mangrove jet ski tours, eagle-feeding and macaque monkey management. Our case study conceded certain limitations linked to the fledgling nature of the ranger system and the inherent transferability issues that surround single-site case studies. We were also unable to interview rangers directly, but findings did draw on primary data from their logbooks and monthly reports. The study therefore contributes to the debate on 'greenwashing', paving the way for follow-up research to gain further insights into the human resource dimension of visitor management at geoparks and other vulnerable destinations which are seeking more sustainable development paths. Strengthened ranger personnel and job conditions, pro-active conservation and improved inter-agency collaboration are seen as the key to a more robust stewardship style that could help make mass tourism more sustainable on Langkawi and across Southeast Asia.

Acknowledgements

This study draws on fieldwork conducted by the author together with Natalia Syura, a Master's student at Meiji University from 2012–2014. Many thanks to the interviewees, also to the reviewers, Dr. A. Chakraborty and RDJ, for their constructive criticism.

References

Aguiló, E., Riera, A. & Rosselló, J. (2005). The short-term price effect of a tourist tax through a dynamic demand model: The case of the Balearic Islands. *Tourism Management* 26(3), 359–365.

Boo, E. (1990). *Ecotourism: The potentials and pitfalls. Vol. 2: Country case studies.* Washington, DC: World Wildlife Fund.

Bouchon, F. (2014). Truly Asia and global city? Branding strategies and contested identities in Kuala Lumpur. *Place Branding & Public Diplomacy* 10(1), 6–18.

Bramwell, B., Higham, J., Lane, B., & Miller, G. (2017). Twenty-five years of sustainable tourism and the Journal of Sustainable Tourism: looking back and moving forward. *Journal of Sustainable Tourism* 25(1), 1–9.

Dodds, R. (2012). Eco-tourism for education and marine conservation: The Chumbe Island Coral Park in Zanzibar. *Téoros* 31(3), 91–97.

Eijgelaar, E., Thaper, C., & Peeters, P. (2010). Antarctic cruise tourism: The paradoxes of ambassadorship, last chance tourism' and greenhouse gas emissions. *Journal of Sustainable Tourism* 18, 337–354.

Farsani, N.T., Coelho, C., & Costa, C. (2012). Geotourism and geoparks as gateways to socio-cultural sustainability in Qeshm Rural Areas, Iran. *Asia Pacific Journal of Tourism Research* 17(1), 30–48.

Habibi, F., & Ahmadzadeh, K. (2015). Tourism development, trade openness and economic growth: The case of Malaysia. *European. Journal of Economics, Finance and Administrative Sciences* 78, 129–139.

Henderson, J.C. (2008). Tourism destination development: The case of Malaysia. *Tourism Recreation Research* 33(1), 49–57.

Hose, T.A. (1995). Selling the story of Britain's stone. *Environmental Interpretation* 10(2), 16–17.

Hunter, C. (1997). Sustainable tourism as an adaptive paradigm. *Annals of Tourism Research* 24, 850–867.

International Monetary Fund (IMF) (2018). World economic outlook. Retrieved from: https://www.imf.org/en/publications/weo.

Langkawi Development Authority (LADA) (2011). *The Langkawi tourism blueprint 2011–2015.* Langkawi: LADA.

Langkawi Development Authority (LADA) (2018). Tourist arrival statistics. Retrieved on Sept. 25, 2019 from: https://www.lada.gov.my/en/information/statistics/tourist-arrival-statistics?style=blue.

Lee, M. (2013). The reality of balancing tourism development and protecting the nature heritage of Langkawi Island, Malaysia. *Journal of Ecotourism* 12(3), 197–203.

Ling, O.G. (2006). Mahsuri's curse – globalisation and tourist development in Pulau Langkawi. *GeoJournal* 66(3), 199–209.

Manning, R., Valliere, W., Wang, B., & Jacobi, C. (1999). Crowding norms: Alternative measurement approaches. *Leisure Sciences* 21(2), 97–115.

Mohammed, S.L., Kamarulzaman, A.G., Ibrahim, K., & Norhayati, A. (2010). *Langkawi Geopark*. Kuala Lumpur: Percetakan Watan Sdn. Bhd.

Newsome, D., Moore, S.A., & Dowling, R.K. (2013). *Natural area tourism, ecology, impact and management* (2nd ed.). Bristol: Channel View.

Newsome, D., & Dowling, R.K. (2010). *Geotourism: the tourism of geology and landscape*. Wallingford: Goodfellow Publishers.

Omar, S.I., Othman, A.G., & Mohamed, B. (2014). The tourism life cycle: An overview of Langkawi Island, Malaysia. *International Journal of Culture, Tourism and Hospitality Research* 8(3), 272–289.

Peeters, P. (2012). A clear path towards sustainable mass tourism? Rejoinder to the paper 'Organic, incremental and induced paths to sustainable mass tourism convergence' by David B. Weaver. *Tourism Management* 33(5), 1038–1041.

Dowling, R.K., & Newsome, D. (2005). *Geotourism*. Oxford: Elsevier.

Syura, N. (2013). *The role of park rangers in visitor management: A case study of rangers at Langkawi Geopark, Malaysia*. Unpublished Master's Thesis, Meiji University's Graduate School of Governance Studies.

UNWTO (2017). Tourism Highlights 2017. Retrieved from: https://www2.unwto.org/publication/unwto-tourism-highlights-2017.

Tisdell, C., & Wilson, C. (2012). *Nature-based tourism and conservation: New economic insights and case studies*. Cheltenham: Edward Elgar Publishing.

Thompson, B.S., Gillen, J., & Friess, D.A. (2018). Challenging the principles of ecotourism: Insights from entrepreneurs on environmental and economic sustainability in Langkawi, Malaysia. *Journal of Sustainable Tourism* 26(2), 257–276

Tyler, L. (2014). Trouble in Paradise. Aug. 24, 2014 edition of the South China Morning Post's weekend magazine, *Post Magazine*. Retrieved from: http://www.leisatyler.com/trouble-in-paradise-langkawi-struggles-to-hold-onto-unesco-geopark-status.

Usui, R., Sheeran, L.K., Li, J.-H., Sun, L., Wang, X., Pritchard, A.J., DuVall-Lash, A.S., & Wagner, R.S. (2014). Park rangers' behaviors and their effects on tourists and Tibetan macaques (Macaca thibetana) at Mt. Huangshan, China. *Animals* 4, 546–561.

Weaver, D.B. (2012). Organic, incremental and induced paths to sustainable mass tourism convergence. *Tourism Management* 33(5), 1030–1037.

WCED (1987). *Our common future: Report of the World Commission on Environment and Development*. G. H. Brundtland, (Ed.). Oxford: Oxford University Press.

Wong, P.P. (1998). Coastal tourism development in Southeast Asia: Relevance and lessons for coastal zone management. *Ocean & Coastal Management* 38(2), 89–109.

6 Collaborative conservation on small islands

Towards community empowerment and sustainable tourism in Kepulauan Seribu, Jakarta

Devi Roza Kausar, Fahrurozy Darmawan and Riza Firmansyah

Introduction

Since the 2000s, collaborative approaches to natural resource management have been promoted as ways to deal with complex environmental issues (Conley & Moote, 2001). The growing recognition of inherent uncertainty in managing ecological systems, including in the face of global stressors such as climate change, has led to emerging shifts in management paradigms from a scientific or mechanistic worldview to an ecosystem, collaborative, and adaptive worldview (Leong, Emmerson, & Byron, 2011). These new paradigms are in line with changes in governance from top-down to participatory governance, involving different government agencies, the local communities, and non-governmental organisations (NGOs). Collaborative conservation finds its root in collaborative governance where values such as interdependence, decentralisation, horizontal networks, cooperation, common interests, shared beliefs, transparency, trust, relationship building, learning, flexibility, and adaptation prevail (Leong et al., 2011). The collaborative conservation approach, according to Leong et al. (2011), refers to multi-party natural resource management projects, programs, or decision-making processes using a participatory approach. Among the multi-party, community is an important part; hence, according to Conley and Moote (2001), community participation and conservation carried out by the community are among the key concepts entailed in collaborative conservation. The collaborative conservation approach draws on partnerships, defined by Gray (1989) as a process through which parties who see different aspects of a problem can constructively explore their differences and search for solutions that go beyond their often-limited vision of what is possible.

This chapter aims to discuss the collaborative program titled 'Save Our Small Islands' (SOSIS) carried out by several parties from 2017 to 2018 and aimed at addressing environmental, conservation, and tourism issues in

Kepulauan Seribu Regency. The Regency is a chain of islands off the north coast of Jakarta, the capital of Indonesia. Kepulauan Seribu, literally meaning the Thousand Islands, consists of approximately 110 islands. Some of its areas form part of a designated national park with the name of Kepulauan Seribu Marine National Park. Thus, it is the only national park located in the nation's capital. The Ministry of Tourism includes it as one of 10 priority destinations in the country and it is also designated as a National Strategic Tourism Area (KSPN), as stipulated in the Government Regulation No. 50, 2011, in the National Master Plan for Tourism Development (Republik Indonesia 2011a, 2011b).

Environmental and socioeconomic issues

Being one of the alternative tourist destinations in the capital city, the Islands, however, face certain issues that need to be tackled. One of the most critical issues is garbage. Some of the islands located in proximity to the mainland are hit by daily waves of trash from the capital city of Jakarta (Asia Sentinel, 2011). Efforts to reduce the impact of the megacity Jakarta with 10 million inhabitants on the coastal environment of Kepulauan Seribu have been made, for instance by working with local communities on alternative approaches to solid waste management and assisting islanders in developing new income-generating livelihoods (UNESCO, 2000). On the other hand, in addition to waves of trash from Jakarta mainland, tourism and local communities living on the Islands have also been identified as contributors of garbage and waste, partly due to poor waste management on the Islands. Other issues faced by the Islands are degradation of coral reef, dispute in access to natural resources when companies operate in residential islands (Christian, Satria, & Sunito, 2018), the need to improve human resources capacity as stressed by the head of the Tourism Office (Haq, 2017), and limited tourism infrastructure (Rahman, 2019).

On the issue of dispute to natural resources, for instance, an agrarian conflict due to a land dispute between a company and residents has been taking place in Pari Island, one of the islands in Kepulauan Seribu (Christian, Satria, & Sunito, 2018). The lives and livelihoods of residents who have lived there for four generations have come under threat in recent years as their customary land rights have been denied when a developer claimed ownership of much of the island (Chandran, 2018). According to the Jakarta Ombudsman office, there is an indication of maladministration in the issuance of land ownership certificates and right to build certificates used by a private enterprise to claim land ownership in Pari Island (The Jakarta Post, 2018). Faulkenberry et al. (2000) argued that a struggle for control over land and other valued resources often forms part of the key impact of tourism when used as a development tool for local economies. Hence, it is worth questioning the distribution of the benefits of tourism.

Shifting towards community-based tourism

With private companies operating on some of the islands, certain local communities only gain minor income and suffer from a polluted environment amid the vast majority of cash-flows from tourism activities directed to companies. This situation has led to a shift towards community-based tourism (CBT) as an approach for tourism on the islands, especially on residential islands. The initiation of a Tourism Awareness Group by community members involved in tourism on residential islands such as Untung Jawa and Harapan Island marked the will towards an alternative approach to tourism which benefits the communities. CBT centres on the involvement of the host community in planning and maintaining tourism development (Blackstock, 2005; Okazaki, 2008). CBT enterprises, owned and managed by communities, have started to grow since early 2000, for instance in Tangkahan, North Sumatra, where ecotourism is managed by the community (Kausar & Suhandi, 2004) and in Candirejo Village near the iconic Borobudur Temple World Heritage Site, Central Java, where village tourism is managed by communities themselves (Fatimah & Kanki, 2008).

The SOSIS Project carried out with the spirit of collaborative conservation, aims to empower the communities to take part in addressing environmental issues in a bid to achieve sustainable tourism in the Islands. The collaborative project is led by the Biodiversity Foundation (Yayasan Kehati) as an NGO responsible to the donors and involves several other NGOs, private operators and academia. The project is implemented in coordination with the local government of Kepulauan Seribu Regency and National Park management and encompasses a range of activities.

Under the project, amongst other things, an app-based diving operator called e-Nyelam (nyelam means diving in English) tries to reduce the use of Styrofoam by providing reusable meal boxes to local caterers who provide food and beverages to scuba diving groups. The operators also make sure that only local guides are involved in diving trips. Divers Clean Action, a youth NGO which focuses on identifying locations with marine debris, works together with e-Nyelam to organise waste collection through diving. Plastic waste collected is used to make eco-bricks for building blocks; this activity is led by Indonesian Divers Society (MASI). In addition, the Center for Tourism Studies and Development (PKPP) – Universitas Pancasila, is making a contribution to the SOSIS project by conducting baseline research on the socioeconomic condition of the Islands' community, working to increase the community's awareness of health, hygiene, and nutrition, as well as improving home economics skills, especially for women. The Center also raises community awareness on waste reduction. All activities carried out by different parties will be discussed later in this chapter, as well as their impact and lessons that can be learned from this collaborative project. The remainder of this chapter will contain the following: a general description of Kepulauan Seribu Regency, a section discussing community empowerment, and a dedicated section on achieving sustainable tourism on the Islands before reaching to a conclusion.

General description of Kepulauan Seribu

Kepulauan Seribu Islands is situated at the Jakarta Bay, bordering the Java Sea in the North and East; North Jakarta, West Jakarta and Tangerang Regency in the South; and Lampung Province in the West. The Regency consists of two districts, namely Kepulauan Seribu Utara and Kepulauan Seribu Selatan, or Northern and Southern Kepulauan Seribu, respectively. The northern part encompasses three islands known as Panggang, Kelapa, and Harapan. All three islands are administratively run as villages with the same name as the island. The southern part consists of three villages named after the island, i.e. Untung Jawa, Tidung and Pari. The district of Northern Kepulauan Seribu covers 5.65 square km, while the Southern covers 3.05 square km. Being closer to the capital Jakarta, however, the population density of Southern Kepulauan Seribu District is bigger.

The Islands, like other tropical archipelagos, are blessed with mild to warm temperatures with an average of 26.5–28.5 degrees Celsius, although the highest temperature can reach 32.9 degrees Celsius. The best time to visit the Islands is between May and October during the dry season. Around 5,008 families live on the 11 residential islands, originating from different ethnic groups, such as Buginese, Javanese, Sundanese, and Betawinese. The presence of many ethnic groups in Kepulauan Seribu is inseparable from the history of Kepulauan Seribu. The existence of the Bugis ethnic group can be traced back to the presence of pirates who used to live in Kepulauan Seribu and these pirates' descendants spread throughout the Islands. The presence of Sundanese ethnic groups in Kepulauan Seribu is mainly due to the area once being part of the Kingdom of Banten.

Community empowerment through SOSIS?

Sadan (1997) defined empowerment as a process of transition from a state of powerlessness to a state of relative control over one's life, destiny and environment. Besides, Rappaport (1987) mentioned that empowerment consists in the ability of people, organisations, and communities to gain mastery over their affairs. As Choi and Murray (2010) stated, if residents fail to be empowered, the success of tourism development and sustainability cannot be guaranteed. In addition, Scheyvens (2003) differentiates between four dimensions of empowerment. The economic gains of tourism that are well documented in the tourism literature are signs of economic empowerment, whereas psychological empowerment comes from self-esteem and pride in cultural traditions. Social empowerment happens when increased community cohesion occurs as members of a community are brought together through a tourism initiative while political empowerment is about a shift in the balance between the powerful and the powerless, between the dominant and the dependent. As reported by Talib et al. (2018), community empowerment is the process of enabling communities to increase control over their lives.

This section will discuss the SOSIS project, which is aimed at community empowerment, particularly on Harapan Island, situated within the Kepulauan Seribu Marine National Park, in a bid to achieve sustainable tourism. Carried out by several parties to address environmental, conservation and tourism issues, the project is conducted with the spirit of collaborative conservation and aimed to empower the communities to take part in addressing environmental issues. The main focus of this program is balancing and harmonising communities' economic improvement with biodiversity conservation through coral reef and mangrove rehabilitation activities, capacity building in community-based ecotourism and environmental education. Tourism has brought other economic opportunities for residents of Kepulauan Seribu, whose main livelihoods are fishing and trading, and like several other island destinations, Harapan Island has thriving tourism activities with popular snorkelling and diving spots. The local community of Harapan Island provides services to visitors in the form of homestays, food, boat rental services for snorkelling and swimming, and others.

However, in addition to the positive impact of increasing residents' income, tourism also brings problems such as waste and pressure on the marine ecosystem. Some tourists care very little about garbage disposal or snorkel carelessly which often results in damaged coral. The problems that occur on Harapan Island may be solved by improving visitors' environmental awareness and by improving the capacity of local communities in managing and running more environmentally friendly tourism activities through training and assistance. At present, much of the damaged coral reefs are caused by impromptu diving and snorkelling. Local tour guides with little information and knowledge of guiding often bring tourists directly to conservation zones that should be off limits to visitors, especially when the number of visits is high.

Other problems that occur include waste and polluted water due to the high number of visitors who usually bring food from the city, leading to increased waste on the island. Both household waste and waste from tourism activities are threats to biodiversity on Harapan Island. Such problems concur, as Farhan and Lim (2012) stated, when the development of tourism causes ecological crises and becomes the primary concern in regards to sustainability in developing countries, including Indonesia.

The results of a survey conducted by the Indonesian Diving Society Association (MASI) and Divers Clean Action – a youth NGO – in May 2017 on Harapan Island show that on certain national holidays such as Eid and New Year, tourists who come to Harapan Island can reach up to 3,000 people or more. This number of tourists visiting the island is worrying due to the amount of pressure they put on the ecosystem, particularly through solid waste, mainly related to plastic and Styrofoam, which threatens coral reef ecosystems. The survey results from the island show that tourists' waste can reach approximately 0.28 kg per tourist per week, which means that with, for example, 3,000 tourists, 840 kg of garbage are produced every week.

Acknowledging these problems, and in order to empower the community, MASI has launched a campaign for tourists and the local community to build awareness and to reduce waste as well as invite local communities to reduce plastic waste through waste recycling training. MASI also shares knowledge on waste management to local partners, namely boat owners, catering, tour guides, and homestay owners. For boat owners, for instance, the efforts to reduce waste begin on board the vessel by providing trash bins, using reusable lunch boxes and tumblers for tourists, and providing the ship owners assistance to dispose of waste at Harapan Island landfill. Divers Clean Action (DCA), on the other hand, organises diving trips in which divers collect plastic waste to be used for making eco-bricks for building blocks or souvenirs. The eco-brick is a reusable building block created by inserting clean and dry used plastic into a plastic bottle to a set density.

In addition to the above-mentioned campaigns initiated by MASI and DCA, another NGO called Monitoring Network (JARMON) played its part in the SOSIS project through coastal ecosystems (coral reefs and mangroves) rehabilitation on Harapan Island. The rehabilitation activities include planting coral reefs and mangroves and monitoring coral reefs as well as reef fish. Healthy corals are vital for activities such as snorkelling, which according to Rangel et al. (2015), can be a popular tourist attraction as it allows tourists to visit natural and cultural structures of the underwater world, and to interact directly with the environment such as coral reefs, reef fish and other marine flora and fauna. Snorkelling can also serve as an excellent environmental educational tool, as it allows tourists to observe marine species and learn about the coastal and marine environment. However, snorkelling also puts pressure on these vulnerable corals, thus rehabilitation efforts are necessary. The activities involve local communities, such as the fishing communities and boat owners on Harapan Island. Community involvement aims to raise awareness about the conservation of natural resources since the communities themselves are also key tourism actors working as tour guides and running boat rental businesses besides working as fishermen. Kamaruddin, Ahmad, and Alwee (2016) posited that the level of participation in an environmental program could be an indicator for measuring the level of awareness of the environment. These tour guides and boatmen who have been involved in guiding and interpretation training can play their part in raising awareness of the importance of conservation of natural resources by sharing information and stories with the visitors. This is in line with Ap and Wong's (2001) suggestion that tour guides, through their knowledge and understanding of a destination and their communication skills, have the power to transform simple visits into deeper experiences and that they can mediate between tourists, locals, and the environment.

Aside from the NGOs who engage in the SOSIS projects, an academic institution also participates in SOSIS. The Center for Tourism Studies and Development (PKPP) based at Universitas Pancasila acts as a strategic partner in conducting socioeconomic monitoring surveys, organising workshops for the community and becoming a liaison centre for communication and coordination between all parties involved in the projects. Activities carried out by PKPP are as follows:

1)   A workshop on nutrition and household expenditure in which the communities, especially women from Harapan Island, participate. This workshop aims to promote a healthy lifestyle and nutritious food for the family and train the communities to utilise their home gardens and other arable lands for planting vegetables and other productive plants. Additionally, the workshop also taught the communities to process organic waste into compost that can be used as environmentally friendly fertilisers to grow these vegetables. All of these activities can be expected to lead to long-term productive economic activities for families on the island since the harvested vegetables can be used for their own consumption or for tourists' consumption. Moreover, this 'green' movement can be the start of a green tourism village, which can turn into an additional tourist attraction. At the household level, dietary diversity captures the economic ability of a household to access a variety of foods (Seymour et al., 2019). More importantly, the overall quantity of food consumed by the household or the nutritional adequacy of individual household members' diets are useful for assessing changes in diets over time or differences across households. Dietary diversity is a particularly important concern among poor populations from the developing world, whose diets tend to be low in several vital micronutrients as a result of being predominantly comprised of starchy staples and only few animal source foods or fresh fruits and vegetables (Seymour et al. 2019).

2)   The household level Socioeconomic Monitoring Survey on Harapan Island. This survey was targeted at the households on Harapan Island. It was conducted based on the identified need to monitor socioeconomic changes before and after the SOSIS project. Increasing welfare at the household level, while preserving biodiversity as a source of life and economic growth, was the main idea behind this project. Hence understanding the socioeconomic conditions of the communities on Harapan Island before and after the project was necessary to evaluate the project.

In addition to the workshop on nutrition and household expenditure and the socioeconomic monitoring survey, PKPP was also in charge of arranging multi-stakeholder coordination meetings attended by parties involved in the project. These meetings had been important for the continuation of the SOSIS program due to some issues that concerned different parties with differing interests and tasks. For instance, the environmental damage in parts of Kepulauan Seribu affected several stakeholders such as the National Park management, whose main interest is conservation, as well as the Regency Tourism Office, whose main interest is the promotion of tourism. Regular multi-stakeholder coordination meetings are needed to facilitate the collaboration of all relevant stakeholders in ensuring that tourism does not cause further environmental damage.

Another organisation involved in the project is Green Indonesia Community (KIH), which integrates learning about resilience and adaptation to climate change on small islands through informal education curricula (kindergarten, elementary, middle school and high school). Public awareness of biodiversity conservation and climate change adaptation on Small Islands needs to be communicated through outreach and environmental education activities. Hence, KIH's role in developing 'Records of Educational Activities for Sustainable Development on Harapan Island, Kepulauan Seribu', which is a module containing learning material for sustainable development with the theme of biodiversity, disaster risk reduction, climate change, and sustainable consumption. The organisation also develops 'Learning Implementation Plans' that have been adapted to the schools' curriculum and can be used as a learning reference for teachers, both those who participated and those who do not participate in the training.

Increasing public awareness, for instance through learning modules, is one of the aims of SOSIS in improving public awareness of preserving the island and its surrounding environment. For achieving sustainable tourism in the long run, environmental awareness among the younger generations is vital since there is a high chance some of them will be involved in the tourism sector, a sector which has been growing since 2012 (Kompas, 2015).

Towards sustainable tourism in Kepulauan Seribu

Community participation is considered necessary in order to obtain support from the community since the project aims to empower them to take part in addressing environmental issues to achieve sustainable tourism. When sustainable tourism is achieved through this development project, the benefit can fulfil community needs as posited by Cole (2006). This could be seen in the SOSIS project, where communities are beginning to play a vital role in achieving sustainable tourism. Under the program, school children participated in environmental education. Guides, caterers and rental boat owners were involved in reducing plastic and Styrofoam commonly used for food served to scuba divers and tourists in general. Homestay owners and the community at large were given knowhow on waste management and to plant their vegetables.

However, as with any project-based activity, it is interesting to look further into the level of community participation and to the magnitude of empowerment that the program brings. Empowerment is recognized as a higher level of community participation where residents are not only included in the planning process but have control over it as well (Boley & McGehee, 2014). In this project, the Tourism Awareness Group – formed by the community – continues to promote the initiatives that have been started through the project among its member, hence the initiatives such as using reusable lunch boxes or home farming activities are ongoing.

Nevertheless, being a collaborative project funded by donors, the projects and their outputs, have been planned when the program proposal was submitted to donors in a bid for funding. Thus, communities' involvement in planning is low, or using Pretty's (1995) typology of participation, it is at the level of functional participation, which happens when external agencies see community participation as a means to achieve project goals, and people can participate in meetings with predetermined objectives (Pretty, 1995). Nonetheless, the fact that increasingly more rental boat owners and guides are involved in reducing plastic and Styrofoam, and that they are more active in waste collection in waters and coastal areas, is a sign of how the communities have begun to empower themselves. This may be due to the community's increasing conformity with the fact that environmental problems may threaten their livelihoods and awareness of sustainable tourism as a common purpose between them and organisations involved in the project. Schusler and Decker (2003) suggested that agreeing to a common purpose and the transformation of relationships – in this case, from participants of the project to advocates who continue to promote the initiatives – are a form of social learning generated by the collaborative conservation project. Schusler and Decker's (2003) statement on common purpose as an important element of a collaborative natural resource management supports Gray's (1989) theory of collaboration, which mentions setting common purpose and agreeing on common problems as part of the requisites for collaboration to work.

Signs of empowerment among the community may be the answer to concerns over the project's continuity and long-term broader impact. This concern is due to the project's dependency on donors, thus its continuity may be questioned and its long-term impacts still need further investigation. In addition, in achieving sustainable tourism through collaborative SOSIS projects, there have also been some challenges in the communication process between parties involved. These challenges occurred in communication between organisations involved directly in the program, and between organisations in SOSIS and the local government or National Park management. The results of activities conducted by different organisations have also been varied. Activities such as capacity building in planting vegetables, waste management, and guiding were attended by quite a significant number of community members. However, concerning visitors, the number of tourists involved in the waste collection while joining a scuba diving program, for instance, was limited. This is due to the cost of participating, which is quite high for Indonesian standards (about GBP 93 for a divers' volunteering program) and a specific diving qualification which is needed to join the activities.

Moreover, the nature of the SOSIS program as a collaborative conservation activity also brings a specific challenge in presenting recommendations to the government. The compilation of reports from each project is presented from the SOSIS project as a whole to relevant parties such as the local government of Kepulauan Seribu Regency, the management of Kepulauan Seribu Marine National Park, and the provincial government of Jakarta. However, there has yet to be a clearly defined recommended list of priorities for a future action plan. To develop such recommendations there should be further discussion and a process of joint decision making, as implied by Gray (1989), who argues that collaboration involves joint decision making among key stakeholders about the future of a domain in which they have shared interests. It is, therefore, necessary to bring SOSIS as a multi-stakeholder program to the next level, where not only does each party do its part but also engages more intensely in the process of joint decision making to develop Kepulauan Seribu into a more sustainable tourism destination.

Conclusion

This chapter aimed to describe SOSIS, a collaborative conservation program carried out by several parties to address environmental, conservation and tourism issues in Kepulauan Seribu Regency. Being one of the alternative tourism destinations in the capital city, the islands – with part of them belonging to a marine national park – however, face certain issues that need to be tackled. Some of the most critical issues are garbage and waste disposal, to which tourism and local communities' general consumption contribute, and the degradation of coral reefs.

Through the program, communities are beginning to play a vital role in achieving sustainable tourism. This becomes obvious through environmental education for students as potential future tourism actors; a movement for reducing plastic and Styrofoam by guides, caterers and rental boat owners; and waste management and utilisation of home gardens for productive plants – all of which contribute to sustainable tourism.

Looking at the level of community participation and the magnitude of empowerment that the program brings, it can be concluded that community participation in Kepulauan Seribu is at Pretty's (1995) level of functional participation, also called participation in meeting predetermined objectives. This observation relates to the nature of the program itself as one which is entirely dependent on donors, hence a proposal and expected outputs that are predetermined by another stakeholder, not the community itself. Nevertheless, there have been some early signs of communities beginning to use the opportunities at hand to empower themselves. Although they began as participants of the project, some of them are continuing the initiatives on their own with the support from the local Tourism Awareness Group formed by the community themselves.

As a collaborative conservation activity, there is also a specific challenge in terms of presenting the output as a recommendation for an action plan to the government. While a compilation of outputs is available, a clearly defined plan containing recommended priorities for the future has yet to be produced. The projects within SOSIS are set to achieve the broader aim of sustainable tourism, despite being put into practise by separate organisations targeting different participants. Therefore, this chapter suggests a joint decision-making process to determine priority recommendations through more effective communication and cooperation between stakeholders in a bid to make Kepulauan Seribu a more sustainable tourist destination.

References

Ap, J., & Wong, K. (2001). Case study on tour guiding: Professionalism, issues and problems. *Tourism Management* 22(5), 551–563.

Asia Sentinel (2011). Indonesia's Trash Island. *Asia Sentinel*, July 22 2011. Retrieved from: https://www.asiasentinel.com/society/indonesias-trash-island.

Blackstock, K. (2005). A critical look at community-based tourism. *Community Development Journal* 40(1), 39–49.

Boley, B.B., & McGehee, N.G. (2014). Measuring empowerment: Developing and validating the resident empowerment through tourism scale (RETS). *Tourism Management* 45, 85–94.

Chandran, R. (2018). Indonesian islanders fight developer with snorkels and homestays. Reuters, 9 October 2018. Retrieved from: https://www.reuters.com/article/us-indonesia-landrights-tourism/indonesian-islanders-fight-developer-with-snorkels-and-homestays-idUSKCN1MJ01L.

Choi, H.C., & Murray, I. (2010). Resident attitudes toward sustainable community tourism. *Journal of Sustainable Tourism* 18(4), 575–594.

Christian, Y., Satria, A., & Sunito, S. (2018). Political economy of agrarian conflict of small island: Case study in Pari Island, Seribu Islands, Capital province of Jakarta. *Sodality: Jurnal Sosiologi Pedesaan* 6(1), 71–78.

Cole, S. (2006). Information and empowerment: The keys to achieving sustainable tourism. *Journal of Sustainable Tourism* 14(6), 629–644.

Conley, A., & Moote, A. (2001). *Collaborative conservation in theory and practice: A literature review.* Tucson: Udall Center for Public Policy, the University of Arizona.

Fatimah, T., & Kanki, K. (2008). A Study on the realization process of community based green tourism in Candirejo Village, Borobudur, Indonesia. *Journal of the City Planning Institute of Japan* 43(3), 517–522.

Farhan, A.R., & Lim, S. (2012). Vulnerability assessment of ecological conditions in Seribu Islands, Indonesia. *Journal of Ocean Coast Management* 65, 1–14.

Faulkenberry, L.V., Coggeshall, J.M., Backman, K., & Backman, S. (2000). A culture of servitude: The impact of tourism and development on South Carolina's coast. *Human Organization* 59(1), 86–95.

Gray, B. (1989). *Collaborating: Finding common ground for multiparty problems.* San Francisco: Jossey-Bass Inc.

Haq, M.F.U. (2017) Tingkatkan pariwisata, warga Kepulauan Seribu akan diberi pelatihan [Trainings for community in a bid to improve Tourism]. *Detik News.* Retrieved from: https://news.detik.com/berita/d-3723247/tingkatkan-pariwisata-warga-kepulauan-seribu-akan-diberi-pelatihan.

Kamaruddin, S.M., Ahmad, P., & Alwee, N. (2016). Community Awareness on Environ Manag through Local Agenda 21 (LA21). *Procedia – Social and Behavioral Sciences* 222 (June 2016), 729–737.

Kausar, D., & Suhandi, A. (2004). Participatory ecotourism planning in Tangkahan, Leuser Ecosystem Region, North Sumatra. Proceedings of the 10th Annual Conference Asia Pacific Tourism Association (APTA). 5–7 July, Nagasaki, Japan.

Kompas (2015). Wisata Pulau Harapan menggeliat [Emerging tourism on Harapan Island]. *Kompas Newsletter*, 25 January 2015. Retrieved from: https://travel.kompas.com/read/2015/01/28/132500127/Wisata.Pulau.Harapan.Menggeliat.

Leong, K.M., Emmerson, D.P., & Byron, R. (2011). The new governance era: implications for collaborative conservation and adaptive management in department of the interior agencies. *Human Dimensions of Wildlife* 16(4), 236–243.

Okazaki, E. (2008). A community-based tourism model: Its conception and use. *Journal of Sustainable Tourism* 16(5), 511–529.

Pretty, J.N. (1995). Participatory learning for sustainable agriculture. *World Development* 23(8), 1247–1263.

Rahman, M.R. (2019) Kementerian PUPR bangun infrastruktur pariwisata Kepulauan Seribu [Ministry of Public Works and Housing develops tourism infrastructure in Kepulauan Seribu]. *Antara News.* Retrieved from: https://www.antara news.com/berita/820315/kementerian-pupr-bangun-infrastruktur-pariwisata-kepula uan-seribu.

Rangel, M.O., Pita, C.B., Gonçalves, J.M.S., Oliveira, F., Costa, C., & Erzini, K. (2015). Eco-touristic snorkelling routes at Marinha beach (Algarve): Environmental education and human impacts. *Marine Policy* 60, 62–69.

Rappaport, J. (1987). Terms of empowerment/exemplars of prevention: Toward a theory for community psychology. *American Journal of Community Psychology* 15 (2), 121–148.

Republik Indonesia (2011a). Peraturan Presiden No. 50 Tahun 2011 tentang Rencana Induk Pembangunan Kepariwisataan Nasional. Sekretariat Kabinet RI. Jakarta.

Republik Indonesia (2011b). Peraturan Presiden No. 93 Tahun 2017 tentang Perubahan atas Peraturan Presiden Nomor 19 Tahun 2015 tentang Kementerian Pariwisata. Sekretariat Kabinet RI. Jakarta.

Sadan, E. (1997). *Empowerment and community planning: Theory and practice of people-focused social solutions.* Tel Aviv: Hakibbutz Hameuchad Publishers.

Seymour, G., Masuda, Y.J., William, J., & Schneider, K. (2019). Household and child nutrition outcomes among the time and income poor in rural Bangladesh. *Global Food Security* 20, 82–92.

Scheyvens, R. (2003). *Tourism for development, empowering communities.* Upper Saddle River: Prentice Hall.

Schusler, T.M., & Decker, D.J. (2003) Social learning for collaborative natural resources management. *Society and Natural Resources* 15, 309–326.

The Jakarta Post (2018). Issuance of land certificates on Pari Island flawed, Ombudsman finds. *The Jakarta Post,* 9 April. Retrieved from: https://www.thejakartapost. com/news/2018/04/09/issuance-of-land-certificates-on-pari-island-flawed-ombudsma n-finds.html.

Talib, I.F.A., Takim, R., Mohammad, M.F., & Hassan, P.F. (2018). Community Empowerment through Rehabilitation and Reconstruction in Social Sector of Kuala Krai, Kelantan, Malaysia. *Procedia Engineering* 212, 294–301.

UNESCO (2000). *Reducing megacity impacts on the coastal environment: alternative livelihoods and waste management in Jakarta and the Seribu Islands.* Jakarta: UNESCO.

Part III

Tourism, development, and local communities

7 What is the economic impact of ecotourism for the poor in Lao PDR?

Saithong Phommavong and Dieter K. Müller

Introduction

It has been argued that local elites or multinational corporations are receiving major benefits from tourism development in developing countries (Ghosh & Ghosh, 2018; Taylor, 2017; Telfer & Sharpley, 2008; Turegano, 2006). In a similar vein, Hall and Lew (2009, p. 103) state that 'high-end tourism developments, which are often built by multi-national corporations, tend to have very high leakage rates'. Accordingly, leakage of tourism income largely results from expenses for imported food, beverages, equipment and transportation services. In particular, profit repatriations by foreign-owned firms increase propensity of tourism revenue leakage from the local economy (Williams, 2009, p. 101). One of the major criticisms towards tourism development is that it widens inequalities between developed nations in tourist generating regions and developing countries in tourist destination regions (Britton, 1982; Brohman, 1996; Walpole & Goodwin, 2000). Specifically, it suggests that economic capital and control stemming from outside sources result in leakage, external dependency, and unequal distribution of benefits and costs. While local elites may benefit greatly from tourism development, the majority of local residents may have to bear the consequences resulting from negative environmental and cultural impacts of tourism development without experiencing a considerable share of the economic benefits (Lacher & Nepal, 2010).

Having recognised this potential inequality in tourism income distribution, various donor organizations and governments in tourist destination countries, including Laos, put effort into increasing the share of incomes from tourism for local communities in those tourist destinations. One of these initiatives is 'pro-poor tourism', which is widely discussed and contested in the academic literature (Hall, 2007; Scheyvens, 2011; Holden & Novelli, 2011; Truong, Slabbert, & Nguyen, 2016; Ly & Bauer, 2016). In many destinations, exotic nature and culture offer opportunities for ecotourism aimed at boosting local economies and combating inequality and dependency (Brohman, 1996; McNeely, 1988; Walpole & Goodwin, 2000). However, the outcomes of ecotourism largely remain untested (Walpole & Goodwin, 2000, p. 561). However, little empirical work has been carried out regarding ecotourism's income and employment generation effect for the poor (Healy, 1994; Park et al., 2017; Sinclair, 1991; Wells, 1992; Walpole & Goodwin, 2000; Zapata et al., 2011). Many of the tourism development initiatives are dependent on the ambitions of donor agencies and governments (Sciortino, 2017; Telfer & Sharpley, 2008), and participation patterns may influence the projects in many different ways (Ounmany, 2014; Park et al., 2017, 2018). A lack of local community participation may be the result of sceptical attitudes toward tourism projects. Thus, an important question to be addressed is whether the potential to ease poverty differs among various approaches to ecotourism development?

Ecotourism has been developed in Laos since the late 1990s in the northern provinces of Luangnamtha and Borkeo with the purpose of 'sustaining culture and nature as well as for poverty reduction' and it has been promoted as a form of pro-poor tourism (Phommavong, 2011a, 2011b). The Laos government and international organizations including UNDP, UNESCO, and state donors, such as New Zealand Official Development Assistance (NZ ODA), set up community-based ecotourism projects by investing in facilities and training locals. This is done in order to enable local villagers in Nam Ha National Protected Area (NHPA) to participate in ecotourism activities by providing services to tourists trekking in the area to experience rural nature and culture (Schipani, 2008). The project was then extended to other provinces including Luangprabang, Khammuan, Savannakhet, and Champasak with financial support from international organizations, such as the Asian Development Bank.

The authors of this study argue that the economic impact of community-based ecotourism projects is largely unknown and thus, there is a need to assess such impact on the local level. By comparing the economic impact of two ecotourism projects in Laos, one privately owned and one publicly owned, this study examines: 1) whether the re-distribution of economic income is different between privately and publicly owned tourism enterprises; and 2) whether the re-distribution of tourism income is different among ethnic groups and classes. The chapter starts with a literature review of tourism and economic impact before moving on to the methodology, findings, and discussion.

Measuring the economic impact of tourism

Despite the fact that the tourism-development nexus has been at the centre of interest for a considerable time, not least since the Millennium Development Goals were launched, most assessments have not shown much interest in the economic outcomes of tourism development in host communities (Saarinen, Rogerson, & Manwa, 2011). Instead political and ideological struggles have dominated the debate often disqualifying neoliberal approaches to development (Schilcher, 2007; Hunt, 2011; Scheyvens, 2011). As a consequence, different attempts to contribute to local development are judged based on their ideological assumptions rather than on the outcome of the attempts. This appears to be particularly the case regarding development at the local level. For instance, Mitchell and Ashley (2007, p. 4) contend that there is a 'surprising' research gap related to the 'quantification of how pro-poor policy interventions affect the shares of revenue reaching the poor' (see also Mitchell & Ashley, 2010). An exception to this is a contribution by Harrison and Schipani (2007) who quantify the economic outcomes of different tourism development projects. Remote villages, state control, language barriers and other cultural constraints are some of the reasons hindering an assessment of economic impact. Certainly, a major reason for the lack of studies quantifying economic outcomes of tourism development projects is limited access to reliable data. Moreover, a lack of benchmark data makes it difficult to assess the actual impact of tourism development on local communities.

Thus, assessment of the economic impact of tourism remains an important task for tourism research, particularly in developing countries where tourism has been employed as a tool for economic development, employment generation, and poverty reduction (Telfer & Sharpley, 2008). However, data for such a context is usually limited and also the generation of new data is complicated owing to reasons related to low statistical standards. Economic impacts of tourism commonly involve the calculation and application of economic multipliers (Archer, 1982; Wall, 1997), which negatively correlate to the size of the area under study; the larger the size of the study area, the smaller will be the leakage and the larger will be the multiplier. Thus, the economic impact on locals has to be seen in relation to the study area.

Lee (2009) points out that the majority of economic impact studies demonstrate positive results from tourism development in an area (Archer & Fletcher, 1996; Fletcher 1989; Huse, Gustavsen, & Almedal, 1998). The measure of the importance of tourism usually includes assessments of the community's ability to retain income within the local economy, the level of employment generated and the equal distribution of economic benefits (Lee, 2009). Blake, Arbache, Sinclair and Teles (2008, p. 108) argue that 'there is little economy-wide research evidence to suggest that tourism does reduce poverty nor studies that quantify the interactions between it and poverty'. Taylor (2017) supports this claim in arguing that increasing income inequality often entails growing conflict over policies between rich and poor, on national and local levels, sometimes creating a split within communities. Thus, an analysis of the channels through which tourism affects households, in particular the poor ones, is necessary.

Several studies apply macroeconomic methods to assess economic impact of tourism. In regard to calculation methods, Smeral (2005) claims an inadequacy of survey data and advocates the use of using Tourism Satellite Accounts (TSA) instead. Alternative approaches were suggested by Riddington et al. (2010), who use geographic information system (GIS) and contingent valuation (CV) to assess the economic impact of wind farms on tourism. Their argument is that these methods can show how economic theory and computer-based techniques can resolve ongoing policy disputes between two government objectives. Wanhill (1994) uses computable general equilibrium (CGE) models in assessing economic and distributional impact of tourism in Brazil. The method is used to quantify the effects on income distribution and poverty reduction that occur via price, earning and government revenue. The results reveal unequal income distribution between households. Deller (2010) proposes geographically weighted regression (GWR) to explore the role of tourism development to assess changes in poverty rates and suggests that the jobs created do not influence poverty levels; instead they provide benefit to others than the poor.

The Gini index, which measures the deviation of a distribution from a perfect equal distribution, has grown to be a popular method for the assessment of tourism income distribution. For example, Lee (2009) uses Gini coefficient and quintile share analysis to examine the patterns and trends of tourism inequality for the United States, and concludes that despite tourism development, income inequality still prevails. Wen & Sinha (2009) employ Gini coefficients in their study of the regional and provincial distribution of international tourism in China. The result of the study reveals a reduction in regional concentration of international tourism. The 'spread effect' of tourism growth may have enabled remote areas to catch up with the coastal area and help to reduce economic disparity in the inland areas. This is also confirmed by Suwei and Changchun (2018) who point to the potential of ecotourism to alleviate poverty in rural China. Other studies applying Gini coefficients, however, indicate that community-based ecotourism in Cambodia in fact did not contribute to decrease income differences (Lonn et al., 2018), or provide increasing benefits for the better-off; indeed, it led to increased local inequalities (Llorca-Rodríguez, Casas-Jurado, & García-Fernández, 2017).

Quantitative approaches to studying economic impacts dominate in tourism literature. While quantitative macroeconomic techniques such as input-output analysis are applicable for large-scale cases, they are inappropriate for local levels where significant data is often unavailable (Smith, 1989; Walpole & Goodwin, 2000). In the meantime, qualitative approaches for tourism's economic impact research are limited. For example, Campbell (1999), Hunt (2011), and Haralambopoulos and Pizam (1996) assess residents' perceptions of tourism impacts rather than measuring actual impacts. Qualitative approaches usually fail to provide comprehensive information on the economic situation but manage to highlight perceived impacts. Thus, impacts remain non-quantified. Although various studies have been conducted, economic impact assessments of tourism in developing countries have been largely absent owing to difficulties related to data acquisition. In particular, studies on economic impacts of tourism in discrete localities are still valuable, particularly when it involves comparative analyses between cases.

Study methods

This study analyses tourism's economic impact at both the household and the village level, defined as community level. These impacts are identified by direct estimations from micro data sources and some secondary data sources. The set of micro data is a result of a larger research project supported by a Swedish research fund addressing the issue of tourism and poverty reduction that had been carried out continuously during 2008–2010. Although the data is somewhat dated, similar community-based ecotourism projects are still in place and thus the analysis is considered a good representation of the economic impact of community-based ecotourism even today. Other components of the data concentrating on the implementation of the ecotourism project and the gender dimension have been done simultaneously during that period (Phommavong, 2011a; Phommavong & Sörensson, 2014).

Two villages, Namtalan and Lao Khao, in the Lungnamtha district and Sing district, Luangnamtha province, were selected for this research. The villages are selected as qualified ecotourism sites because they were classified as 'the first community-based ecotourism project in Laos' which implied that they have to follow the Nam Ha Ecotourism Project (NHEP) Eco-guide for tourist services (Nam Ha NPA, 1998, n.p.). The villages are located in the buffer zone of the national protected area where natural forests are still abundant and rich in biodiversity. Furthermore, the area is home to many ethnic minority groups. Tourism in the villages is developed according to the criteria outlined in the NHEP Eco-guide and services include forest trekking, river trips, and village homestays. Tourism development is expected to contribute economic benefits for local people, sustain cultural heritage and raise funds for environmental conservation. The research sites have been chosen to illustrate two specific ecotourism projects operated by government and private sectors, respectively. The first case, Namtalan village and originally home of the Khmu ethnic group, joined the Mekong Tourism Development Project (MTDP) in 2005, which is a part of the 'best practices' of the second phase of the NHEP (2003–2007) (Schipani, 2005). Now, the project is owned and operated by the provincial tourism office and thus considered as publicly owned project. The village was later merged with the nearby Lanten ethnic village as part of the national village consolidation policy. The Lao Khao village, located in the Sing district and home of the Akha ethnic group, is the second village for this study. The ecotourism project, or the Akha Experience (AE) was set up as an international donor aid-led project financed by the German Agency for Technical Cooperation (GTZ) (Cohen, 2009). Ecotourism activities and services for tourists are major offerings. Different from the first case, the AE was transferred to Exotissimo, a private ecotourism company and operated by them for 15 years. It is run entirely privately (Mumm & Tuffin, 2007). Therefore, the study sites represent two distinctive modes of operation for ecotourism.

Simple random sampling was applied and thus each unit of the population has an equal probability of inclusion in the sample (Bryman, 2008). The sample of 35 households in Lao Khao (64% of all involved households) and 47 households in Namtalan (85%) were surveyed. In total, the study covered 82 out of 110 households, which represents roughly 75% of the population in the two villages. The study employed a survey questionnaire as the data collection tool. The instrument was pilot tested in these two villages and other villages prior to the final survey. The survey questionnaires were administered by the researcher and the research assistants in the Lao language. The data was encoded for computer analysis and translated into English for interpretation.

Gini coefficients and quintile share analysis are used as an analytical method to compare the incomes of two different groups in tourism (Lee, 2009; Lonn, Mizoue, Ota, Kajisa, & Yoshida, 2018; Llorca-Rodríguez et al., 2017; Wen & Sinha, 2009). Usually the method is applied for measuring the distribution of economic impact of tourism among members of local communities or spatial units, respectively. Wen and Sinha (2009) add that Gini coefficients can be used to measure the relative degree to which a population deviates from the state of perfect equality.

Wen and Sinha (2009) define the Gini coefficient as follows: $G=1+(1(n)-(2/(n \times n \times y0) \times (y1+2y2+3y3+\ldots+nyn))$. Here, G represents the Gini coefficient, n is the number of observations, $y0$ is the mean of observations, and $y1, y2, \ldots$ to yn represent individual observations in decreasing order of size of the relevant variable, y. This study examines the local distribution of tourism income on the village level in order to measure how tourism income varies within the two villages. The Gini coefficient is interpreted in the following way: the larger the Gini coefficient, the greater the degree of inequality.

The quintile share analysis is used as complementary to the Gini coefficient. The method is usually used with cross-sectional analysis. However, it is applied to compute the degree of economic inequality at a single point in time, too (Lee, 2009). In this study, quintile share analysis is used to compare the ecotourism income of different groups of people. This is done to determine how the distribution of income affects different groups in a specific place at a single point in time.

Results

Tourist expenditure

The major concern in this section is to demonstrate the relative importance of different offers rather than discussing the overall development of tourism. Table 7.1 compares the ecotourism earnings account for the two villages, categorized by types of expenditure in 2009 and provided as the official record by the tourism service unit (TSU). The data was derived from an overview of tourist expenditure recorded by the relevant offices and village tourism managers. The categories of expenditure for some items are different for the two villages. For instance, massage, village activities, cooking fees, and entertainment are unavailable in Namtalan. Expenditure for food in both cases accounts for about 40%, followed by guide fees accounting for about 39% for Namtalan and lodging and cooking fees accounting for 21% for Lao Khao. An explanation for this is a growing linkage to food providers within the village instead of food imports into the village.

Table 7.1 Average direct tourist expenditure in Namtalan and Lao Khao villages by category of expenditure (2009)[1]

Category of expenditure	Namtalan (public)		Lao Khao (private)	
	Total expenditure (Kip)	Percentage	Total expenditure (Kip)	Percentage
Village fund	4,105,043	9.3	1,090,000	3.1
Food	17,520,000	39.6	14,460,000	41.2
Lodging	3,240,000	7.3	7,520,000	21.4
Handicrafts	1,404,000	3.2	580,000	1.7
Massage	0	0	2,460,000	7
Village activities	0	0	20,000	0.1
Cooking fees	0	0	7,620,000	21.7
Entertainment	0	0	1,320,000	3.8
Guide fees	17,320,000	39.1	0	0
Lodge services	530,000	1.2	0	0
Security fees	130,000	0.3	0	0
Total	44,249,043	100	35,070,000	100

Source: Tourism service unit (TSU), Luangnamtha tourism department

In both cases, tourists spent money for similar services, such as food, accommodation, and handicrafts. Contributions to village funds are mandatory in order to provide the village collective with economic resources for future investments in common services. Apart from this fund, the figures reveal that the NHEP-ecotourism model generates incomes for providers of basic services. However, some items such as security and cooking fees were reported differently between two villages.

Household incomes

Table 7.2 shows household incomes of the two villages based on a survey conducted by the research team. The income from rice, vegetables/fruits, meat and selling jar wine equals 38.3% of the total income. This figure is similar to food expenditure in Table 7.1 amounting to 39.6% and containing the categories of food (rice, vegetables/fruits, meat). However, the villagers received only half of the amount spent for village guides – about 18% for Namtalan in contrast to 39.1% on the official record (see Table 7.1). This difference is perhaps caused by an overestimation by official statistics. Compared with the official records, the primary survey of incomes reveals diverging information for other income categories too. The incomes from accommodation (lodge and lodge services) collected as primary data and presented in Table 7.2 correspond to about 20% for Namtalan and only 3.5% for Lao Khao. This figure is lower in the official record (TSU) for Namtalan with 8.5% (lodging 7.3% and lodge service 1.2%).

Table 7.2 Average direct household incomes in Namtalan and Lao Khao village by category of income (2009)

Category of income	Namtalan (public) (n=47)		Lao Khao (private) (n=35)	
	Mean household income (Kip)	Percentage	Mean household income (Kip)	Percentage
Rice	45,578	6.8	31,743	3.7
Vegetables/fruits	72,701	10.9	57,219	6.7
Meat (chicken, duck)	84,710	12.7	80,000	9.3
Guide fees	121,935	18.2	274,667	31.9
Cooking fees	81,885	12.2	164,000	19.0
Lodge services	135,000	20.2	30,000	3.5
Massage	0	0	59,231	6.9
Cultural shows	0	0	164,286	19.1
Jar wine	53,647	8.0	0	0
Handicrafts	74,143	11.1	0	0
Total	669,599	100	861,146	100

Source: Author's survey

Similarly, handicraft sales account for 11% in Namtalan in Table 7.2, but only for 3.2% in Table 7.1. These differences indicate that public records for Namtalan show higher earnings for some items, including food and guide fees, than the survey data. This applies also to the privately owned ecotourism operation in Lao Khao, where the official record for food and lodging services reports higher incomes than the survey data.

Table 7.2 also shows household incomes in Lao Khao. The income received by households for food combining the first three items (rice, vegetable, meat) is about 19%. This amount is much lower than from the official tourism record (41.2%). A comparison with tourist expenditure (Table 7.2) indicates that almost half of the amount spent on food leaks out of the local economy. According to a local manager, this happened when the rotation system for making meal services in the village failed to provide sufficient food for tourists; he then had to purchase food from the market in town. Income from guide fees scored the highest proportion of household incomes for the villagers, about 32%. Other categories including cooking fees and cultural shows had a similar proportion of about 19% each.

Table 7.2 presents a different structure of income distribution compared to those presented in Table 7.1. The publicly owned tourism venture resulted in higher food incomes from rice, vegetables/fruits, and meat, corresponding to 30.4%. This is about twice the share raised by the privately owned company where only 19.7% can be related to food sales. This is partly owing to the ethnic practice of the Khmu who still make jar-wine that can add value to their food and drink sales. In Lao Khao, fees for local Akha guides accounted for about 32% of the household incomes. The guides take tourists to the village and accompany them during their trekking. In contrast, the public tourism enterprise has the strategy of recruiting guides from all villages involved in the trek. Thus, in Namtalan only about 18% of the household income is dependent on guiding. The private tourism company also pays higher fees for cooking than its public counterpart – 19% and 12.2% of the household income, respectively, can be attributed to this, but the opposite is the case for the lodging services, where the corresponding figures are about 4% and 20%. The commodification of ethnic practices creates surplus values for the village households. Products including massage, cultural shows, jar wine, and handicrafts all raise significant income for the villagers. In summary, results from the two cases indicate that privately organized tourism generates higher revenue for the households than publicly organized tourism. This appears partly to be related to the commodification of ethnic practices. The total mean household income of Lao Khao, regardless of different sample sizes (35/47), is thus higher than Namtalan – 861 146 Kip and 669 599 Kip, respectively.

Income distribution

Although ecotourism projects contribute to these two villages economically, not all households receive an equal level of income. Degrees of inequality between these two villages are shown in Tables 7.3 and 7.4 expressed by Gini index and quintile shares. The Gini index of Namtalan is slightly higher than that of Lao Khao (0.41 and 0.39, respectively); the higher the index, the greater the inequality. This implies that the privately run businesses in Lao Khao share income from tourism to villagers slightly more equally than the publicly run tourism operations in Namtalan. Both values for the Gini index in the two villages are however a little higher than the national average. For example, it was reported that the Gini coefficient for household income in Laos during 2007/2008 was 0.35 (LMPI, 2010), indicating that tourism development increases economic inequality at the local level.

Table 7.3 Gini coefficient and quintile share analysis of household income in Namtalan (2009)

	Namtalan (public)		Mean	Std. Deviation	t-value	P
Gini index		0.41				
Quintile	('000Kip)	%				
1st	0–125	5.1	56,600	42,604.64	0.23	0.82
2nd	125–203	11.0	159,700	27,569.3	0.9	0.38
3rd	203–260	15.9	237,977.78	18,349.78	5.06	0.00
4th	260–400	21.8	325,555.56	51,822.08	0.71	0.49
5th	400–1,727	46.1	688,627.11	399,243.15	−0.19	0.85

Source: calculated from the survey

The quintile analysis of household income points, however, in the opposite direction compared with the Gini indices. The privately owned ecotourism project shows a wider income gap than the government run ecotourism venture. The lowest quintile of the population, in terms of income, received relatively equal shares in Namtalan and Lao Khao, about 5% and 4%, respectively.

The survey results reveal that the privately operated ecotourism enterprises distribute income to all villagers more equally than the publicly operated companies (50.56/46.14). The result of the t-test reveals that only within the group with an income range from169,000 to 215,000 Kip, are household incomes equal in both villages, regardless of different characteristics of village household and ecotourism activities. For all other income categories, there are significant differences between the two the villages. Inequality of income distribution is evident even when the analysis does not reveal whether households in the different income categories partake in different activities. Importantly, the equality dimension of ecotourism income was not on track to be pro-poor, and this widens the gap between lowest and highest income groups.

Conclusion

Although it is argued that using non-governmental organizations (NGOs) and the public sector to establish best practice models and act as mediators to ensure that putting 'equitable benefits-sharing mechanisms' in place are most prominent (Harrison & Schipani, 2008, p. 184), results of this study show that, in practice, inequality in distributional effects of tourism income is still prevailing, both in cases of publicly and privately run ecotourism ventures. If the idea of handing over the ecotourism project to communities themselves is promoted, it remains uncertain if benefits are equally distributed. This is because the poorest group is hindered in its participation in

Table 7.4 Gini coefficient and quintile share analysis of household income in Lao Khao (2009)

	Lao Khao (private)		Mean	Std. Deviation	t-value	P
Gini index		0.39				
Quintile	('000Kip)	%				
1st	0–127	4.4	51,500	41,822.24	0.23	0.82
2nd	127–169	10.4	149,500	13,351.03	1.01	0.33
3rd	169–215	13.6	194,142.86	15,507.29	5.17	0.00
4th	215–408	21.1	302,257.14	78,672.29	0.68	0.51
5th	408–1,304	50.6	724,200	349,721.65	−0.19	0.85

Source: calculated from the survey

tourism by many factors such as their level of education, business compe-
tence, and various socioeconomic factors, as has been argued by Park et al.
(2018). Besides these factors, income inequality can also be linked to tourism policy, transparency in the management of tourism and village funds, as
well as to gender issues (Phommavong, 2011a; Phommavong & Sörensson,
2014; Trupp & Sunanta, 2017).

The strategy for tourism development in Laos generally states that tourism
has to combat poverty, but a specific strategy to assist the poorest group has
not been realized (Phommavong et al., 2010). In the case of Namtalan, home
for both ethnic groups, the Khmu and Lanten, the majority of the Lanten
people withdrew from working in ecotourism because of a mistrust regarding
the tourism manager, a member of the Khmu people, and his ability to
manage the village fund in a transparent way (Phommavong, 2011a). In the
case of Lao Khao, some ethnic beliefs and practices govern, particularly the
role of women in the family and society, and thus contribute to inequality
(Phommavong & Sörensson, 2014). The results from the Gini coefficient and
the quintile share analysis indicate that the incomes of class three are significantly more equally distributed. This means that particularly the middle-
income groups are benefitting from tourism independent of village context.
For the poorest and the richest households, benefits from tourism differ. In
the case of Lao Khao, the poorest families cannot supply food for tourists
and serve at the lodge due to the constraints of their family assets. Even richer
families are inclined to resist involvement in tourism since they are often
bound to their own large agricultural activities.

In summary, it is noted that place-based strategies for tourism development as a tool for equal income distribution, particularly to the poor, have
not succeeded. This study supports the academic criticism concerning the
ability of current pro-poor tourism approaches to actually make a difference for the poorest. Thus, the growth in employment opportunities
caused by tourism is not including the poor to any greater degree (Deller,
2010). This implies that the efforts of the government in directing tourism
to reach the poor are only successful to a certain extent, in that even this
group may benefit somewhat from tourism. However, tourism development
in itself seems to accentuate differences within the villages, offering a better
life for some households, while at the same time leaving the poorest further behind. Moreover, the study clearly indicates that compared to the
publicly run companies often promoted by donors and academics, privately run companies do not perform worse in creating income and dis-
tributing it equally to households at the village level despite companies'
interests in accumulating capital. Indeed, private companies perform
slightly better in this respect. Thus, strategies to create backward linkages
for local tourism development and to involve the poorest groups in society
should be mandatory for all development projects, independent of whether
they are organized as private or public companies.

Acknowledgements

We would like to thank Assoc. Prof. Aina Tollefsen of the Department of Geography, Umeå University, Sweden, for reading and offering valuable comments on this paper. This study was financially supported by the Swedish International Development Agency (Sida). We thank the staff of the Faculty of Social Sciences, National University of Laos for their contributions to the fieldwork.

Note

1   The exchange rate was LAK8,522 per US$1 in 2009.

References

Archer, B.H. (1982). The values of multipliers and their policy implications. *Tourism Management* 3, 236–241.

Archer, B., & Fletcher, J.E. (1996). The economic impact of tourism in Seychelles. *Annals of Tourism Research* 2, 32–47.

Blake, A., Arbache, J.S., Sinclair, M.T., & Teles, V. (2008). Tourism and poverty relief. *Annals of Tourism Research* 35, 107–126.

Britton, S.G. (1982). The political economy of tourism in the Third World. *Annals of Tourism Research* 9, 331–358.

Brohman, J. (1996). New directions in tourism for Third World development. *Annals of Tourism Research* 23, 48–70.

Bryman, A. (2008). *Social Research Methods.* Oxford: Oxford University Press.

Campbell, L.M. (1999). Ecotourism in rural developing communities. *Annals of Tourism Research* 26, 534–553.

Cohen, P.T. (2009). The post-opium scenario and rubber in northern Laos: Alternative Western and Chinese models of development. *International Journal of Drug Policy* 20, 424–430.

Deller, S. (2010). Rural poverty, tourism and spatial heterogeneity. *Annals of Tourism Research* 37, 180–205.

Fletcher, J.E. (1989). Input-output analysis and tourism impacts studies. *Annals of Tourism Research* 16, 514–529.

Ghosh, P., & Ghosh, A. (2018). Is ecotourism a panacea? Political ecology perspectives from the Sundarban Biosphere Reserve, India. *GeoJournal* 84(2), 345–366.

Hall, C.M. (2007). Pro-poor tourism: Do 'tourism exchanges benefit primarily the countries of the south'? *Current Issues in Tourism* 10, 111–118.

Hall, C.M., & Lew, A.L. (2009). *Understanding and managing tourism impacts: An integrated approach.* Abingdon: Routledge.

Haralambopoulos, N., & Pizam, A. (1996). Perceived economic impacts of tourism: The case of Samos. *Annals of Tourism Research* 3, 503–526.

Harrison, D., & Schipani, S. (2007). Lao tourism and poverty alleviation: Community-based tourism and the private sector. *Current Issues in Tourism* 10, 194–230.

Harrison, D., & Schipani, S. (2008). Tourism in the Lao People's Democratic Republic. In M. Hitchcock, V.T. King, & M. Parnwell (Eds.), *Tourism in Southeast Asia: Challenges and New Directions* (pp. 165–188). Copenhagen: NIAS Press.

Healy, R.G. (1994). Tourism merchandise as a means of generating local benefits from ecotourism. *Journal of Sustainable Tourism* 2, 137–151.

Holden, A., & Novelli, M. (2011). The changing paradigms of tourism in international development: placing the poor first – Trojan horse or real hope? *Tourism Planning & Development* 8, 233–235

Hunt, C. (2011). Passport to development? Local perceptions of the outcomes of post-socialist tourism policy and growth in Nicaragua. *Tourism Planning & Development* 8, 265–279.

Huse, M., Gustavsen, T., & Almedal, S. (1998) Tourism impact comparisons among Norwegian towns. *Annals of Tourism Research* 25, 721–738.

Lacher, R.G., & Nepal, S.K. (2010). Dependency and development in northern Thailand. *Annals of Tourism Research* 37(4), 947–968.

Lao Ministry of Planning and Investment (LMPI) (2010) *Poverty in Lao PDR 2008.* Vientiane: LMPI.

Lee, S. (2009). Income inequality in tourism services-dependent counties. *Current Issues in Tourism* 12, 33–45.

Llorca-Rodríguez, C.M., Casas-Jurado, A.C., & García-Fernández, R.M. (2017). Tourism and poverty alleviation: An empirical analysis using panel data on Peru's departments. *International Journal of Tourism Research* 19(6), 746–756.

Lonn, P., Mizoue, N., Ota, T., Kajisa, T., & Yoshida, S. (2018). Evaluating the contribution of community-based ecotourism (CBET) to household income and livelihood changes: A case study of the Chambok CBET program in Cambodia. *Ecological Economics* 151, 62–69.

Ly, T.P., & Bauer, T. (2016). Ecotourism in mainland Southeast Asia: Theory and practice. *Tourism, Leisure and Global Change* 1(1), 61–80.

McNeely, J.A. (1988). *Economics and biological diversity: Developing and using economic incentives to conserve biological resources.* Gland: IUCN.

Mitchell, J., & Ashley, C. (2007). *Can tourism offer pro-poor pathways to prosperity? Examining evidence on the impact of tourism on poverty.* Overseas Development Institute Briefing Paper 22. London: ODI.

Mitchell, J., & Ashley, C. (2010). *Tourism and poverty reduction: Pathways to prosperity.* London: Earthscan.

Mumm, M.M., & Tuffin, W. (2007). The Akha Experience: The first community-based tourism public-private partnership in the Lao PDR. *UNDP-Laos, Juth Pakai* 9, 52–66.

Nam Ha NPA (1998). Nam Ha National Protected Area – an ASEAN natural heritage site. Retrieved from: http://www.namha-npa.org/info/eco_tourism_in_namha_npa.htm.

Ounmany, K. (2014). *Community-based ecotourism in Laos: Benefits and burdens sharing among stakeholders.* Doctoral Dissertation, BOKU University of Natural Resources and Life Sciences, Vienna.

Park, E., Phandanouvong, T., & Kim, S. (2018). Evaluating participation in community-based tourism: A local perspective in Laos. *Current Issues in Tourism* 21(2), 128–132.

Park, E., Phandanouvong, T., Xaysena, P., & Kim, S. (2017). Empowerment, participation and barriers: ethnic minority community-based ecotourism development in Lao PDR. In I.B. de Lima and V.T. King (Eds.), *Tourism and ethnodevelopment: Inclusion, empowerment and self-determination* (pp. 139–152). Abingdon: Routledge.

Partridge, M.D., & Rickman, D.S. (2007). Persistent pockets of extreme American poverty and job growth: Is there a place-based policy role? *Journal of Agricultural and Resource Economics* 32, 210–224.

Phommavong, S., Müller, D.K., & Tollefsen, A. (2010). Tourism policy for poverty reduction. *International Journal of Culture and Tourism Research* 3, 131–150.

Phommavong, S. (2011a). Tourism and the question of poverty. In C. Minca & T. Oakes (Eds.), *Real tourism: Practice, care, and politics in contemporary travel culture* (pp. 183–202). Abingdon: Routledge.

Phommavong, S. (2011b). *International tourism development and poverty reduction in Lao PDR*. Doctoral Dissertation, Umeå University, Sweden. GERUM 2011:4.

Phommavong, S., & Sörensson, E. (2014). Ethnic tourism in Lao PDR: Gendered divisions of labour in community-based tourism for poverty reduction. *Current Issues in Tourism* 17(4), 350–362.

Riddington, G., McArthur, D., Harrison, T., & Gibson, H. (2010). Assessing the economic impacts of wind farms on tourism in Scotland: GIS, surveys and policy outcomes. *International Journal of Tourism Research* 12, 237–252.

Saarinen, J., Rogerson, C., & Manwa, H. (2011). Tourism and millennium development goals: Tourism for global development? *Current Issues in Tourism* 14, 201–203.

Scheyvens, R. (2011). *Tourism and poverty*. New York: Rotledge.

Schilcher, D. (2007). Growth versus equity: The continuum of pro-poor tourism and neoliberal governance. *Current Issues in Tourism* 10, 166–193.

Schipani, S. (2005). *The Nam Ha ecotourism project in Luang Namtha: Best practice 1999–2002 & current practice January 2003-March 2005*. Report to UNESCO Bangkok Office.

Schipani, S. (2008): *Impact: the effects of tourism on culture and the environment in Asia and the Pacific: Alleviating poverty and protecting cultural and natural heritage through community-based ecotourism in Luang Namtha, Lao PDR*. Bangkok: UNESCO.

Sciortino, R. (2017). Philanthropy in Southeast Asia: Between charitable values, corporate interests, and development aspirations. *Austrian Journal of South-East Asian Studies* 10(2), 139–163.

Sinclair, M.T. (1991). The economics of tourism. *Progress in Tourism, Recreation and Hospitality Management* 3, 1–27.

Smeral, E. (2005). The economic impact of tourism: Beyond satellite accounts. *Tourism Analysis* 10, 55–64.

Smith, S.L.J. (1989). *Tourism analysis: A handbook*. Harlow: Longman.

Suwei, G., & Changchun, Z. (2018). Exploration of poverty alleviation based on ecotourism in minority areas of Yunnan Province. *Ekoloji* 27(106), 1105–1113.

Taylor, S.R. (2017). Issues in measuring success in community-based indigenous tourism: Elites, kin groups, social capital, gender dynamics and income flows. *Journal of Sustainable Tourism* 25(3), 433–449.

Telfer, D.J., & Sharpley, R. (2008). *Tourism and development in the developing world*. London: Routledge.

Truong, V.D., Slabbert, E., & Nguyen, V.M. (2016). Poverty in tourist paradise? A review of pro-poor tourism in South and South-East Asia. In C. M. Hall and S. J. Page (Eds.), *The Routledge handbook of tourism in Asia* (pp. 121–138). Abingdon: Routledge.

Trupp, A., & Sunanta, S. (2017). Gendered practices in urban ethnic tourism in Thailand. *Annals of Tourism Research* 64, 76–86.

Turegano, M.A.S. (2006). Dependency and development patterns in tourism: A case study in the Canary Islands. *Tourism and Hospitality Planning & Development* 3, 117–130.

Wall, G. (1997). Scale effects on tourism multipliers. *Annals of Tourism Research* 24, 446–450.

Walpole, M.J., & Goodwin, H.J. (2000). Local economic impacts of Dragon tourism in Indonesia. *Annals of Tourism Research* 27, 559–576.

Wanhill, S. (1994). The measurement of tourist income multipliers. *Tourism Management* 15, 281–283.

Wells, M.P. (1992). Biodiversity conservation, affluence and poverty: Mismatched costs and benefits and efforts to remedy them. *Ambio* 21, 237–243.

Wen, J.J., & Sinha, C. (2009). The spatial distribution of tourism in China: Trends and impacts. *Asia Pacific Journal of Tourism Research* 14, 93–104.

Williams, S. (2009). *Tourism geography: A new synthesis.* Abingdon: Routledge.

Zapata, M.J., Hall, C.M., Lindo, P., & Vanderschaeghe, M. (2011). Can community-based tourism contribute to development and poverty alleviation? Lessons from Nicaragua. *Current Issues in Tourism* 14(8), 725–749.

8 Migration into tourism micro-entrepreneurship

Socioeconomic advancement or mobility trap?

Alexander Trupp

Introduction

Tourism and migration are essential contributors to the social and economic development of many developing or transforming societies in Southeast Asia. Migrants can be seen as a development resource whose income and remittances sustain their own livelihoods as well as those of their left-behind family members (Hugo, 1983; Toyota, Yeoh, & Nguyen, 2007). Equally, evidence suggests that tourism development can lead to socioeconomic betterment as a tool to create jobs and empower communities (Dolezal, 2015; Hipsher, 2017). In particular, the notion of tourism micro-entrepreneurship, defined as businesses employing five people or less, offers prospects of self-determination, female empowerment, income and further career outlooks (Çakmak, Lie, & McCabe, 2018; Morais, Ferreira, Nazariadli, & Ghahramani, 2017). Microbusinesses in Southeast Asia often operate in a context of competition, risk and insecurity, and entail conflict with authorities (Endres, 2013; Trupp, 2015a). At the same time, tourism development in Southeast Asia has also been criticised for creating uneven development and transforming host communities into the passive 'toured' (Cohen, 2003; Dolezal & Trupp, 2015).

Along these intersecting fields of tourism, migration and micro-entrepreneurship, this chapter discusses opportunities and challenges for ethnic minority souvenir vendors in Thailand's tourist areas, whereby the following questions arise: Can migration into self-employment make a positive contribution to the socioeconomic development of the migrating actors and their areas of origin, or do they increase or lead to precarious and insecure working relationships? Does ethnic entrepreneurship offer opportunities for advancement and sustainable career prospects or does it prove to be a development blockade in the sense that economic and social advancement is made more difficult?

These broad questions can be answered if both the structural embedding of actors and their possibilities for action are considered. Taking Thailand's ethnic minorities as a case study, the mixed embeddedness (Kloosterman, Van der Leun, & Rath, 1999) of ethnic businesses in social, economic and political-legal structures in the context of internal migration are analysed and their motivations, strategies for action and restrictions in the field of tourist economies are shown. This article draws on extensive fieldwork including semi-structured interviews and participant observation among predominantly female souvenir vendors who are members of the highland ethnic minority group Akha. The research was conducted between 2008 and 2016 in Thailand's urban and beach-side tourist areas, such as Chiang Mai, Bangkok, Ko Samui and Pattaya.

Migration and micro-entrepreneurship

An ethnic economy consists of self-employed people, employers and their employees from an ethnic minority (Light & Gold, 2007). The economic activities of individuals or companies that are related to the particularities of ethnic groups in their general business structure and strategy, in their specific system of production and/or in relation to their service and production structures, are understood as ethnic entrepreneurship (Goebel & Pries, 2006). Actors belonging to an ethnic group may share a common cultural heritage, or a common origin, language or religion but at the same time, these references are also known and visible to people who do not see themselves as part of this group (Dabringer & Trupp, 2012).

Ethnic entrepreneurship arises in response to discrimination and marginalisation in the labour market and by mainstream society (Portes & Rumbaut, 1996) or in response to the demand for specific services and products provided by the ethnic group. In such niche economies, ethnic entrepreneurs vertically network along value chains and thus create jobs for members of their own group (Nee & Sanders, 2001). The interactionist model explains ethnic economies through the interaction between the opportunity structures and obstacles of the host society (market conditions, competition between companies, migration policies) and the resources and group characteristics (goals, experiences and skills of entrepreneurs, mobilisation of social and ethnic resources) of ethnic entrepreneurs (Waldinger, Aldrich, & Ward, 1990). The value of social capital is defined as the ability to secure resources through networks or larger social structures (Portes & Sensenbrenner, 1993), which is emphasised by numerous studies and development organisations such as the World Bank or the OECD (Woolcock & Narayan, 2000).

A considerable proportion of the self-employed and small businesses operate in the informal sector which has been associated with work-intensive production, simple technology, low income, low entry barriers, a lack of access to social security systems and unregistered and non-formalised economic activities (Chen, 2007). Studies on street vending in Asia conclude that governments have more or less failed to recognise street vending as legal activity and that they are viewed as obstacles to modern urban development (Kusakabe, 2006).

Research on ethnic economics and migration in Asia is dominated by transnational and international approaches, while forms and effects of internal migration are hardly discussed (Elmhirst, 2012). The scientific discourse on rural-urban migration first became popular in the 1970s in connection with the problems of rapidly increasing urbanisation and regional disparities. In 2017, the urban population in Thailand was 49.2% (World Bank, 2019). The decline of agricultural activities and the associated migration to urban centres is a diversification strategy of rural households in the region (Rigg, 1998). Household diversification is based on different preconditions and objectives (Rigg, 2003): High-income households, which are usually also characterised by a higher education of their members, strive to achieve high levels of investment, e.g. in transportation companies or wholesale, and tend to accumulate further capital. Middle-income households often try to send their household members as employees to the city, or to engage in retailing, and thus to consolidate or strengthen their socioeconomic status, often through personal contacts.

For the category of low-income and poor (and mostly landless) households, migrating and being employed as micro-traders, mobile street vendors or garbage collectors is a survival strategy. Households with a high socio-economic status especially benefit from internal migration processes. Other studies point to the development potential for poor internal migrants (Deshingkar, 2005). People can build knowledge, contacts and self-confidence in the context of their migration experiences and thus make their economic activities more successful, for example by avoiding expensive and often exploitative intermediaries and middlemen. For instance, in a study on north-eastern India, Rao (2001) shows that internal migration developed from a survival strategy in the 1970s to a strategy of consolidation and additional diversification in the 1990s. Moreover, remittances play a central role in internal migration (Deshingkar, 2005). Results of the National Migration Survey in Thailand show that 16% of Thai households receive material support from migrants, while only just under 5% of migrants receive support from their 'home' households (Osaki, 1999).

Minorities and internal migration in Thailand

Thailand formally recognised nine highland ethnic minority groups, which are also called *chao khao* (in English, hilltribe). This categorisation, which was introduced by the Thai authorities in 1959, not only refers to a topographical dimension in which highland inhabitants are distinguished from lowland inhabitants, but also reflects a political and social dimension. The term hilltribe can be pejorative or perceived as being associated with characteristics such as wild, primitive and uncivilised, thus illustrating the low status of minority groups in Thailand's social hierarchy (Winichakul, 2000). From the late 1950s, the so-called hilltribes became part of the interest of the Thai nation state. In the context of the East-West conflict, they were suspected of sympathising with communist ideologies and collectively identified as enemies of the state. Added to this was the strategic importance of their settlement areas in the difficult-to-access and uncontrollable mountain and border areas. After the end of the East-West conflict, economic-ecological factors came to the fore. The ethnic minorities were held liable for environmental destruction and drug trafficking partly connected with opium cultivation (Laungaramsri, 2003). These developments contributed to a negative image of ethnic minorities that has survived in large parts of the Thai society, especially in urban centres. However, since the early 2000s, a shifting of ethnoscapes and terminologies 'from "hilltribes" and "ethnic groups", as labelled by outsiders, to "Indigenous Peoples", based on self-definition, emerged' (Leepreecha, 2019, p. 58).

The region and the inhabitants of northern Thailand's mountain and hill country have experienced profound economic and socio-cultural transformation processes. Moreover, conflicts with the nation state regarding land and hunting rights, citizenship rights and assimilation policies, as well as conflicts between Christianised and 'traditional' minority groups that favour new hierarchies and power relations in the villages continue (Tooker, 2004). One of the main consequences of these transformation processes led to increasing migration to urban centres.

From a spatial perspective, the economic and tourist centres such as the capital Bangkok and the surrounding central and southern regions of the country are experiencing migration gains, while the northern and north-eastern regions have a negative migration balance (IOM, 2019). However, statistical census data should be viewed with caution, as it only covers permanent forms of migration, but ignores various forms of circular or multi-local migration. The increase and diversification of forms of mobility in the context of internal migration has benefited from the development of transport and telecommunications infrastructure and economic developments. The fact that temporary migrants usually cannot be registered in the migration destination area is a further complication of the statistical recording of internal migration. It is even more difficult to find concrete data on the migration of ethnic minorities because the criterion of ethnicity is not part of the questions asked.

However, existing studies indicate an increasing importance of ethnic minority migration in Thailand. For example, the ethnologist Alting von Geusau estimated in 1997 that one of seven Akha no longer lives in their home villages (Toyota, 1998). The number of Akha migrant women in the northern city of Chiang Mai increased from 50 in the late 1970s (Toyota, 1998) to about 2,000 in the 1990/2000s (Boonyasaranai & Chermue, 2004). The withdrawal of customary land and hunting rights, the ban on logging and the lack of training opportunities in the areas of origin along with village conflicts, the allure of urban lifestyles, and the desire for independence are the driving forces behind rapidly increasing migration (Buadaeng, Boonyasaranai, & Leepreecha, 2002). In the urban and tourist migration destinations, ethnic minorities are mainly employed in wage work such as construction, filling stations, gastronomy, hotels, and the entertainment industry. A further group of migrants are pupils and students who migrate to the cities due to a lack of training opportunities in their areas of origin; this educational migration is often supported by scholarships from Christian or Buddhist organisations. A third group consists of self-employed people who trade in agricultural products or are active in tourism as guides, tour operators or in the art and souvenir trade. In the following sections, the development of the urban souvenir trade and the associated possibilities and barriers are outlined using the example of the independent Akha souvenir vendors.

Tourism and development of the Akha souvenir trade

Tourism-led souvenir business

The business with handicrafts and souvenirs began in the 1960s in the Northern Thai village areas, when international tourists in search of adventure and authenticity increasingly visited the mountain region (Cohen, 2001). The commercialisation of artworks into souvenirs was not initiated by the minorities themselves but by external actors, such as business operators in Chiang Mai (Cohen, 1983).

The sales products of the individual Akha souvenir vendors are composed of self-produced and purchased goods, whereby an increase of the latter can be observed in recent years. Various bracelets or bags are produced in-house and the necessary raw materials are purchased from Bangkok's wholesalers or, in the case of natural decorative materials (e.g. job's tears seeds), in the village areas. The street vendors work for their souvenir production before and after their everyday sale activities as well as during the visits to their home villages. The production is not organised in a village or family association, but is highly individualised, as in almost all cases every salesperson is responsible for his or her own production. Other products such as chains, bracelets or wooden frogs are bought from non-Akha traders or large markets and then resold. The Akha are therefore owners, managers, vendors and partly producers of their own business or goods. Their sales target group is not members of their own ethnic group as in the classic niche model, but mainly international tourists. Three types of micro-businesses can be distinguished with regard to mobility in the sales area and business size (Smith & Henderson, 2008; Gantner, 2011): mobile street vendors represent the largest group in terms of numbers. They have no fixed sales location and carry their goods with them in a strapped basket. Semi-mobile vendors place their goods on sidewalks, but they have to change locations frequently due to 'order controls' of the municipal police (Trupp, 2014). Immobile salespeople have fixed stalls at markets or small business premises.

Gendered practices

The vast majority of Akha souvenir sellers are female. With very few exceptions, the group of mobile street vendors in particular is made up of women. In the field of semi- and immobile sales, men are somewhat more strongly represented. Akhazhaw, the Akha's philosophy of life, which has been handed down orally for generations, prescribes a strict gender-based division of labour in the Akha society, in which women are responsible for the production of clothing in addition to working in agriculture and the household (Kammerer, 1988). The women themselves explain this unequal distribution by the fact that men simply do not sell so well as they do. Men are deemed too shy as mobile vendors to speak to tourists, and one interviewee said that men are too lazy. Akha women's migration and participation in tourism has reconstructed gender inequality but it has also advanced their economic status as breadwinners of the household and opened up new horizons (Trupp & Sunanta, 2017).

Spatial expansion

With the establishment of Chiang Mai as a tourist centre in Northern Thailand, opportunity structures were created of which Thailand's highland ethnic minorities could make use. The opening of Chiang Mai Night Bazar as part of the national development plan enabled Akha traders and producers to sell their products and goods to international tourists. In 1975 the first Akha opened a stand at the famous night market in Chiang Mai and since then many have followed her example (Toyota, 1998). In the same decade, the Old Chiang Mai Cultural Center was opened by a private business entrepreneur, in which cultural shows and dance performances by Northern Thai and minority groups took place. This was the second point of contact for Akha sellers in the early phase of tourism development. In the course of infrastructural and tourist developments in Northern Thailand and the previously outlined processes of change in the village areas, the number of Akha souvenir sellers in Chiang Mai increased steadily. At the daily night market about 100 Akha work as ambulatory street vendors and dozens rent a sales stand (Fuengfusakul, 2008). In recent years, three different daily markets have also been opened, offering Akha small entrepreneurs additional sales opportunities.

However, the expanded sales opportunities and the tourist upswing in Chiang Mai led to increased competition and poorer profits for the individual Akha sellers. Therefore, in the 1990s the first Akha souvenir traders began to migrate to the capital Bangkok and later to the mass tourism destinations along the coasts of Hua Hin and Pattaya or on the islands of Phuket and Koh Samui. The pioneers of the 1990s were very successful because they were able to sell their products quickly and at a good price in the new destinations. After the stock of souvenirs was sold, the Akha returned to their village and informed relatives and villagers about these new opportunities. The emergence of migration networks that provide (potential) migrants with information, as well as differentiated means of transport and communication, have also encouraged migration over greater geographical distances (Trupp, 2015b, 2017).

Life and work perspectives

The Akha migrants represent different types of rural-urban directed mobility processes in developing countries (Hugo, 1983). First, seasonal migrants work in the high tourist season or, in the case of students, during the semester break and return to the villages for agricultural activities. Second, working life migrants move for the entire duration of their working life and then intend to return to the village. Indeed, the majority of the Akha micro-entrepreneurs stresses a wish to return to their home village in the future with sufficient savings. Permanent migrants live and work mainly in the northern city of Chiang Mai, where in recent decades spatial concentrations of residential areas of minority groups have formed (Rabibhadana & Jatuworapruk, 2007). The majority of seasonal and working migrants are female, migrate alone and leave family members behind in the village. Children are rarely taken along. Men almost never migrate independently into the souvenir economy but accompany their wives. The Akha sellers migrate not only between the area of origin and the target area, but also between different sales areas and provinces. Experienced souvenir sellers have migration and business experience in all major tourist destinations in Thailand. For many of the Akha interviewed, the desire for self-employment is also at the centre of the migration decision. The possibility to become one's own boss allows a free division of work and independence from other employers with whom bad experiences have sometimes been had (Trupp, 2017).

While the majority of interviewed vendors only choose the ethnic economy as a professional field until they can permanently return to the minority villages with sufficient savings or other possibilities, others hope to achieve further socioeconomic advancement by expanding the souvenir business or migrating abroad. It is above all the young generation of Akha salespeople who can imagine a permanent life in an urban context.

The role of social networks

Social networks in migration contexts are usually viewed positively, as they connect people with information, ideas, goods or financial resources, thus reducing risks and costs and making a positive outcome to migration more likely. For the analysis of social relationships of Akha entrepreneurs, a distinction is made here between 'insider relationships' in the sense of *bonding social capital* and 'outsider relationships' in the sense of *bridging social capital* (Putnam, 2000).

Within insider relationships, a *bounded solidarity* (Portes & Sensenbrenner, 1993) can be observed within the Akha sellers, which is based on identification with the group – characterised by a common language (Akha), a common regional origin, a similar socioeconomic status and similar experiences of discrimination, and thus leads to the transfer of resources. Most Akha migrate to tourism centres to receive a better job and to be independent of Thai employers. Their sales work begins in the early afternoon and usually ends at or after midnight. The time before and after is still used for the production of souvenirs. Information on the organisation of souvenir sales, accommodation and transport facilities, etc. is shared among Akha vendors. This solidarity is also based on habituated, internalised values and norms that motivate people to build and maintain relationships. Experienced entrepreneurs and salespeople feel obliged to help other family members or villagers, as they have to support the others as older and experienced Akha. In general, it can be said that although conflicts, i.e. negative social capital, exist within Akha sellers, they remain limited. Fuengfusakul (2008, p. 122) comes to a similar conclusion in her study on mobile sellers at the Chiang Mai Night Bazar: 'they [the conflicts] do not accumulate into antagonism because all of them share the same fate of being the lowest group of vendors and have often been looked down upon by Thai stall holders'. In some cases, negative dimensions of social capital could be observed when, for example, newcomers were given false information about sales and transport opportunities in the new migration destination area. Nevertheless, it can be summarised that social relations at the horizontal level between actors with similar socioeconomic status are strong and have a positive impact on the network members. At the same time, however, the vertical relationships between Akha who are differently equipped with status and capital are rather weak. There are few contacts between the 'elite Akha' with high socioeconomic status and the 'ordinary saleswomen'. An Akha woman with a successful shop expressed her shame for the street vendors who – in her opinion – sell inferior souvenir products.

Another important dimension in relation to bonding social capital and development is the link between migration destinations and areas of origin. Most migrants return to the village when they get sick, for their children during their holidays and on important religious holidays, usually two to four village visits per year. In addition to the personal village visits, Akha migrants and their left-behind family members are in regular contact via mobile phones. Women provide a significant portion of the household income for the families left behind in the villages. The remittances are mainly used for the education of the children and the maintenance costs of grandparents and in-laws. In the case of high incomes, investments are also made in larger purchases such as motorcycles, cars or house building. Money is also spent on status symbols such as jewellery or new mobile phones.

In addition to insider relationships, the Akha micro-entrepreneurs maintain networks with external actors, such as tourists, foreigners living in Thailand and members of the Thai majority society. This form of bridging social capital primarily arises in the context of daily sales activities in the international tourism centres. Some Akha sellers establish lasting business relationships with Western tourists and small entrepreneurs who import Akha souvenirs to Europe, Australia or the USA. This ability to 'bridge' social capital to outsiders is, however, only possible for those actors who have good communication skills and a basic knowledge of the English language. The young generation of salespeople especially uses the daily contact with tourists to practice and improve English and other languages. In this context, transnational relations between Akha women and international tourists arise at times, which in some cases lead to marriage and international marriage migration. However, they also report conflicts with tourists, for example, in the course of price negotiations for a product, but also in connection with sexual harassment (Trupp, 2017).

The economic and political-legal context of souvenir street vending

Economic and political-legal structures at the local and national level also play an important role in the success or failure of Akha souvenir businesses. In order to start a small souvenir business, Akha vendors need to have a starting capital of approximately 5,000–10,000 Baht (currently approximately 140–280 Euro) which is needed for initial transport, accommodation, and production costs. This corresponds to approximately one month of salary as a wage worker in construction or agriculture. Therefore, young souvenir vendors with few savings usually receive financial support from their mother. Although the economic barriers to entering the souvenir business are comparatively low, the study also shows that it is not the socioeconomically weakest actors who migrate. In addition to social and economic resources, incorporated cultural capital (Bourdieu, 1986) in the form of languages, communication skills and the skill of sewing and embroidery is important for souvenir production.

The market situation for Akha entrepreneurs is characterised by high competition and dependence on international tourists. In the early established sales areas of Chiang Mai and Bangkok, competition among salespeople is fierce and the competition for customers is less along the lines of the quality of the offered goods, but rather in terms of flexibility, sales strategy and duration of sales time. Those who still work after midnight are exposed to less competition. Experienced Akha entrepreneurs know very well about the different economic possibilities resulting from the range of clients and travel times and migrate between different sales locations within one year. Accordingly, most street vendors in Chiang Mai or Kaosan Road earn 8,000–15,000 Baht per month, while in the newer coastal regions three to four times the income is possible.

So far, however, very few have been able to use the experience and capital accumulation in the context of migration and tourism micro-entrepreneurship to further socioeconomic advancement opportunities. Bigger savings for future investments or entrepreneurial advancements in the sense of upgrading their business (e.g. from a mobile to a fixed stand) is hardly possible.

On the political, legal and social level, Akha entrepreneurs are confronted with numerous barriers. Thus, their low status and the reproduced negative image of the Akha within mainstream Thai society mean that they do not have access to the domestic tourist market. Many of the Akha interviewed emphasised that they can count their Thai buyers of recent years on one hand, despite the booming domestic tourism. Moreover, purchase preferences and a sense of authenticity of products differ between Western and domestic tourists. Similarly, Husa (2019) states that souvenir purchases in the highland area of Northern Thailand play a rather minor role for domestic tourists.

An unclear citizenship policy as well as unclear information on the legal situation and urban policy regarding the regulation of street sales are further challenges. The political developments in Thailand from the 1960s onward, which viewed the Akha and other highland minority groups as rather recent immigrants, led to the fact that a large part of the minority groups is still denied Thai citizenship (Sakboon, 2011). Citizenship in Thailand does not only depend on the place of birth, but also on the residence status or the parents' place of birth. It must be proven that at least one parent was born in Thailand. Since many do not have an official document such as a birth certificate, this proof is usually very difficult to produce. Toyota (2006) assumes that every second member of an ethnic minority group in Thailand with a legitimate right to citizenship has not yet received it. The numbers of ethnic minority members without citizenship is lower today but reliable data on this issue is rare to non-existent (Trupp, 2017). Those who do not hold citizenship also have no or only very limited access to basic state services and are excluded from electoral and labour laws. It is also not possible for undocumented migrants to rent a sales stand, as residence permits are also required for this. They are forbidden from leaving the province they live in and approvals must be obtained for each trip. This restricts affected Akha vendors in their legal mobility and exposes them to great dangers and penalties if they do migrate to tourist centres. Therefore, many Akha sellers from this group avoid the long and risky journey to the newer and economically promising sales destinations in the south of the country. Such people are marginalised within an already marginalised group (Ishii, 2012).

While the granting of citizenship is regulated at national level, the rules for street sales are determined and enforced at regional and local level. A study by Kusakabe (2006) on street sales in Bangkok shows that the policy of recent years towards street vendors has been characterised by strict law enforcement, which provides for penalties and arrests of vendors/ sole traders without a licence.

Since 2014 Thailand has been ruled by a military government (Schaffar, 2018) which demonstrates a kind of law and order agenda featuring the 'clean up' of popular street vending areas which create an atmosphere of strong uncertainty among vendors, and which has led to evictions of small businesses. The spatial reorganisation plan of the Bangkok Metropolitan Administration (BMA) ignored street vendors' livelihoods and rights (Boonjubun, 2017) and led to the removal of 20,000 vendors from 478 locations since 2016 (Lefevre, 2018).

There is no official license for the Akha mobile street vendors in any of the sales zones, but this regulation is also handled differently in different zones and regions. Akha sellers emphasise that they have few problems with control bodies and community authorities at the night market in Chiang Mai but are regularly controlled and punished in Bangkok, especially in the newer migration and sales areas. The penalty for selling without a license is the income of one to three days of sales. The regulations for street sales also apply to other 'Thai' traders, but Akha traders, according to their own statements, are checked more often, since they are quickly identified and classified as *hilltribe* due to their clothing and appearance – with suspicion of unlawful residence.

Conclusion

This chapter analysed the migratory movements of predominantly female Akha ethnic minority vendors into urban tourism micro-entrepreneurship. Results demonstrate that the Akha souvenir economies have expanded geographically from the northern city of Chiang Mai to the capital of Bangkok and further south to coastal and island destinations. The author further assessed whether migration into self-employment makes a positive contribution to the socioeconomic development of the migrating actors and their areas of origin and whether tourism micro-entrepreneurship offers opportunities for advancement and sustainable career prospects.

Findings show that internal social capital serves as important pillar for surviving in the marketplace. For Akha micro-entrepreneurs, the mobilisation of insider social capital has served as a prerequisite for gaining information, establishing security, cohesion and sociality, and reducing expenses. Trust has been identified as an essential component of marketplaces in Southeast Asia (Widiyanto, 2019). For Akha vendors, social cohesion is based on collective experiences of discrimination in the context of previous migrations and work as well as on a similar socioeconomic status. Strong social relationships with outsiders or actors of higher socioeconomic status, however, are rather rare and the absence of such powerful relationships often limit entrepreneurial upward mobility. The difficulty in linking vertical social capital has also been documented for micro-entrepreneurs in other Southeast Asian cities such as Hanoi (Turner & Nguyen, 2005). Despite the important role of social relations within the Akha group, large parts of the Akha souvenir economies are highly individualised. The procurement of materials, production and sales are not collectively organised and micro-entrepreneurs are responsible for themselves in almost all business steps.

Economically, most Akha micro-entrepreneurs earn more as self-employed vendors than as workers in construction or agriculture. However, competition has increased sharply, especially in the sales areas that have been established for some time. A shift to newer destinations is currently leading to higher profits, but competition is also expected to increase there in the near future. The pioneers in the urban Akha souvenir business were able to sell their products at a high price in a short time and thus improve their economic status and living conditions as part of an accumulation strategy. Capital accumulation, which enables further investments in the areas of origin – such as house building or the purchase of a car – in addition to covering one's own basic living costs and those of the family members left behind, is becoming increasingly difficult in many destinations due to the highly competitive situation and the saturation of the tourist market. In this competitive atmosphere, self-exploitation through long and late working hours, physical exertion in mobile street vending, a difficult working environment in centres of mass tourism and work in the non-legally secure informal sector is often the only possibility for economic success. The souvenir economy in the 'old' destinations such as Chiang Mai and Bangkok is more of a survival strategy, while in the newer coastal and island destinations higher profits are currently possible in the sense of an accumulation strategy. Thus, for many street vendors in the long-established destinations, tourism entrepreneurship leads into a mobility trap of stagnation.

Dependencies on international tourists, disregard by domestic tourists and Thai vendors as well as impediments by national and local authorities, are observed in all sales areas except the Northern region. Akha entrepreneurs receive no support from authorities at the national or local level. An incomprehensible citizenship policy hampers mobility rather than promotes it, and the recent government 'clean-up' of vending areas have made souvenir selling more difficult. Local urban policies focus more on legal controls and penalties than on the provision of information and support for entrepreneurs at the fringes. Urban space across Southeast Asia gets increasingly contested and privileges certain forms of movements (such as 'modern' transportation) and spaces (such as shopping areas) over 'traditional' mobilities of street vendors and places for petty trade (Eidse, Turner, & Oswin, 2016). Such developments point to a reproduction of marginality and social segregation in urban and tourist contexts that contradict a positive development perspective.

On the other hand, Akha entrepreneurs emphasise the positive effects of independence, namely not having to report to superiors and having the freedom to visit family and friends at any time. The young generation is also looking for opportunities to improve their language and communication skills through daily contact with international tourists which can lead to greater self-determination.

The chapter shows that tourism micro-entrepreneurs can mobilise their social and cultural capital by carving out their own niches in the tourism industry. Their activities create employment for themselves and other members of their own ethnic group and – to a minor extent – can support the livelihoods of their left-behind families. Yet, the majority of Thailand's ethnic micro-entrepreneurs in the souvenir business come from socioeconomically marginalised regions and remain at the fringes of a business niche in urban and beach-side tourism hotspots that do not offer sustainable career prospects.

References

Boonjubun, C. (2017). Conflicts over streets: The eviction of Bangkok street vendors. *Cities* 70, 22–31.

Boonyasaranai, P., & Chermue, M. (2004). *Akha: LakLay chiwit cak chumchaw su muanng* [in Thai language]. Chiang Mai: Social Research Institute, Chiang Mai University.

Bourdieu, P. (1986). The forms of capital. In J.G. Richardson (Ed.), *Handbook of theory and research for the sociology of education* (pp. 241–258). New York: Greenwood Press.

Buadaeng, K., Boonyasaranai, P., & Leepreecha, P. (2002). *A study of the socio-economic vulnerability of urban-based tribal peoples in Chiang Mai and Chiang Rai, Thailand.* Chiang Mai: Social Research Institute, Chiang Mai University.

Çakmak, E., Lie, R., & McCabe, S. (2018). Reframing informal tourism entrepreneurial practices: Capital and field relations structuring the informal tourism economy of Chiang Mai. *Annals of Tourism Research* 72, 37–47.

Chen, M.A. (2007). Rethinking the informal economy: Linkages with the formal economy and the formal regulatory environment. In DESA working paper 46. New York: United Nations Department of Economic and Social Affairs.

Cohen, E. (1983). The dynamics of commercialized arts: The Meo and Yao of Northern Thailand. *Journal of the National Research Council of Thailand* 15(1), 69–82.

Cohen, E. (2001). *Thai Tourism: Hill Tribes, islands and open-ended prostitution.* Bangkok: White Lotus.

Cohen, E. (2003). Contemporary tourism and the host community in less developed areas. *Tourism Recreation Journal* 28(1), 1–9.

Dabringer, M., & Trupp, A. (Eds.). (2012). *Wirtschaften mit Migrationshintergrund. Zur soziokulturellen Bedeutung „ethnischer" Ökonomien in urbanen Räumen.* Vienna: Studienverlag.

Deshingkar, P. (2005). Background paper: Maximizing the benefits of internal migration for development. Presented at the Regional Conference on Migration and Development in Asia.

Dolezal, C. (2015). The tourism encounter in community-based tourism in Northern Thailand: Empty meeting ground or space for change? *Austrian Journal of South-East Asian Studies* 8(2), 165–186.

Dolezal, C., & Trupp, A. (2015). Tourism and development in Southeast Asia. *Austrian Journal of South-East Asian Studies* 8(2), 117–124.

Eidse, N., Turner, S., & Oswin, N. (2016). Contesting street spaces in a socialist city: Itinerant vending-scapes and the everyday politics of mobility in Hanoi, Vietnam. *Annals of the American Association of Geographers* 106(2), 340–349.

Elmhirst, R. (2012). Methodological dilemmas in migration research in Asia: Research design, omissions and strategic erasures. *Area* 44(3), 274–281.

Endres, K. (2013). Traders, markets, and the state in Vietnam: Anthropological perspectives. *Austrian Journal of South-East Asian Studies* 6(2), 356–365.

Fuengfusakul, A. (2008). Making sense of place: A case study of vendors and small entrepreneurs in the Chiang Mai Night Bazar. In S. Tanabe (Ed.), *Imagining communities in Thailand. ethnographic approaches* (pp. 107–134). Chiang Mai: Mekong Press.

Gantner, B. (2011). Schattenwirtschaft unter Palmen: Der touristisch informelle Sektor im Urlaubsparadies Patong, Thailand. *Austrian Journal of South-East Asian Studies* 4(1), 51–80.

Goebel, D., & Pries, L. (2006). Transnationalismus oder ethnische Mobilitätsfalle? Das Beispiel des „ethnischen Unternehmertums". In F. Kreutzer, & S. Roth (Eds.), *Transnationale Karrieren* (pp. 260–282). Wiesbaden: VS Verlag für Sozialwissenschaften.

Hipsher, S. (2017). *Poverty reduction, the private sector, and tourism in Mainland Southeast Asia.* Singapore: Springer.

Hugo, G. (1983). New conceptual approaches to migration in the context of urbanization: A discussion based on the Indonesian experience. In P.A. Morrison (Ed.), *Population movements: Their forms and functions in urbanization and development* (pp. 69–114). Liege: Ordina.

Husa, L.C. (2019). The 'souvenirization'and 'touristification'of material culture in Thailand–mutual constructions of 'otherness' in the tourism and souvenir industries. *Journal of Heritage Tourism*, May 2019, 1–15. DOI: doi:10.1080/1743873X.2019.1611835.

IOM (2019). *Thailand migration report 2019.* Bangkok: IOM.

Ishii, K. (2012). The impact of ethnic tourism on hill tribes in Thailand. *Annals of Tourism Research* 39(1), 290–310.

Kammerer, C.A. (1988). Shifting gender assymetries Among Akha of Northern Thailand. In N. Eberhardt (Ed.), *Gender, power, and the construction of the moral order: Studies from the Thai periphery* (pp. 33–51). Madison: Center for Southeast Asian Studies, University of Wisconsin.

Kloosterman, R., Van der Leun, J., & Rath, J. (1999). Mixed embeddedness: (In)formal economic activities and immigrant businesses in the Netherlands. *International Journal of Urban and Regional Research* 23(2), 252–266.

Kusakabe, K. (2006). *Policy issues on street vending: An overview of studies in Thailand, Cambodia and Mongolia.* Bangkok: International Labour Office. Retrieved from: http://www.ilo.org/wcmsp5/groups/public/—asia/—ro-bangkok/documents/publication/wcms_bk_pb_119_en.pdf.

Laungaramsri, P. (2003). Ethnicity and the politics of ethnic classification in Thailand. In C. MacKerras (Ed.), *Ethnicity in Asia* (pp. 157–173). London, New York: Routledge.

Leepreecha, P. (2019). Becoming indigenous peoples in Thailand. *Journal of Southeast Asian Studies* 50(1), 32–50.

Lefevre, A. (2018, September 17). Bangkok's street vendors decry evictions as authorities clean up. *Reuters.* Retrieved from: https://www.reuters.com/article/us-thailand-streetvendors-idUSKCN1LX2NH.

Light, I., & Gold, S.J. (2007). *Ethnic economies.* Bingley: Emerald Publishing.

Morais, D.B., Ferreira, B.S., Nazariadli, S., & Ghahramani, L. (2017). Tourism microentrepreneurship knowledge cogeneration. In N. Scott, M. van Niekerk, & M. di Martino (Ed). *Knowledge transfer to and within tourism: Academic, industry and government bridges* (pp. 73–95). Bingley: Emerald Publishing Limited.

Nee, V., & Sanders, J. (2001). Trust in ethnic ties: Social capital and immigrants. In K. S. Cook (Ed.) *Trust in society* (pp. 374–392). New York: Russel Sage Foundation.

Osaki, K. (1999). Economic interactions of migrants and their households of origin: Are women more reliable supporters? *Asian and Pacific Migration Journal* 8(4), 447–471.

Portes, A., & Rumbaut, R.G. (1996). *Immigrant America: A portrait* (2nd ed.). Berkeley, London: University of California Press.

Portes, A., & Sensenbrenner, J. (1993). Embeddedness and immigration: Notes on the social determinants of economic action. *American Journal of Sociology* 98(6), 1320–1350.

Putnam, R.D. (2000). *Bowling alone. The collapse and revival of American community.* New York: Simon & Schuster.

Rabibhadana, A., & Jatuworapruk, T. (2007). Impact of tourism upon local communities: Changes in an urban slum area and a rural village in Chiang Mai. In M. Kaosa-ard (Ed.), *Mekong tourism: Blessings for all?* (pp. 61–81). Chiang Mai: Social Research Institute, Chiang Mai University.

Rao, B.G. (2001). *Household coping/survival strategies in drought-prone regions: a case study of Anantapur District, Andhra Pradesh, India.* New Delhi: Society for Promotion of Wastelands Development. Retrieved from: ftp://ftp.solutionexchange.net.in/public/wes/cr/res-15061002.pdf.

Rigg, J. (1998). Rural-urban interactions, agriculture and wealth: A southeast Asian perspective. *Progress in Human Geography* 22(4), 497–522.

Rigg, J. (2003). *Southeast Asia: The human landscape of modernization and development.* London: Routledge.

Sakboon, M. (2011). The borders qithin: The Akha at the drontiers of national integration. In C. Vaddhanaphuti, & A. Jirattikorn (Eds.), *Transcending state boundaries: Contesting development, social suffering and negotiation* (pp. 205–244). Chiang Mai: The Regional Center for Social Science and Sustainable Development (RCSD), Chiang Mai University.

Schaffar, W. (2018). The iron silk road and the iron fist: Making sense of the military Coup D'Etat in Thailand. *Austrian Journal of South-East Asian Studies* 11(1), 35–52.

Smith, R.A., & Henderson, J.C. (2008). Integrated beach resorts, informal tourism commerce and the 2004 tsunami: Laguna Phuket in Thailand. *International Journal of Tourism Research* 10(3), 271–282.

Tooker, D.E. (2004). Modular modern: Shifting forms of collective identity among the Akha of Northern Thailand. *Anthropological Quarterly* 77(2), 243–288.

Toyota, M. (1998). Urban migration and cross-border networks: A deconstruction of Akha-identity in Chiang Mai. *Southeast Asian Studies* 35(4), 197–223.

Toyota, M. (2006). *Securitizing border-crossing: The case of marginalized stateless minorities in the Thai-Burma Borderlands.* Singapore: Institute of Defense and Strategic Studies.

Toyota, M., Yeoh, B.S., & Nguyen, L. (2007). Bringing the 'left behind' back into view in Asia: A framework for understanding the 'migration–left behind nexus'. *Population, Space and Place* 13(3), 157–161.

Trupp, A. (2014). *Migrating into tourist business. Agency and mixed embeddedness of ethnic minority street vendors in Thailand.* Vienna: University of Vienna

Trupp, A. (2015a). Agency, social capital, and mixed embeddedness among Akha ethnic minority street vendors in Thailand's tourist areas. *SOJOURN: Journal of Social Issues in Southeast Asia* 30(3), 779–817.

Trupp, A. (2015b). The development of ethnic minority souvenir business over time and space. *International Journal of Asia Pacific Studies* 11(Suppl. 1), 145–167.

Trupp, A. (2017). *Migration, micro-business and tourism in Thailand: Highlanders in the city.* Abingdon: Routledge.

Trupp, A., & Sunanta, S. (2017). Gendered practices in urban ethnic tourism in Thailand. *Annals of Tourism Research* 64, 76–86.

Turner, S., & An Nguyen, P. (2005). Young entrepreneurs, social capital and Doi Moi in Hanoi, Vietnam. *Urban Studies* 42(10), 1693–1710.

Waldinger, R., Aldrich, H.E., & Ward, R. (Eds.). (1990). *Ethnic entrepreneurs. Immigrant business in industrial societies.* Newbury Park, London, New Delhi: Sage.

Widiyanto, D. (2019). The third wave of Indonesia's food market: Practices at small community markets in Yogyakarta. *Austrian Journal of South-East Asian Studies* 12 (1), 49–67.

Winichakul, T. (2000). The others within: Travel and ethno-spatial differentiation of Siamese subjects 1885–1910. In A. Turton (Ed.), *Civility and savagery: Social identity in Tai States* (pp. 38–62). Richmond: Curzon.

Woolcock, M., & Narayan, D. (2000). Social capital: Implications for development theory, research, and policy. *The World Bank Research Observer* 15(2), 225–249.

World Bank (2019). *Urban Population.* Retrieved from: https://data.worldbank.org/indicator/SP.URB.TOTL.IN.ZS?locations=TH.

9 Fishermen into tour boat operators

Tourism development in Labuan Bajo, Indonesia

Aldi Lasso and Heidi Dahles

Introduction

Studies on sustainable tourism underpin the importance of the local community's role, with tourism often being proposed as a tool to enable the enhancement of local communities (Anderson, 2015; Croes & Vanegas, 2008; Mensah & Amuquandoh, 2010). However, most studies in sustainable tourism development focus on finding ways to make tourism development successful in local communities rather than critically assessing the possible impact on host communities (Blackstock, 2005). As a result, sustainable tourism development is shallowly viewed from a tourism-centric perspective (Hunter, 1995) that stresses the sustainability of tourism itself (Sharpley, 2009).

In communities where tourism development occurs, residents commonly depend on various sources of income. Consequently, the introduction of tourism to local communities implies a two-sided impact on local livelihoods. Tourism can either co-exist with or disrupt existing forms of livelihood (Fabinyi, Knudsen, & Segi, 2010; Ghosh, 2012). In coastal areas, tourism has often been suggested as a potential livelihood that would reduce pressures on fishing resources (Fabinyi et al., 2010; Porter, Orams, & Lück, 2015; Su, Wall, & Jin, 2016). However, the initiation of tourism development often leads to a livelihood transformation that might put local people at risk (Tao & Wall, 2009a). Contributing a case study to the discussions on the interrelatedness of tourism development and sustainable livelihoods, this paper provides evidence for such a transformation in a fishing community in the coastal area of Labuan Bajo, East Nusa Tenggara, Indonesia.

Labuan Bajo is the capital of the district of Manggarai Barat (West Manggarai) and is located at the most western tip of the island of Flores. A six-hour boat trip from Komodo Island, Labuan Bajo is the main gate to the Komodo National Park, the only place in the world where Komodo dragons, the world's rarest and largest lizards, live (Map 9.1). Since 2011, the popularity of Komodo dragons has significantly increased, resulting in growing numbers of visitors to the island (Erb, 2015). In Labuan Bajo retail and service enterprises have been established specifically targeting foreign tourists (Walpole & Goodwin, 2001). Thus, Labuan Bajo has become the centre of local tourism business activity and has seen rapid development of its tourism industry.

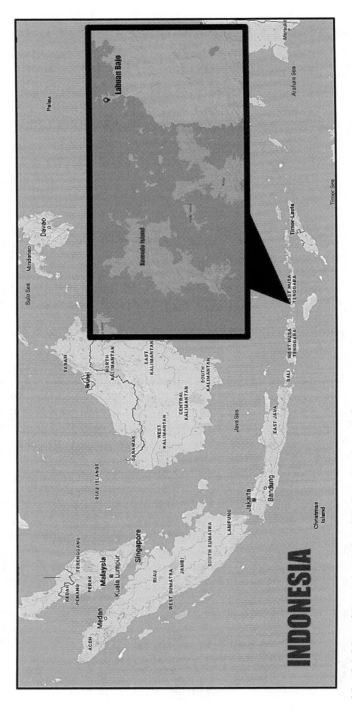

Map 9.1 Map of Komodo National Park and Labuan Bajo
Source: Adapted from Google (Cartographer) (2017).

Eventually, this transition resulted in the replacement of traditional livelihoods with tourism-based occupations and complete dependency on the new business. Instead of providing them with a better life, the former fishermen have come to encounter new challenges resulting from tight competition, high dependence on tour operators, and fluctuations in tourist arrivals. The sustainability of their new livelihood is thus in doubt. In studying the consequences of the transition to a tourism-based livelihood, this chapter contributes to the debate on the implications of tourism development for the sustainability of local livelihoods.

The position of tourism in sustainable development

Debates on 'sustainable tourism development' have been ongoing in both academic and professional literature for decades. In an attempt to bring livelihood improvements to local communities, tourism scholars have come to view tourism as a main strategy to reduce poverty in local communities (Croes & Vanegas, 2008; Scheyvens & Hughes, 2018). Consequently, many studies in sustainable tourism development suggest ways to ensure the success of tourism development in local communities rather than critically evaluating tourism as a development strategy (Blackstock, 2005; Dolezal, 2015). It has been proposed that scholars should be mindful of this lapse and that, instead of 'sustainable tourism development', they should advocate 'sustainable development through tourism' (Beeton, 2006; Sharpley, 2000, 2009).

In developing countries, the implementation of sustainable development through tourism has faced particular challenges (Tosun, 2001). Macroeconomic problems have tempted governments to adopt tourism without proper consideration of the possible consequences to local livelihoods and the potential damage to the sustainability of development. The top-down approach applied by most governments in developing countries (Tosun, 2001) often results in the initiation of tourism development without consulting local communities (Dolezal & Trupp, 2015; Nost, 2013; Sindiga, 1995; Suchet & Raspaud, 2010). Further, government-led tourism development may obstruct or even destroy local businesses and weaken existing livelihoods (Dahles, 2003).

As the term 'livelihood' refers to all activities undertaken in order to fulfil human needs (Chambers & Conway, 1992), people commonly engage in a range of such activities, both tourism-related and non-tourism-related (Shen, Hughey, & Simmons, 2008). To obtain sustainable livelihoods, people depend on secure access to natural, financial, human, social, and institutional resources (Department for International Development [DFID], 1999; Shen et al., 2008). In the context of tourism, these resources are prone to disruption (such as political conflicts), seasonality (causing fluctuations in income and employment), consumer volatility (rapid changes in tastes and preferences affecting tourist arrivals to destinations), and institutional change: variations in formal and informal rules (Trupp, 2016). Thus, to achieve a measure of sustainability, local communities have to continuously adapt their livelihood strategies in response to challenges that leave them vulnerable (Shen et al., 2008).

When tourism is introduced to a local community, livelihoods are inevitably affected (Shen et al., 2008) as tourism may swiftly come to dominate the economy of the community (Tao & Wall, 2009a). There are different ways in which tourism becomes embedded in local economies. Tourism can be employed as a diversification strategy which may complement existing livelihoods and improve the capability of local people to secure an income. This approach is promoted as an adaptive strategy to disperse risks and increase per capita income (Tao & Wall, 2009a). A number of studies show the positive effects of implementing this diversification strategy (Anup & Thapa Parajuli, 2014; Iorio & Corsale, 2010). Su, Wall, and Jin (2016) present a case of livelihood changes in Long Islands in Shandong Province, China, induced by *Yujiale* tourism, a special type of coastal tourism. The authors found that local livelihoods are enhanced through the incorporation of *Yujiale* tourism which uses existing marine-based resources to generate jobs and increase income to supplement traditional livelihoods.

However, tourism also has the potential to disadvantage local livelihoods. Tourism pushed by governments as an engine of rapid growth can make existing livelihoods obsolete (Tao & Wall, 2009a). Mbaiwa (2011) witnessed changes in livelihood activities and lifestyles in the Okavango Delta, Botswana, that increased livelihood insecurity for local communities. Local livelihoods transform into 'tourism livelihoods' characterised by an extreme, if not complete, dependence on income generated through tourism-based activities. Such tourism livelihoods are particularly vulnerable to visitor volatility and external events (Dahles & Prabawa, 2013; Liu, 2003).

Following Butler (1993), it is argued in this chapter that tourism should be developed in a manner that does not damage, hamper or destroy the livelihood resources and activities available to local people. Tourism is only one optional strategy which may or may not become a tool for local people to secure the sustainability of their livelihoods (Tao & Wall, 2009a). Sustainable tourism strategies, we argue, should not revolve around the sustainability of tourism as such, but should advance local development with tourism as a tool for economic diversification.

Research strategy and methods

This chapter is based on ethnographic fieldwork in Labuan Bajo, Indonesia, in 2015. The first author took up residence in Labuan Bajo and engaged in participant observation, which entailed repeated intensive interaction with 11 former fishermen recruited through snowball sampling, in the period from February to August 2015. The daily interaction included interviewing, observing, listening to and sharing information in order to co-produce an understanding of the local experience of tourism development and its context (Hammersley & Atkinson, 2007). The participants in this research, all former fishermen, had given up their traditional lifestyle and were making a living by operating tour boats for tourist transportation. The interviews were tape recorded and the recordings were transcribed and manually analysed to generate major themes, which were subsequently coded and systematised in matrices, and then matched with observation-based field notes for cross-comparison. The final step in the analysis consisted of data interpretation by comparing and contrasting the initial findings with the outcome of an elaborate review of academic literature on tourism impacts on community development (Tracy, 2013). Ethical guidelines were implemented prudently throughout the research process. Participants' consent was obtained and data sources have been anonymised in accordance with the protocol of research ethics.

From fishing to tour boat business

The early Labuan Bajo settlement was established at the beginning of the 19th century by sea-faring people from other islands in the archipelago, such as Bajau, Bimanese, Buginese and Endenese natives (Fox, 1977), who came to gather *trepang* (sea-cucumber). Most of the current residents of this coastal area are their descendants. Being highly skilled in boat-handling, sailing and fishing, the local fishermen successfully adopted *bagan* fishing in 1980s which swiftly became their most important source of income.

The coastal area of Labuan Bajo accommodates four small villages located side by side along the coast: Kampung Ujung, Kampung Tengah, Kampung Cempa and Kampung Air. In these villages, fishing has long been the main livelihood for local people. Traditional fishing was conducted with small open boats and employed nets, hooks, traps and gillnets. More recently, local fishermen sometimes resorted to rather unsustainable methods, such as bombs and poison. In the 1980s, *bagan* fishing came to dominate local livelihoods. *Bagan* is a fishing technique using large nets and portable lights or kerosene lanterns to attract squid, the main catch (Secretariat of the Pacific Community, 2011). Fishing has always been complemented by *meting*, a gathering activity targeting shellfish on the beaches and in estuaries during low tide.

With the port of Labuan Bajo within reach, these *bagan* fishermen did not have any difficulty selling their catch. Native Manggarai people from all over the area came to the local fish auction, currently called *Tempat Pelelangan Ikan* (TPI), to buy the fresh catch of squid and fish, and Labuan Bajo became the fish market centre. Although fishing satisfied their needs, local people considered this livelihood challenging. *Bagan* fishing demands hard work and long working hours including night shifts and many days at sea. The availability of crews, the price of fuel and the unpredictability of the catch caused considerable income fluctuations for the local fishermen.

In the 1990s, when the number of tourists to Komodo National Park (KNP) slowly increased, the *bagan* fishermen of Labuan Baju started to get involved in tourism. At the time, trips to Komodo Island could be conducted via different entrances such as Bali, Lombok, Sape and Labuan Bajo. Only a small number of tour boats operated in Labuan Bajo as the demand was relatively low. As Mr. Baco, a 59-year-old tour boat operator, explained: 'In

Table 9.1 Number of visitors to KNP

Year	International visitors	Domestic visitors	Total
1993	NA	NA	19,472
1995	NA	NA	28,175
1997	29,842	2,467	32,309
1999	15,814	2,005	17,819
2001	12,612	1,476	14,088
2003	10,305	1,282	11,587
2005	16,904	1,742	18,646
2007	19,307	762	20,069
2009	34,954	1,580	36,534
2011	41,833	6,177	48,010
2013	54,147	9,654	63,801
2015	76,195	19,215	95,410
2017	76,612	48,457	125,069

Source: Komodo National Park, 2009; Statistics Indonesia (BPS) 2013, 2016; Liputan 6, 2018

1990s, tourism started to develop but was not too crowded. Tourism began to be busier in 1995'. When the number of tourists soared in 1996 and 1997 (Table 9.1), more fishermen were tempted to join the tour boat business, although the number of tourist arrivals fluctuated in the following years.

In 2003, when West Manggarai became an independent district, Labuan Bajo, as its capital, turned into the main recipient of government-led development measures. The local government promoted visits to Komodo Island departing from Labuan Bajo, while the national government in Jakarta initiated an intensive international marketing campaign to enhance the popularity of this destination. As a result, the number of arrivals to this area, in particular international arrivals, increased in proportion to the number of visits to Komodo National Park. This situation caused a significant increase in tour boat demand. Encouraged by the success story of the early entrepreneurs who developed the tour boat business, more fishermen shifted from fishing to tour boat operations. The most affordable way to join the tour boat services was by modifying their *bagan* boats into tour boats. The conversion of the vessels was relatively easy and inexpensive. The large boat hands (big logs on each side of boat) were removed and on-board facilities were added, such as a cockpit, toilets, cabins, a deck, a small kitchen, and couches or chairs for the comfort of the passengers.

For the local fishermen, the tourism business held the promise of a better life, easy money and a lighter workload. As Mr. Sahrul, a former fisherman, claimed: 'The workload in tour boat business is lighter [than *bagan* fishing] because operating the tour boat does not require immense stamina'. He contended that he could earn a much higher income from *bagan* fishing than by operating a tour boat, but the increasing risks of this livelihood activity drove his decision to give up fishing. Among these risks were the growing uncertainty of the catch as squid was becoming scarce, the challenge of finding skilled crew members to operate the *bagan* boats, and the high operational cost, particularly in view of rising fuel prices. As Sahrul put it: '... if we have been at sea for a week and we have not succeeded to obtain any catch, we begin to be highly anxious because the operational costs continue while we have zero income'. The mounting problems affecting *bagan* fishing made the decision to convert to the tour boat business easy. The prospect of a lighter workload and regular working hours was appealing, and the remarkable increase in visitors to Komodo Island since 2009, in particular the boom in international tourist arrivals, nurtured expectations of a regular and substantial income.

When the local fishermen modified their *bagan* boats for the purpose of servicing tourists, they significantly reduced, if not eliminated, the option of returning to fishing. They would require a relatively large amount of money to convert their boats back to *bagan* fishing vessels. In addition, although they may still maintain their skills as helmsmen, their fishing skills and physical stamina may have decreased significantly over time. Most importantly, however, their fishing grounds, mooring places, crew members and trading networks have been taken by other fishermen coming into Labuan Bajo from neighbouring islands. Restoring their proper place in the community of *bagan* fishing people would take considerable effort and time and would critically impede their capability to return to fishing. Thus, a transformation has occurred as these people made a substantial and irreversible livelihood modification (Chapin et al., 2010).

Emerging challenges to the tour boat business

The Labuan Bajo tour boat business is commonly a family business and offers employment to members of extended family networks. Some tour boat operators own or co-own the boats, while others are employed to work for owners who are not involved in operating the boat. The owners are those who converted their *bagan* vessels into tour boats; their employees are often former *bagan* vessel crew members. As former fishermen, these people still preserve their sailing skills in operating the new business. As is common practice in family businesses, family members, in particular wives, engage in the management, particularly the financial administration. Some wives also contribute to their household income by selling snacks. Although small, these additional earnings support the family in meeting their daily needs, especially when the demand for boat rental is low.

Preparations for a boat trip begin when the tour boat operators receive a trip reservation. A day before departure, these tour boat operators make relevant arrangements, including ensuring the availability of safety equipment and sufficient fuel, as well as shopping for groceries for cooking meals on board during the tour. Captains or crew commonly perform regular maintenance of the vessel. Some boat owners allow the crew members or hired captains to live on the boats.

This is a mutually beneficial relationship between owners and employees as the latter perform maintenance tasks in return for free lodging.

Although the tour boat business seems to provide an adequate income to the former fishermen of Labuan Bajo, new challenges are emerging which potentially imperil the sustainability of this tourism-based livelihood. The tour boat operators heavily depend on local tour operators and independent tour organisers to sell boat trips to Komodo Island. Most tourists visiting the area arrive on package tours offered by local tour operators or independent tour guides. In the high season, tour operators and tour guides actively approach the tour boat operators due to a lack of tour boats available for rent. This is when the tour boat operators are in a good position to get a good price for boat rental. However, during the low season, the tables are turned. As only a limited number of tour packages are sold, the tour boat operators have no other option but to accept reduced rental prices. Worse, the absence of pricing standards has led to fierce competition among the local tour boat operators, reducing their earnings even more.

As more local fishermen and outside investors join the business, the tour boat operators have to deal with increasing competition. As the word of the Komodo tourism boom is spreading, people from other parts of Indonesia, particularly from saturated tourism destinations such as Bali, are attracted to Labuan Bajo to share in the tourism bonanza. These external investors are commonly equipped with experience and financial capital, which detrimentally affects the competitiveness of the local businesspeople. Surrounded by more experienced businesspeople in the tourism industry, the local community is losing market share. In the low season, they feel more like onlookers instead of players in the rapid tourism development – a frequent remark expressed by the local tour boat operators. Tensions through business competition are increasing even more as a number of diving tour operators have initiated new tour packages, combining diving activities with snorkelling and a visit to Komodo National Park. This is an encroachment on the market share of the local tour boat operators as snorkelling tours and Komodo Park visits happen to be their core business. In this situation it has become difficult for local people to maintain their livelihood.

The long low tourist season is another challenge these tour boat operators have to face. The high tourist season when earnings are substantial only lasts two months a year. The money made during this short period of time has to support local families during the remaining 10 months of the year. Mr. Sahrul revealed that in the low season, he sometimes stays at home for days without an income, while he has to support his crew members and keep up the maintenance of his boat. Another local tour boat operator confirmed that he experienced times when he had only two customers in six months.

Efforts to maintain livelihoods

Despite the challenges, particularly the intensifying business competition and the protracted low tourist season, only a small number of participants diversified their tourism-based livelihood. Among the few who did, the diversification strategies remained in the realm of the tourism industry, such as renting out rooms to visitors.

To anticipate problems that might be caused by the high dependency on local tour operators and tour guides, local tour boat operators have implemented a number of strategies. One strategy revolves around maintaining a good relationship with important suppliers of customers such as travel agencies and independent guides. The tour boat operators put much effort into making friends in the industry for the purpose of obtaining boat renting jobs. They often visit tour operation offices for a chat and a cup of tea in order to maintain good relationships with the tour operators and their office staff. Mr. Baco explained: 'We will have difficulties [in getting tour jobs] if we do not know many guides. We also have many friends in "office" (the term used to call tour operators)'. To rent boats for their tour packages, these tour operators or tour guides commonly prioritise the tour boat operators they know. Equally significant are attempts to find effective marketing strategies. One distinctive strategy is building a personal relationship with customers by continuing communication after the tour has finished. Boat operators usually ask the customers' phone numbers, email addresses, or social media accounts for further communication. If customers are satisfied with the service, they most likely recommend the boat to their connections. Word-of-mouth promotion appears to be a significant contributor to business success. As Mr. Manjailing, one of our participants, pointed out:

> I sometimes got a tour job directly from old customers. Those who have known me for a long time and we have maintained good relationship. For example, tourists from France and Italy sometime went directly to my house [asking for a full tour package]. I usually offered them whether they wanted to stay at my house or on the boat. ... I tried to give them the best service because [through their recommendation] either their parents or friends might come [as my customers] in the future.

This strategy also enables Mr. Manjailing to make more money out of a tour as he receives the full payment from the customers cutting back on fees and commissions for tour operators and tour guides. Similarly, networking with close business associates, relatives and extended family, living on other islands, is strategically used to promote their tour boat business and market their tours directly to potential customers in order to reduce their reliance on tour operators and tour guides.

Connections with government institutions appear to significantly increase the local business people's capacity to weather the low tourist season. Four of our participants benefit from an unwritten agreement with the local government to rent out their boats on a monthly basis providing them with a regular monthly income. Consequently, these tour boat operators are relatively unaffected by the (seasonal) fluctuation in the number of visitors. As one of the beneficiaries, Mr. Irfan, explained: 'For me, my [economic] condition is still safe in both high or low [season] because I have a contract with KNP. It is really helpful [for me]'. His connection with KNP has so far delivered three boat renting jobs each month.

To some extent, the above strategies have assisted the local tour boat operators in maintaining their businesses. They do not just sell a transportation service, they also offer tour packages and start to develop into independent tour organisers. This strategy reduces their dependency on tour operators and tour guides and, at the same time, increases the possibility of generating more income. Smart financial management also improves the ability of local business people to anticipate the low season. They have come to understand that saving a portion of their income generated during high season enhances their financial resilience in the low season. However, despite all their efforts, their reliance on tourism still remains high.

Discussion

The increase in tourist visits, which created a rise in demand for tour boat rentals, has been a trigger for a comprehensive livelihood transformation in the coastal area of Labuan Bajo. Experiencing the alleged blessings of tourism development first-hand has motivated local fishermen to embrace the tour boat business. Most local fishermen modified their *bagan* vessels to make them suitable for tourist transport. The transition, however, did not significantly improve their capacity to sustain their livelihood. A number of factors underlie this failure. At face value, the seasonality of tourism is responsible for the new livelihood challenges faced by local people. Due to their dependence on tour guides and tour operators for customer demand, the local tour boat operators struggle to keep their business going during the long low season. However, a closer look reveals that the boat operators have neglected to develop strategies to effectively deal with the seasonality of their industry. An important strategy would be one that diffuses such risks by way of diversifying their sources of income. As the engagement with tourism intensifies, local people become more and more dependent on this single source of income while relinquishing their traditional skills and livelihood opportunities. There is only limited evidence of attempts at livelihood diversification or business innovation. Alternative sources are hardly explored or remain within the realm of the tourism industry.

The dependence on tourism significantly reduces the capability of local people to maintain their livelihood in view of new challenges emerging in the tourism industry. One of these challenges is the increasing competition emanating from newcomers with business experience and financial capital who are better equipped to capitalise on new opportunities. The local tour boat operators' reliance on tourism as the sole source of income has significantly increased their vulnerability as the tourism industry is prone to rapid and drastic changes (Dahles & Susilowati, 2015; Shen et al., 2008; Telfer & Sharpley, 2008). In the case of a sudden decrease in tourist arrivals – which is not unlikely in this volatile industry – local people would have very limited alternatives to sustain their livelihoods.

However, the transition to the tour boat business has left intact the locals' most valuable asset: their boats, which are converted fishing vessels. The tour boat business that the former fishermen are currently running still requires their helmsman skills and this means that they preserve their human capital (Department for International Development [DFID], 1999; Scoones, 1998). Yet, a return to *bagan* fishing would not be a straightforward escape route if times get rough in the tourism industry as others have taken their place in the local fishing industry. However, recent developments in tourism demand has come to revitalise traditional fishing techniques. More and more travel agencies hire local boat operators and fishermen to demonstrate their traditional skills and provide well-paying anglers from all over the world with a unique fishing experience. Other future opportunities may materialise from a growing international interest in traditional knowledge, environmental protection and coastal management where demand of local caretakers is emerging.

Conclusion

Although the transition to using tourism as a new livelihood enables former fishing communities in Labuan Bajo to generate a relatively satisfactory income, it would be premature to conclude that tourism is an appropriate strategy to provide sustainable livelihoods for local people. Tourism development is commonly promoted to contribute to poverty alleviation while providing long-term socioeconomic benefits including stable income opportunities to ensure sustainable livelihoods (Scheyvens & Hughes, 2018). In Labuan Bajo, people are often struggling to make ends meet as tourism turned out to be an unbalanced income provider, particularly due to seasonal fluctuations and increasing competition. Depending on tourism as the sole source of income has significantly increased the vulnerability of Labuan Bajo villagers. Tourism replaced the former fishing-based livelihood without offering the same prosperity that *bagan* fishing did in its glory days. Consequently, tourism has not improved the capacity of local people to sustain their livelihood, but instead has weakened it.

Tourism is a fickle industry (Dahles & Susilowati, 2015; Liu, 2003), and local communities depending on this for their income are at risk of falling into extreme poverty if tourism declines. Labuan Bajo could easily become yet another case of a tourism-based livelihood that proves unsustainable (Su, Wall, & Xu, 2016; Tao & Wall, 2009b, 2009a). Stakeholders in Labuan Bajo tourism, particularly the Indonesian government and international travel agencies, have a role to play in creating opportunities for livelihood diversification. Education in matters such as financial administration, foreign languages, environmental protection and coastal management would greatly enhance the capacity of local people to benefit from business opportunities in the tourism industry and beyond. After all, local people are not mere spectators but agents of development.

References

Anderson, W. (2015). Cultural tourism and poverty alleviation in rural Kilimanjaro, Tanzania. *Journal of Tourism and Cultural Change* 13(3), 208–224.

Anup, K.C., & Thapa Parajuli, R.B. (2014). Tourism and its impact on livelihood in Manaslu conservation area, Nepal. *Environment, Development and Sustainability* 16(5), 1053–1063.

Beeton, S. (2006). *Community development through tourism*. Collingwood: Landlinks Press.

Blackstock, K. (2005). A critical look at community-based tourism. *Community Development Journal* 40(1), 39–49.

Butler, R.W. (1993). Tourism- An evolutionary perspective. In J.G. Nelson, R. Butler, & G. Wall (Eds.), *Tourism and Sustainable Development: Monitoring, Planning, Managing* (pp. 27–44). Waterloo: Heritage Resources Centre, University of Waterloo.

Chambers, R., & Conway, G. (1992). *Sustainable rural livelihoods: Practical concepts for the 21st century*. Brighton: Institute of Development Studies.

Chapin, F.S., Carpenter, S.R., Kofinas, G.P., Folke, C., Abel, N., Clark, W.C., Olsson, P., Stafford Smith, D.M., Walker, B., Young, O.R., Birkes, F., Biggs, R., Grove, J. M., Naylor, R.L., Pinkerton, E., Steffen, W., & Swanson, F.J. (2010). Ecosystem stewardship: Sustainability strategies for a rapidly changing planet. *Trends in Ecology & Evolution* 25(4), 241–249.

Croes, R., & Vanegas, M. (2008). Cointegration and causality between tourism and poverty reduction. *Journal of Travel Research* 47(1), 94–103.

Dahles, H. (2003). Tourism, small enterprises and community development. In D. Hall, & G. Richards (Eds.), *Tourism and sustainable community development* (pp. 154–169). New York: Routledge.

Dahles, H., & Prabawa, T.S. (2013). Entrepreneurship in the informal sector: The case of the pedicab drivers of Yogyakarta, Indonesia. *Journal of Small Business and Entrepreneurship* 26(3), 241–259.

Dahles, H., & Susilowati, T.P. (2015). Business resilience in times of growth and crisis. *Annals of Tourism Research* 51, 34–50.

Department for International Development [DFID] (1999). DFID Sustainable livelihood guidance sheets. Retrieved from: https://www.ennonline.net/dfidsustainableliving.

Dolezal, C. (2015). The tourism encounter in community-based tourism in Northern Thailand: Empty meeting ground or space for change? *Austrian Journal of South-East Asian Studies* 8(2), 165–186.

Dolezal, C., & Trupp, A. (2015). Tourism and development in South-East Asia. *Austrian Journal of South-East Asian Studies* 8(2), 117–124.

Erb, M. (2015). Sailing to Komodo: Contradictions of tourism and development in eastern Indonesia. *Austrian Journal of South-East Asian Studies* 8(2), 143–164.

Fabinyi, M., Knudsen, M., & Segi, S. (2010). Social complexity, ethnography and coastal resource management in the Philippines. *Coastal Management* 38(6), 617–632.

Fox, J.J. (1977). Notes on the Southern voyages and settlement of the Sama-Bajau. *Bijdragen tot de Taal-, Land- en Volkenkunde* 133(4), 459–465.

Ghosh, T. (2012). Sustainable coastal tourism: Problems and management options. *Journal of Geography and Geology* 4(1), 163–163.

Google (Cartographer) (2017). Retrieved from: https://www.google.com.au/maps/@-8.6154954,119.7010758,10.38z?hl=en.

Hammersley, M., & Atkinson, P. (2007). *Ethnography: Principles in Practice.* Abingdon: Routledge.

Hunter, C.J. (1995). On the need to re-conceptualise sustainable tourism development. *Journal of Sustainable Tourism* 3(3), 155–165.

Iorio, M., & Corsale, A. (2010). Rural tourism and livelihood strategies in Romania. *Journal of Rural Studies* 26(2), 152–162.

Komodo National Park (2009). *Visitor statistics.* Labuan Bajo: Komodo National Park.

Liputan 6 (2018). Turis AS Paling Banyak Berkunjung ke Pulau Komodo. *Liptuan 6.* Retrieved from: https://www.liputan6.com/regional/read/3547338/turis-as-paling-ba nyak-berkunjung-ke-pulau-komodo.

Liu, Z. (2003). Sustainable tourism development: A critique. *Journal of Sustainable Tourism* 11(6), 459–475.

Mbaiwa, J.E. (2011). Changes on traditional livelihood activities and lifestyles caused by tourism development in the Okavango Delta, Botswana. *Tourism Management* 32(5), 1050–1060.

Mensah, E.A., & Amuquandoh, F.E. (2010). Poverty reduction through tourism: Residents' perspectives. *Journal of Travel and Tourism Research (Online)* 77.

Nost, E. (2013). The power of place: Tourism development in Costa Rica. *Tourism Geographies: An International Journal of Tourism Space, Place and Environment* 15(1), 88–106.

Porter, B.A., Orams, M.B., & Lück, M. (2015). Surf-riding tourism in coastal fishing communities: A comparative case study of two projects from the Philippines. *Ocean & Coastal Management* 116, 169–176.

Scheyvens, R., & Hughes, E. (2018). Can tourism help to "end poverty in all its forms everywhere"? The challenge of tourism addressing SDG1. *Journal of Sustainable Tourism* 27(7), 1–19.

Scoones, I. (1998). Sustainable rural livelihoods: A framework for analysis. In IDS Working Papers 72. Brighton: Institute of Development Studies.

Secretariat of the Pacific Community (2011). Bagan fishing in Majuro, Marshal Islands. Retrieved from: http://www.spc.int/DigitalLibrary/Doc/FAME/InfoBull/ FishNews/136/FishNews136x_14_Bagan.pdf.

Sharpley, R. (2000). Tourism and sustainable development: Exploring the theoretical divide. *Journal of Sustainable Tourism* 8(1), 1–19.

Sharpley, R. (2009). The myth of sustainable tourism. CSD Working Papers Series 2009/2010 – No.4. Retrieved from: https://ysrinfo.files.wordpress.com/2012/06/csd_ working_paper_4_sustainable_tourism_sharpley.pdf.

Shen, F., Hughey, K.F.D., & Simmons, D.G. (2008). Connecting the sustainable livelihoods approach and tourism: A review of the literature. *Journal of Hospitality and Tourism Management* 15(1), 19–31. DOI: doi:10.1375/jhtm.15.19.

Sindiga, I. (1995). Wildlife-based tourism in Kenya: Land use conflicts and government compensation policies over protected areas. *Journal of Tourism Studies* 6(2), 45–55.

Statistics Indonesia (BPS) (2013). *Komodo District in Figures.* West Manggarai: BPS, Statistics of West Manggarai Regency.

Statistics Indonesia (BPS) (2016). *Komodo District in Figures.* West Manggarai: BPS, Statistics of West Manggarai Regency.

Su, M.M., Wall, G., & Jin, M. (2016). Island livelihoods: Tourism and fishing at Long Islands, Shandong Province, China. *Ocean & Coastal Management* 122, 20–29.

Su, M.M., Wall, G., & Xu, K. (2016). Tourism-induced livelihood changes at mount Sanqingshan world heritage site, China. *Environmental Management* 57(5), 1024–1040.

Suchet, A., & Raspaud, M. (2010). A case of local rejection of a heritage tourism policy: tourism and dynamics of change in Abondance, French Alps. *International Journal of Heritage Studies* 16(6), 449–463.

Tao, T.C.H., & Wall, G. (2009a). Tourism as a sustainable livelihood strategy. *Tourism Management* 30(1), 90–98.

Tao, T.C.H., & Wall, G. (2009b). A livelihood approach to sustainability. *Asia Pacific Journal of Tourism Research* 14(2), 137–152.

Telfer, D.J., & Sharpley, R. (2008). *Tourism and development in the developing world.* Abingdon: Routledge

Tosun, C. (2001). Challenges of sustainable tourism development in the developing world: the case of Turkey. *Tourism Management* 22, 289–303.

Tracy, S.J. (2013). *Qualitative research methods: Collecting evidence, crafting analysis, communicating impact.* Oxford: John Wiley & Sons.

Trupp, A. (2016). *Migration, micro-business and tourism in Thailand: Highlanders in the city.* Abingdon: Routledge.

Walpole, M.J., & Goodwin, H.J. (2001). Local attitudes towards conservation and tourism around Komodo National Park, Indonesia. *Environmental Conservation* 28 (2), 160–166.

10 Modernity, globalisation, and development in the Philippines

Implications for the cultural landscape, authenticity, and tourism of Ifugao Province

Yukio Yotsumoto

Introduction

Ifugao Province in the Philippines has a splendid cultural landscape of rice terraces attracting tourists who search for 'authentic' tourism experiences. However, preserving the authentic culture and landscape has been a challenge for the local and national governments. In this chapter, the question as to why it is challenging to preserve traditional culture and landscape despite a demand from The United Nations Educational, Scientific and Cultural Organization (UNESCO) and international tourists will be discussed by looking closely at two macro social processes: modernity and globalisation. Modernity is a social process described by secularisation, rationalisation, democratisation, individualisation and a scientific way of thinking, all of which are distinct from traditional societies (Giddens & Sutton, 2017, p. 10). Globalisation, on the other hand, is 'the compression of the world and the intensification of consciousness of the world as a whole' (Robertson, 1992, p. 8). These concepts are especially useful when it comes to understanding the transformation of the Ifugao cultural landscape.

In 2010, the Ifugao Province received 87,802 tourists, who came to appreciate the traditional cultural landscape (Ifugao Post, 2012) representing the past primitive life. These landscapes were important images for both tourists and the local tourism sector, influenced by popular culture media forms (Salazar, 2009, pp. 50–51). The media, governments and the tourism industry in the Philippines tried to preserve these images to attract more tourists. However, in 2014, the number of tourists decreased to 65,965 (Republic of the Philippines, Department of Tourism, 2014), which may be related to the degradation of traditional cultural landscapes. The traditional raised-floor houses with thatched roofs, which I call 'authentic landscapes' here, are disappearing in the province as local people begin to favour houses made of concrete and galvanised sheet iron like in other ethnic tourism destinations such as in Northern Thailand (Trupp, 2014, p. 68). In addition, the erosion of rice terraces is widespread, which poses a threat to the attraction. It does have at least some influence on the popularity of the destination, as an example shows: A Western male traveller made a comment on TripAdvisor about 'inauthentic village life' in Ifugao, saying that 'there really is not much of authentic Ifugao village life to see' (TripAdvisor, 2014) which might influence tourists' perceptions of Ifugao as a destination. To deal with the issue of a lack of authenticity, the Municipality of Banaue started a beautification project in April 2017. In this project, the rooftops and walls of houses in the villages of Batad and Bocos got painted with green and earth like colours to match the cultural landscape of traditional rice terraces (Empian, & Rao, 2017).

Despite these efforts, I argue that maintaining the authentic Ifugao cultural landscape is difficult due to forces of modernity, globalisation and broader development processes. I base my discussion on fieldwork conducted in the municipalities of Banaue and Kiangan (specifically, Nagakadan village) in 2008 and 2011, and the analysis of secondary data such as official statistics and newspaper articles. The fieldwork includes observations and both formal and informal interviews with provincial government staff, municipality staff, museum staff, jeepney drivers, inn owners, hotel staff and farmers. Formal interviews were mainly conducted with public officials and farmers which took 30–60 minutes each. I also visited farmers along the village road and interviewed them inside their houses. Informal interviews were carried out with private businesses, which took less than 20 minutes. The interview memos were recorded, typed, and classified into topics for concept charting. However, before delving into the data of this research, it is important to review the literature on modernity and globalisation, ethnic tourism, and cultural landscapes.

Modernity and globalisation

Indigenous communities including Ifugao people are increasingly influenced by macro social processes of modernity and globalisation that originate from outside their villages. With modernity in the mid-18th century Enlightenment until around the mid-1980s (Giddens & Sutton, 2017, p. 11) came changes in the economic, political, and cultural aspects of social arrangement as well as how individuals interact with one another and form their identity (Roberts & Hite, 2000, pp. 9–10). Most importantly, modernity (or 'modernisation') became a project to assist developing countries in becoming more 'similar' to developed countries (Western nations) through a shift from traditional values and institutions to values based on rationality and bureaucratic institutions.

As opposed to modernity, globalisation is defined as 'the compression of the world and the intensification of consciousness of the world as a whole' (Robertson, 1992, p. 8). The accelerated process of globalisation began to be noticed since the 1970s (Giddens & Sutton, 2017, p. 7) and the use of globalisation as a concept by scholars increased substantially during the latter half of the 1980s (Robertson, 1992, p. 8). The shrinkage of the world and a sense of belonging to a global community occurred through the movement of people, goods, money, information, and culture across national borders at an accelerated speed. Key players contributing to globalisation are transnational actors, corporations, international governmental organisations, non-governmental organisations (NGOs), global social movements, diaspora and other transnational actors such as migrants, international tourists and professionals (Cohen & Kennedy, 2013, p. 38). Globalisation leads to the decreasing role of the nation-state which was the major actor of modernity.

Having briefly discussed the two concepts at hand, I want to mention the stance this chapter takes regarding the relationship between modernity and globalisation. Therborn (2000) and Eitzen and Zinn (2012) do not see globalisation as a new phenomenon but as one that has existed for over 1,000 years. The idea that globalisation is not a recently developed phenomenon is shared by many scholars, but whether modernity and globalisation can be equated or not is under discussion. In this chapter, I take the position that globalisation is the corollary of modernity (Giddens, 1990). Reasons for this are:

1) the characteristics of modernity, that is, secularisation, rationalisation, democratisation, individualisation and the ascent of science are still intact in the age of globalisation;

2) although the role of the nation-state has declined in comparison to global actors such as transnational corporations and international NGOs, people's life opportunities are still determined by the country in which people are born. Thus, a continuity between modernity and globalisation exists;

3) it is widely observed that, particularly in rural areas of developing countries, people's wish is to escape the hardship of agrarian life and social structure by adopting a modern way of life, of which opportunities are expanding as globalisation advances.

In the past, the main agent of modernity, the nation-state, has helped or forced to 'develop' indigenous communities based on the idea of progress, while oftentimes undermining the tradition of indigenous people through modernisation policy. However, in indigenous and agrarian communities, while the influence of modernity is still strong, there are attempts to preserve and/or revitalise local traditions. A preservation of tradition has been sought by indigenous people themselves but also from outside global actors such as UNESCO. Thus, the traditional cultural landscapes of indigenous communities have been shaped by opposing forces of modernity and globalisation.

UNESCO is an influential global agent that preserves local culture. One of the missions of UNESCO is to identify, protect and preserve cultural and natural heritage around the world. By having the exclusive authority to designate World Heritage status, regarding the preservation of traditional culture, the organisation has a powerful influence over the governments who seek World Heritage recognition, which is also observed in Ifugao Province.

Tourism is also a major agent of globalisation and modernity (Telfer & Sharpley, 2008, p. 57). Multinational tourism companies create international networks of suppliers and provide travel experiences globally to international visitors, which expand flows of capital, human resources and knowledge, as well as interactions between hosts and guests beyond national boundaries. The changes in market economies that tourism facilitates are often accompanied by a loss of authenticity (Bianchi, 2017). At the same time, tourism offers an incentive for the preservation of culture, as is the case in ethnic tourism (Lah, 2014).

Ethnic tourism and authenticity

Several studies have indicated the relationship between ethnic tourism development and a loss of authenticity through commodification (Bilby, 2001; Ballengee-Morris, 2002). Cole (2007, p. 945) summarises this predominant view: 'tourism turns culture into a commodity, packaged, and sold to tourists, resulting in a loss of authenticity'. In a sense, ethnic tourism development in a capitalist economy sows the seeds of its destruction when focused on a type of tourist who looks for the past primitive Other (Cole, 2007; Dolezal, 2015). In order to keep attracting tourists, ethnic tourism destinations, including Ifugao Province, need to put an effort into maintaining authenticity. To maintain the attractiveness of destinations, a contradiction of commodification and a loss of authenticity needs to be overcome. In this regard, Wang's (1999) idea of three types of authenticity in tourist experiences – objective authenticity, constructive authenticity and existential authenticity – finds potential use. In the first type, tourists are concerned with the originality of the toured objects. In the second type, tourists see authenticity in toured objects through their imagery, expectations, preferences and beliefs. In the third type, tourist activities stimulate the existential state of Being so that tourists can *feel* they have authentic experiences (Wang, 1999, p. 352). These ideas will be examined in conclusion when discussing the future of Ifugao Province.

The heritage of cultural landscape

Ifugao's cultural landscape is formed by farming practices that can also be regarded as heritage; consequently, heritage tourism is developed in addition to ethnic tourism. Although there is no universal definition of 'heritage tourism' (Ung & Vong, 2010, p. 159; Balcar & Pearce, 1996, p. 203) as its meaning indicates different matters in different areas of the world (Timothy & Boyd, 2003), 'the present day use of the past' (Graham, Ashworth, & Tunbridge, 2000) is the most commonly used definition of 'heritage' (Timothy & Boyd, 2006).

Cultural landscape as a representation of heritage is the result of the intervention of a cultural group in nature (Sauer, 1925). It represents a connection between tangible and intangible heritage as well as between local communities and their heritage (Rossler, 2006, p. 334). Furthermore, it is created by associating people's livelihoods with nature (Taylor, 2012, p. 273). Cultural landscape consists of built aspects such as houses, paddy fields, irrigation channels, vegetable gardens, roads, and schools that groups of people develop for their daily living (Domosh, Newmann, & Price, 2015, p. 28), as well as non-material aspects, that is, intangible and less tangible aspects such as traditional farming practices and festivals that celebrate harvest.

When it comes to the heritage conservation discussion, a tangible and material characteristic of heritage has been emphasised, while recently, the living dimension of heritage has been recognised (Poulios, 2011). The idea of a living heritage might be more useful in an Asian context as the region emphasises less the material fabric of objects, which indicates that the authenticity of original material objects is less important (Winter, 2014). This idea was recognised in The Nara Document of Authenticity (Taylor, 2004, p. 430) and multiple approaches including the Asian approach to authenticity for the management of cultural heritage are needed as some Asian regions do not have a term for heritage and its concept (Winter & Daly, 2012, p. 8).

Recent popularity in the concept of cultural landscape among scholars stems from its adoption as a category in the World Heritage Convention in 1992 (Wu, 2010, p. 1148). Ifugao's rice terrace landscape is the first property that was inscribed on the UNESCO World Heritage list in 1995 using the cultural landscape category. The designation is a magnet for tourists and visitors and has increased the global prestige (Adie, 2017) which resulted in a growth of international tourists (Santa-Cruz & Lopez-Guzman, 2017).

The cultural landscape of the Ifugao People

The cultural landscape of the Ifugao people is changing as the disappearance of traditional Ifugao houses exemplifies. It is therefore important to have a closer look at the traditional cultural landscape of the Ifugao people as a representation of a traditional way of life.

Cultural landscape as a traditional way of life

The place the Ifugao people inhabit is located on the east side of the Cordillera mountain terrain, consisting of mountains, hills and plateaus. The rice terraces of the Ifugao people are the most visible cultural landscape that demonstrates the traditional way of life in the area (Figure 10.1). More than 80 percent of the slopes are over 30 degrees steep, and in order to be cultivated, they need to develop terraced fields. In such geographical conditions, the Ifugao people lived through paddy field cultivation as a source of income. Therefore, they developed a culture that is essentially related to rice and paddy field work. The rice terraces thus represent the Ifugao people's traditional way of life that, at the same time, attracts many Western researchers and tourists.

On the rice terraces, brown-colour, raised-floor and thatched-roof houses can be noticed. These traditional Ifugao houses are called *Bale*, which are high-story houses built without nails. To enter the room, climbing up a two meter-ladder is necessary. The house only has one room which is typically 4 ×

Figure 10.1 The rice terraces of the Ifugao people
Source: Yotsumoto

6 square meters (Yap, 2005, p. 6). There is a hearth in the corner of the room for cooking and heating. Rice is stored on a ceiling space and rat guards placed on the pillars protect it. Under the house is a dirt-floor where hammocks are hung, woodcarvings are made, and clothes are dried. Since there is no electricity or water inside, candles are used for lightning and washing dishes and the laundry is done outside. The houses are over 100 years old and had a religious significance as a series of feasts were held there in the past (Goda, 2002). Building materials, design, and room arrangement are influenced by the cultural practices and environment of the community. Houses reflect the way of life of local people, that is, they embody a whole range of socio-cultural factors of the locality (Wang, 1997).

The cultural landscape representing modern life

The Ifugao people's internal drive for a better life has been shaped by the government's efforts to modernise Ifugao Province especially in the areas of education and agriculture. Modernity in these two areas changed residents' way of life and the perception of what a 'better' life is. Modern houses therefore are a reflection of people's search for a more comfortable lifestyle. For example, older people do not need to climb a high ladder to get into a house. Still, a stronger need to build modern houses comes from seeking better education, which is a requirement to obtain better jobs, i.e. jobs in the non-agricultural sector. However, if this is not possible and one needs to remain in agriculture, people, understandably, want to avoid strenuous agricultural work. Thus, there are a growing number of agricultural machines in rice terraces. This section discusses modern agriculture and education which have changed the cultural landscape.

Modernising the educational system

A better life in contemporary Ifugao society is possible by doing well in school. In the past, education was not formal as knowledge and wisdom were acquired from older people and through participation in community activities. Since the Ifugao people had no written language, they learned it through folk tales and songs. However, under the governance of the US, a formal educational system was established in the Philippines and it was expanded and refined by the Philippine government after independence. While the nature of colonisation in the Philippines during Spanish rule was exploitative and destroyed the social fabric of communities (Suzuki, 1997), during American rule, the Philippines was managed by Benevolent Assimilation policy under which the American political and educational system was introduced. The Philippines eventually became independent in 1946. American rule changed the Philippines from a communal base society to a nation-state. English became the primary language of instruction and an important factor in improving social status. Consequently, the status of the Ifugao language has declined with the spread of education. As formal education under the nation-state spread, traditional knowledge also began to be increasingly lost and neglected.

Modernising agriculture

For farmers, it is important to provide a supportive study environment for their children so that they can attain professional jobs. To encourage their children to study hard and for their convenience, parents build a modern house with many rooms, electricity and possibly a shower. The traditional inheritance system, which Goda (2002, p. 69) calls the 'rule of ranked bilateral primogeniture', produces many landless farmers who either become tenant farmers or agricultural wage labourers, given that only the two older children inherit land when they marry. The life of tenant farmers is hard. Half of the harvested rice has to be handed over to the owner of farmland. Thus, the traditional inheritance system has created a social class division of haves and have-nots, the former called *Kadangyuans* and the latter called *Lawa.* For *Lawa,* education is very important to escape the hard life. Even for *Kadangyuans,* nowadays, being a teachers or government employee is more attractive than being a farmer. Therefore, they spend money to build modern houses.

For those who remain in farming, it is natural to seek ways to reduce hard work while increasing the yield of rice. The Philippine Department of Agriculture introduced lowland rice in the 1960s, which people call the 'miracle rice'. In the 1980s, the lowland rice came to replace indigenous rice in various parts of Ifugao Province (Crisologo-Mendoza & Prill-Brett, 2009), can be planted twice a year, harvests more than indigenous rice and resists typhoons although it requires chemical fertilisers. The introduction of the agricultural machines also brought changes in farmers' lifestyle. These machines are welcomed by the farmers as it reduces the severe labour and increases productivity.

However, the modernisation of agriculture leads to the disappearance of agricultural rites and the traditional cultural landscape. For instance, the selection of rice species suitable for the land and the use of organic fertiliser has been carried out for several generations in Nagakadan village. The organic fertiliser is made by the traditional practice called *Pingkol* which is a small mound of earth laid on the ground consisting of soil and plants such as straw, waterweed and fern. However, now, the unique traditional cultural landscape of the after-harvest rice terraces with *Pingkol* is observed less and less as the use of chemical fertilisers is increasing.

Although the traditional way of life is attractive to tourists, it is not an easy life for Ifugao farmers. The tradition created landless farmers called *Lawa*, whose life has been very difficult. Modernisation in education and agriculture as discussed above and promoted by the government helped to ease their hard life to a certain extent. Thus, maintaining the tradition means to work against the improvement of tenant farmers' lifestyles. An Ifugao farmer of 68 years old commented that 'life before was so hard' and 'life is a lot easier now' (Agence France-Presse, 2015). Thus, this raises ethical concerns about maintaining the traditional cultural landscape.

Cultural landscape shaped by globalisation

As becomes obvious from the above, modernity has worked to diminish the traditional way of life and cultural landscape. On the other hand, globalisation's relationship to tradition is bifurcated, impacting on tradition in negative ways through processes of Westernisation and, on the other side, maintaining tradition through the realisation of the value of the local. Which direction globalisation takes is determined by who the agent of globalisation is. Three agents of globalisation are at work in Ifugao Province. The first one is international migrants (overseas Filipino workers) who unintentionally contribute to the diminishing of tradition through remittances that are used to build modern houses by their families remaining in Ifugao Province. The second one is an international organisation (UNESCO) that protects tradition. The third one is tourism businesses and international tourists that contribute money to communities and thus facilitate the transformation of the traditional subsistence economy into a monetary economy. The first and the third agents created opportunities to obtain cash that is essential for pursuing a modern life and hence they have changed the traditional Ifugao landscapes while the second agent facilitated the formation of networks (the national government, local governments and NGOs) for the conservation of the traditional Ifugao landscapes. The next three subsections discuss these three agents in detail.

Overseas Filipino workers as globalising agents

The Philippines is well known as a country to send workers overseas. There are also Filipino overseas migrant workers in Nagakadan village and their remittances have influenced the quality of life of residents. In 2013, there are 10,238,614 Filipinos living abroad permanently, temporarily, and illegally without a visa (Commission on Filipinos Overseas, 2013), resulting in 25.4 billion US dollars remitted to the Philippines (Bangko Sentral Ng Pilipinas, n.d.). Families living in the Philippines build houses and buy TV sets with the help of remittances from their family members abroad. Using the remitted money, primarily from female oversea workers, the husbands or family members invest to become tailors and wood carving artisans, establish tire repair shops and Sari-sari (small grocery) stores, and become tricycle and jeepney owners. Moreover, in agriculture, money is invested to produce commercial crops. Vegetables are demanded by tourists and the urban elites, thus, there is a growing number of farm households in the Cordillera that produce these (Lewis, 1992). The remittances of overseas workers became fund for setting up businesses in Nagakadan village, too. For example, a 63-year-old female farmer with a husband and five children have lived as tenant farmers, but now two daughters reside abroad (in Russia and Hong Kong) and send money. The farmer's root is a tenant farmer, but due to her daughters' remittances, this woman was able to become the owner of a Sari-sari store, one of four such stores in Nagakadan village (interviewed on August 11, 2011). For villagers, if even one family member can go overseas, this means an escape from tenant farming and a chance to improve their life and to setup businesses.

UNESCO as a globalising agent

The Rice Terraces of the Philippine Cordilleras were designated as a UNESCO world cultural heritage site in 1995. They were recognised for their unique tradition and an outstanding landscape that shows a traditional human settlement, and land-use and harmonious human interaction with the environment. The rice terraces met three criteria relating to being a 'testimony to a community's sustainable and primarily communal system of rice production', 'a memorial to the history and labour of more than a thousand generations of small-scale farmers', and being an 'example of land-use that resulted from a harmonious interaction between people and its environment' (UNESCO, n.d.). During the selection process and after designation, UNESCO demands that local and national governments conserve and manage the sites, or the sites are relegated to the List of World Heritage in Danger if the conservation is not warranted. For tourists who seek authenticity, this downgrading means a loss of authenticity in the dimensions of originality and authority (Bruner, 2004). However, the World Heritage Committee decided to put the property of Ifugao rice terraces on the List of World Heritage in Danger in 2001 due to concerns relating to lack of government support and international assistance, abandoned terraces due to out-migration and difficult access for tourists (e.g. from Manila) (UNESCO, 2002, p. 32). In 2012, the property of Ifugao rice terraces was removed from the List of World Heritage in Danger (UNESCO, 2012a, p. 40). The national and local governments of the Philippines have accomplished a range of objectives of heritage conservation, such as the recovery of 50 percent of collapsed rice terrace walls, the adoption of conservation standards, the restoration of the main irrigation system, legislation for protection by the national government, the implementation of community-based land-use and zoning plan projects, the establishment of rice terrace owner organisations and others (UNESCO, 2012b, p. 64).

Tourism as a globalising agent

Tourism businesses and tourists can be regarded as a globalising force that undermines the traditional culture to a large extent. They solidified and expanded the monetary economy that was introduced to the community by modernity. The shift from the subsistent economy to the monetary economy is not reversible and jobs to provide cash income have increased. Before the tourism boom in the 1980s, when Ifugao farmers saw the appeal for more income, they worked as construction workers or agricultural wage labourers. However, the growth of tourism opened up tourism-related jobs such as cleaners, waiters, jeepney drivers, souvenir shop assistants and handicraft makers. One example is a 53-year-old female farmer in Banaue, who is a tenant farmer borrowing farmland. She is in need of income because three of her eight children go to college, hence, she works at Banaue Hotel as a housekeeper four days a week. Farming remains her part-time job when is not doing her cleaning role (interviewed on August 7, 2008). Another example is a 47-year-old male farmer in Banaue, who has a wife and four children and is also a tenant farmer. As half of the rice is transferred to landowners, the rice he grows is not enough for his family's livelihood. He and his wife want their children to have a good education, which costs money. Hence, he makes woodcrafts and wicker baskets, and sells them to tourists in a Banaue market. For him, handicrafts became a main source of income and farming now is a side job (interviewed on August 5, 2008). In fact, the regional director of the Department of Tourism, Cordillera Administrative Region acknowledges that tourism had become an industry bigger than agriculture since around 2008 (Ifugao Post, 2012). Work in tourism therefore causes a shortage of farmers which results in the abandonment or insufficient maintenance of rice terraces.

At the same time, some tourists are not satisfied with the modern cultural landscape and their voices are taken into consideration by the government, which wants to develop tourism further. Thus, some measures to preserve the traditional culture are implemented although its effectiveness is questionable.

Conclusion

The World Heritage Committee reviewed the efforts of the Philippine government to protect the rice terraces for 10 years and they concluded that the plan to protect the Ifugao rice terraces is satisfactory and decided to remove it from the List of World Heritage in Danger in 2012. Despite the removal, the rice terraces continue to deteriorate and local people keep building modern houses that result in a loss of authenticity of traditional Ifugao culture for tourists. A newspaper article says the conditions are alarming by stating that 'Ifugao rice terraces may become an urban jungle' (Agence France-Presse, 2015). However, the plan and measures to protect the rice terraces have not worked well. Why is it so challenging to maintain the traditional cultural landscape?

In this chapter, it was suggested that macro social forces of modernity and globalisation transformed the society from a subsistence economy into a market economy and changed people's lifestyle expectations. Local people want to pursue a better life, which is possible by adopting a more modern lifestyle. Although modernity in Ifugao Province originally was introduced from outside (The US and Manila), the quest for a modern lifestyle has been internalised, especially through education since the early 20th century. Opportunities to obtain cash that is necessary for modern life were expanded by globalisation; specifically, remittances from overseas labour migrants and earning from the tourism-related jobs that have been created since the tourism boom in the 1980s.

In particular, the globalising agent UNESCO dedicates itself to the preservation of traditional culture, in combination with local governments and national agencies. The national and local governments of the Philippines also consider the voice of the tourists who look for authenticity in order to develop tourism. Farmers, however, are generally not interested in the preservation of traditional culture, which originated from outside and which reminds them of the past hard life. They have internalised the idea that modern life is a better life. Thus, farmers' pursuit of the modern life continues to undermine the authenticity of traditional culture and landscape which disappoints tourists.

Through the discussion above, it is envisaged that preservation of the traditional culture and landscape is a formidable challenge and difficult to achieve. The main question concerns what the stakeholders of tourism should do in order to guarantee the future of tourism. Wang's (1999) expanded conceptualisation of authenticity might be the key to that question. Objective authenticity and constructive authenticity emerge in reference to toured objects while existential authenticity does not require toured objects as tourist's existential state of Being (existential self) is activated by tourist activities.

Currently, when international tourists, the local and national governments, the media, and the tourism businesses discuss authenticity in Ifugao Province, they refer to the originality of toured objects, i.e. the Ifugao cultural objects and landscape. However, tourism stakeholders in Ifugao Province could consider Wang's (1999) existential authenticity. In other words, activity- and experience-based tourism such as tours involving farming experiences, participation in traditional festival preparation and fixing rice terrace walls with Ifugao farmers should be considered. Here, the originality of traditional farm practices and festival making that seem to somewhat be stuck in time and space in the past is not necessarily important as the Ifugao rice terraces are a living heritage (Poulios, 2011). Even though some aspects of originality are lost in toured objects, Ifugao society as a totality can still provide activities that are different from the home countries of international tourists and that activate tourists' authentic selves.

References

Adie, B.A. (2017). Franchising our heritage: The UNESCO world heritage brand. *Tourism Management Perspectives* 24, 48–53.

Agence France-Presse (2015, June 1). Ifugao rice terraces may become urban jungle. *Inquirer.net*. Retrieved from: http://newsinfo.inquirer.net/695128/ifugao-rice-terraces-may-become-urban-jungle.

Balcar, M., & Pearce, D.G. (1996). Heritage tourism on the west coast of New Zealand. *Tourism Management* 17(3), 203–212.

Ballengee-Morris, C. (2002). Cultures for sale: Perspectives on colonialism and self-determination and the relationship to authenticity and tourism. *Studies in Art Education, A Journal of Issue and Research* 43(3), 232–245.

Bangko Sentral Ng Pilipinas (n.d.). Overseas Filipinos' (OF) remittances. Retrieved from: http://www.bsp.gov.ph/statistics/keystat/ofw.htm.

Bianchi, R. (2017). The political economy of tourism development: A critical review. *Annals of Tourism Research* 70, 88–102.

Bilby, K.M. (2001, December). Maroon autonomy in Jamaica. *Cultural Survival Quarterly Magazine.*

Bruner, E.M. (2004). *Culture on tour: Ethnographies of travel.* Chicago: University of Chicago Press.

Cohen, R., & Kennedy, P. (2013). *Global sociology.* New York: New York University Press.

Cole, S. (2007). Beyond authenticity and commodification. *Annals of Tourism Research* 34(4), 943–960.

Commission on Filipinos Overseas (2013). Stock estimate of overseas Filipinos. Retrieved from: https://cfo.gov.ph/downloads/statistics/stock-estimates.html.

Crisologo-Mendoza, L., & Prill-Brett, J. (2009). Communal land management in the Cordillera region of the Philippines. In J. Perera (Ed.), *Land and cultural survival: The communal land rights of indigenous peoples in Asia* (pp. 35–61). Manila: Asian Development Bank.

Dolezal, C. (2015). The tourism encounter in community-based tourism in Northern Thailand: Empty meeting ground or space for change. *Austrian Journal of South-East Asian Studies* 8(2), 165–186.

Domosh, M., Newmann, R.P., & Price, P.L. (2015). *Contemporary human geography: Culture, globalization, landscape.* New York: W.H. Freeman and Company.

Eitzen, S., & Zinn, M.B. (2012). *Globalization: The transformation of social worlds.* California: Wadsworth Cengage Learning.

Empian, O.C., & Rao. (2017). Modern huts in Banaue to be painted to make them scenic. *Baguio Midland Courier.* May 7, 2017. Retrieved from: http://baguiomidla ndcourier.com.ph/ifugao.asp?mode=archives/2017/may/5-7-2017/ifug1.txt.

Giddens, A. (1990). *The consequences of modernity.* Cambridge: Polity Press.

Giddens, A., & Sutton, P.W. (2017). *Essential concepts in sociology.* Cambridge: Polity Press.

Goda, T. (2002). *Cordillera: Diversity in culture change, social anthropology of hill peoples in Northern Luzon, Philippines.* Quezon City: New Day Publishers.

Graham, B., Ashworth, G.J., & Tunbridge, J.E. (2000). *A geography of heritage: Power, culture and economy.* London: Arnold.

Ifugao Post (2012, February 5). Tourism booming in Ifugao. Retrieved from: http:// ifugaopost.blogspot.com/2012/02/tourism-booming-in-ifugao.html.

Lah, S.C. (2014). Ethnic tourism: A case study of language and culture preservation of the Bateq indigenous group of Orang Asli in peninsular Malaysia. *SHS Web of Conferences* 12, 1–7.

Lewis, M.W. (1992). Agricultural regions in the Philippine Cordillera. *Geographical Review* 82(1), 29–42.

Poulios, I. (2011). Is every heritage site a 'living' one? Linking conservation to communities' association with sites. *The Historic Environment: Policy & Practice* 2(2), 144–156.

Republic of the Philippines, Department of Tourism (2014). Distribution of regional travellers in the Philippines, January–December 2014, Partial report. Retrieved from: http://www.tourism.gov.ph/Tourism_demand/RegionalTravelers2014.pdf.

Roberts, J.T., & Hite, A. (2000). *From modernization to globalization: Perspectives on development and social change.* Malden: Blackwell Publishers.

Robertson, R. (1992). *Globalization: Social theory and global culture.* London: SAGE.

Rossler, M. (2006). World heritage cultural landscapes: A UNESCO flagship programme 1992–2006. *Landscape Research* 31(4), 333–353.

Salazar, N.B. (2009). Imaged and imagined? Cultural representations and the 'tourismification' of peoples and places. *Cahiers d' Etudes Africaines* 49, 49–71.

Santa-Cruz, F.G., & Lopez-Guzman, T. (2017). Culture, tourism and world heritage sites. *Tourism Management Perspectives* 24, 111–116.

Sauer, C.O. (1925). The morphology of landscape. *University of California Publications in Geography* 2(2), 19–54.

Suzuki, S. (1997). *Monogatari: Filipin no rekishi* [An account: The history of the Philippines]. Tokyo: Chuokoron Shinsha.

Taylor, K. (2004). Cultural heritage management: A possible role for charters and principles in Asia. *International Journal of Heritage Studies* 10(5), 417–433.

Taylor, K. (2012). Heritage challenges in Asian urban cultural landscape settings. In P. Daly, & T. Winter (Eds.), *Routledge handbook of heritage in Asia* (pp. 266–279). Abingdon: Routledge.

Telfer, D.J., & Sharpley, R. (2008). *Tourism and development in the developing world.* New York: Routledge.

Therborn, G. (2000). Globalizations: dimensions, historical waves, regional effects, normative governance. *International Sociology* 15(2), 151–179.

Timothy, D.J., & Boyd, S.W. (2003). *Heritage tourism*. Harlow: Prentice Hall.

Timothy, D.J., & Boyd, S.W. (2006). Heritage tourism in the 21st century: Valued traditions and new perspectives. *Journal of Heritage Tourism* 1(1), 1–16.

TripAdvisor (2014, February 18). Not Authentic Village Life. Retrieved from: https://www.tripadvisor.jp/ShowUserReviews-g294249-d4493288-r221918776-Tam_an_Villa ge-Banaue_Ifugao_Province_Cordillera_Region_Luzon.html#.

Trupp, A. (2014). Host perspectives on ethnic minority tourism in Northern Thailand. *Journal of Tourism Consumption and Practice* 6(1), 52–80.

UNESCO (n.d.). Rice terraces of the Philippine Cordilleras. Retrieved from: http://whc.unesco.org/en/list/722.

UNESCO (2002). World heritage 25 com (WHC-01/CONF.208/24). Retrieved from: http://whc.unesco.org/archive/repcom01.htm#riceterraces.

UNESCO (2012a). World heritage 36 com (WHC-12/36.COM/7A). Retrieved from: http://whc.unesco.org/en/decisions/4839.

UNESCO (2012b). World heritage 36 com (WHC-12/36.COM/19). Retrieved from: http://whc.unesco.org/en/decisions/4839.

Ung, A., & Vong, T.N. (2010). Tourist experience of heritage tourism in Macau SAR, China. *Journal of Heritage Tourism* 5(2), 157–168.

Wang, N. (1997). Vernacular house as an attraction: Illustration from hutong tourism in Beijing. *Tourism Management* 18(8), 573–580.

Wang, N. (1999). Rethinking authenticity in tourism experience. *Annals of Tourism Research* 26(2), 349–370.

Winter, T., & Daly, P. (2012). Heritage in Asia: Converging forces, conflicting values. In D. Patrick Daly, & T. Winter (Eds.), *Routledge handbook of heritage in Asia* (pp. 1–35). Abingdon: Routledge.

Winter, T. (2014). Beyond eurocentrism? Heritage conservation and the politics of difference. *International Journal of Heritage Studies* 20(2), 123–137.

Wu, J. (2010). Landscape of culture and culture of landscape: Does landscape ecology need culture? *Landscape Ecology* 25, 1147–1150.

Yap, D.L.T. (2005, August 6–9). Conservation and progress: Bridging the gap, the case of the Ifugao rice terraces. United Nations University global seminar series: Inaugural Shimane-Yamaguchi session, Yamaguchi, Japan.

Part IV

Tourism, development, and governance

11 Tourism development in Myanmar

Dynamics, policies, and challenges

Frauke Kraas, Zin Nwe Myint and Nicole Häusler

Introduction

Having recently experienced rapid growth in the demand for tourism, Myanmar is beginning to diversify its range of tourism products and services. As the benefits of the latest political and socioeconomic transformation processes are now being recognised, Myanmar offers immense potential for tourism development in light of its abundant historical, cultural, and natural heritage, not to mention the genuine hospitality of its people and the exotic appeal of a country hitherto 'unexplored' (at least from a foreign perspective). This potential is augmented by the rising incomes among Myanmar's Asian neighbours, as well as the accompanying surge in interest and investment in foreign travel. Although the 2018/2019 crisis and violence in the Rakhine state at the border with Bangladesh resulted in a decrease in the number of Western tourists, this decline was offset by an increase in the number of Asian tourists, especially from China.

In addition to its major religious and cultural sites – notably the Shwedagon Pagoda in Yangon and the world's largest concentration of pagodas at Bagan (inscribed on UNESCO's World Heritage List in July 2019) – the highly diverse ethnic groups and the broad range of Myanmar's natural and cultural assets offer immense potential for tourism development. Natural attractions include the country's relatively unspoilt beaches, islands, and bays around Ngapali, Chaungtha, and Ngwe Saung; its extensive national parks and nature reserves; the vast Ayeyarwady River and Delta area and the Indawgyi and Inle Lakes; and the Shan Hills as well as the picturesque mountain ranges of Chin, Sagaing, and Kachin. As for its cultural attractions, cities such as Yangon, Mandalay, Kalaw, Mawlamyine, Bago, Sagaing, and Myeik contribute their own unique historical characters, including their Buddhist and colonial heritage. Recently, numerous hotels and restaurants (mainly in the mid- to upper price range) have opened, and global hotel chains are increasingly entering the market (CBI, 2018; Ei Ei Thu, 2018b).

In this study, we analysed and assessed the current situation and potential for tourism development in Myanmar in terms of its phases, regional distribution, characteristics, assets, and challenges. With regard to methodology, we combined a systematic literature review of national and international sources with empirical fieldwork in all states and regions of the country. The first stage of our investigations involved field observation and rapid appraisal methods. Between 2012 and 2019, numerous fieldwork stays, excursions, and research-based university teaching allowed us to conduct 55 expert interviews with key government, administration, private-sector, and civil society actors, as well as 74 conversations and interviews with both national and international tourists and local community members throughout Myanmar. Moreover, as a long-time consultant to both public and private tourism organisations in Myanmar, one of the authors was able to provide information gleaned from her daily work, as well as her attendance at dozens of workshops and conferences that focused on the development of tourism in Myanmar.

In the following sections, we present an overview of tourism structures in Myanmar. Next, we cover tourism policies, focusing on decentralisation and the new Tourism Law. After that, we review recent trends in Myanmar tourism, including community-based tourism (CBT) projects and initiatives for sustainable tourism. The final sections point to challenges and offer recommendations for steps toward achieving more sustainable tourism development in Myanmar.

Overview of tourism structures in Myanmar

In this section, we trace the different phases of tourism development and provide an overview of the regional distribution of the centres and characteristics of tourism, including information about visitors' origins and their arrivals.

Phases of tourism development

So far, tourism development in Myanmar has taken place in three phases, beginning with the British colonial period, followed by the period when a market-based economy was introduced, and finally during the country's most recent transformation process, characterised by growing numbers of domestic and foreign visitors.

Although the pre-colonial visits by explorers and missionaries cannot be described as tourism in its narrower sense, the images and impressions that they conveyed attracted growing numbers of investors and merchants (Ko Ko Thett, 2012, p. 12) and paved the way for the initial phase of early tourism development during the British colonial period (1824–1948). Towards the end of the 19th century, this early interest led to the emergence of international tourism, primarily for the purposes of pursuing culture, education, adventure, and hunting, and was targeted mainly at elites. After Myanmar (then known as Burma) gained its independence in 1948, however, subsequent conflicts and civil war initially limited international visitors' freedom to travel and the length of time they could feasibly remain in the country (Henderson, 2003; Ko Ko Thett, 2012). Travel was then further constrained by the nationalisation of Burmese industries and the national policy of autarchy and isolation from the rest of the world, which were characteristics of the 'Burmese way to socialism' that arose in 1962 (Ko Ko Thett, 2012, p. 13; Kraas, Spohner, & Aye Aye Myint, 2017, p. 132).

It was not until the introduction of a market-based economy after 1988 that a second phase of tourism development could begin. This took place in 1996 with the launch of the 'Visit Myanmar Year' marketing campaign (Henderson, 2003, pp. 107–108), with its systematic objectives of encouraging more openness to tourism in general. Such promotion facilitated the expansion of infrastructure and development in the classic 'quadrangle' comprising Yangon, Bagan, Mandalay, and Inle Lake, with a focus on historic, cultural, and religious sites (referred to as the 'commodification of Buddhism' by Philp and Mercer, 1999). In the 1990s some areas were newly opened up for international tourism in the mountain peripheries (see the detailed maps in Michalon, 2017). However, the country's poor transport and supply infrastructures – hence its inaccessibility – meant that tourism development was virtually impossible in these more peripheral regions. In addition, tourism was distinctly seasonal (with November to mid-April being the busiest, before the start of the monsoon season), thus limiting opportunities for year-round tourism. Furthermore, by the late 1990s, international campaigns against the military's human rights violations resulted in EU and US economic and diplomatic sanctions against the country, led by 'Burma campaign' groups, which caused a decline in the number of international tourists (Hudson, 2007; Ko Ko Thett, 2012; Michalon, 2017). The fact that 'tourists are forced to stay in government owned hotels and [to exchange] a minimum of US$300 [other sources refer to US$200] foreign currency when they enter the airport' (Hall & Ringer, 2000, p. 8) was widely criticised.

The third and most recent phase of tourism development began in 2012 in response to the reforms that took place in the wake of the elections in 2010, and tourism was then further fostered by the change to a democratic government in 2015. The comprehensive reforms comprised a series of political, economic, and administrative reforms that included the release of pro-democracy leader Aung San Suu Kyi from house arrest, which paved the way for the landslide victory of the National League for Democracy (NLD) in 2015; the establishment of the National Human Rights Commission; and much new legislation, which included anti-corruption laws, foreign investment laws, and labour laws. Furthermore, there was a relaxation of press censorship and of the regulations regarding currency practices. The political reforms also led to profound socioeconomic transformation processes (Cheesman, Skidmore, & Wilson, 2012; Egreteau & Robinne, 2016), which strongly affected the growing development of tourism in the country.

Since the above-mentioned changes took place, the number of visitors to Myanmar has increased rapidly (Kraas & Häusler, 2016; Suntikul & Rogers, 2017). Tourism statistics published by the Ministry of Hotels and Tourism (MoHT) (Table 11.1), include day-trippers from neighbouring countries who crossed the border for the purpose of trade or to visit family, as well as tourists making 'visa runs' (to renew temporary visas), and are therefore less reliable.

Table 11.1 Myanmar tourism characteristics, 2011–2018

Year	International tourist arrivals	Total spending (million US$)	Average daily visitor spend (US$)	Average length of stay (days)
2011	816,369	319	120	8
2012	1,058,995	534	135	7
2013	2,044,307	926	145	7
2014	3,081,412	1,789	170	9
2015	4,681,020	2,122	171	9
2016	2,907,207	2,197	154	11
2017	3,443,133	1,969	153	9
2018	3,551,428	1,651	122	9

Source: MoHT, 2019b

Since 2016, the number of daily border crossings has no longer been included in the totals issued by MoHT, and this change has had an impact on the arrival statistics. Domestic tourism – with estimated 2.5 million internal trips in 2015 – plays a comparatively minor role, with weekend pilgrimages or visits to family accounting for most of this activity. After introducing the general tourism characteristics of Myanmar, the next section covers the regional distribution of travel.

Regional distribution: tourism centres and areas

Myanmar has a number of well-established centres of international tourism that boast significant religious, cultural, and historical sites. These sites have attracted visitors for decades and include the 'classic four' destinations: in and around the former capitals Mandalay and Yangon, the pagodas and traditional handicrafts at Sagaing (Khin Khin Soe, Kraas, & Yee Yee Than, 2016), the archaeological site at Bagan (Rich & Franck, 2016), and Inle Lake in Southern Shan State (Ingelmo, 2013). Recently, several new tourist destinations have emerged. In July 2014, three ancient Pyu city-states – Halin, Beikthano, and Sri Ksetra (which were politically significant from about 200 BC to AD 700) – were added to the UNESCO List of World Heritage Sites (Su Su & Win Kyaing, 2016), as was Bagan as of June 2019. For Myanmar, receiving this prestigious designation has revived enthusiasm about developing and promoting historical and cultural tourism.

The cities of Yangon and Mandalay and their surroundings have witnessed a growing demand for resorts to accommodate domestic visitors and provide amenities for weekend tourism, which is becoming increasingly popular among Myanmar's upper-middle class and elites, as well as within the expanding international expatriate community. As a result, a tourism sector that specialises in summer retreats, golfing, and hiking is being developed in the former colonial hill stations, such as Kalaw and Pyin Oo Lwin, and the mountain regions around Taunggyi in Shan State (Kraas & Zin Nwe Myint, 2015).

In addition, there are signs of the nascent development of a tourism sector aimed at international visitors that will focus on nature-based and cultural/heritage attractions. With the completion of a transnational highway, the signing of numerous bilateral agreements (Worrachaddej-chai, 2019), and the opening in August 2014 of international border crossings between Myanmar and Thailand (namely at Tachileik–Mae Sai, Myawaddy–Mae Sot, and Kawthaung–Ranong, and later at Htee Kee–Phu Nam Ron and Mawdaung–Singkhon), border areas have emerged as new destinations (allowing cross-border trade, visits by relatives, and so-called 'visa runs'), especially for tourists and business people from Thailand and those entering Myanmar via Thailand (Ishida, 2013; Kudo, 2013; Kraas, 2014; Kesinee, Suthep, & Pairach, 2015). More recent border openings between Myanmar and India took place in May 2018 (at Tamu–Moreh [to Manipur] and Rihkhawdar–Zokhawthar [to Mizoram]) which will raise the number of tourists coming from the Indian side (e.g. to Rih Lake in Chin State).

For the most part, infrastructure in the peripheral mountain areas in the Sagaing Region and the Chin and Kachin States remains underdeveloped, with the result that these areas are still largely inaccessible; this drawback also applies to the southernmost part of Myanmar with regard to the Myeik Archipelago and Kawthaung. Since 2017, however, both local and foreign investors are now developing tourism in this region, which has led to a dramatic rise in the number of domestic tourists in particular. In the areas around Kyaiktiyo, Thaton, Mawlamyine, Hpa-an, and Kyaikkhami, peace agreements have resulted in a burgeoning weekend tourism segment that attracts mainly domestic tourists and is centred on visits to religious sites; moreover, in the past few years, Mon State has begun to attract growing numbers of international tourists, initiating group tourism from Thailand for those wishing to visit famous religious sites and meditation centres (Lusby & Eow, 2015; Zin Nwe Myint & Kraas, 2017). Areas that were previously conflict-ridden in and around the former colonial hill station at Thandaung Gyi are now establishing a budding community involved tourism (Häusler, Zin Mar Than, & Kraas, 2019).

Furthermore, basic tourism infrastructure is emerging in selected hot spots in Chin State and Shan State (Kraas, Zin Nwe Myint, & Khin Khin Soe, 2016), the Sagaing Region, and Kachin State (Zin Mar Than, 2017; Kraas & Zin Mar Than, 2017). Early signs of tourism development are also evident in the mountain regions around Mogok and Kyatpyin, where mining- and gem-related tourism has begun to emerge (Kraas, 2016; Zin Nwe Myint, Kraas, & Swe Zin Theik, 2017; Zeyar Hein, 2019a). Among the more recent trends are hiking, sports, and wellness- and rehabilitation-oriented tourism (e.g. in Shan State, Mon State, and the Tanintharyi Region), while hotels in Nay Pyi Taw, Yangon, and Mandalay are now offering special packages for MICE tourism (meetings, incentives, conferences, and events) (Phyo Thu, 2015).

Tourism facilities and characteristics

Since 2013, tourist arrivals, facilities, and expenditures have been growing apace owing to increased demand at almost all Myanmar's established and emerging tourist destinations. In 2018, the country was reported to have a total of 1,704 hotels with 68,167 rooms, and 33 foreign investments (totalling US$1,749.992 million) were made in hotels and commercial complexes; 11 projects were under construction, and 20 projects have already received permission for construction from the Myanmar Investment Commission (MIC). The majority of the investors come from Singapore (34 hotels, with an investment of US$2,764.180 million) and Thailand (13 hotels, with an investment of US$497.964 million), with other investors coming mainly from Japan, Hong Kong, and Vietnam (MoHT, 2019b). Furthermore, Myanmar has 2,712 registered tour companies that provide inbound/domestic tourism, of which 41 are joint ventures and only one is owned by a foreign company. In order to offer outbound trips, local companies need a special licence, and about 553 local tour operators are currently able to offer this kind of service in Myanmar (MoHT, 2019b). Nevertheless, Myanmar is currently grappling with hotel oversupply as a swath of properties continues to open up, especially in Yangon, while tourist arrivals fall short of the country's projected targets (Carruthers, 2018). This situation has also led to an abundance of unemployed hotel staff and tour guides.

Unfortunately, statistics on the number of domestic tourists are not publicly available; however, the residents of Myanmar have clearly begun to explore their own country, taking short-term trips that last from two to five days and even longer during the Thingyan water festival. Although local tour operators who are specialised in domestic pilgrimages still offer visits to famous pagodas, the attitude toward travel and tourism is changing. Young Myanmar travellers are more likely to enjoy riding motorbikes or mountain bikes, horseback riding, bamboo rafting, short trekking tours, or renting 4-wheel drive cars to explore remote areas, and beach and snorkelling tourism has also become popular.

The number of international visitors, although small in the past, has increased substantially since 2010 (Table 11.1). Asian nationals (mostly from Thailand, China, and Japan) comprise the largest visitor group (approximately 76%), followed by Western Europeans (13%, mainly from France, the UK, and Germany) and North Americans (5.5%) in 2018. Although the number of tourists arriving from most of the Western countries slightly decreased, the number of tourists coming from Hong Kong/China, Korea, and Japan has increased significantly (by around 135%, 89%, and 24%, respectively) (MoHT, 2019b). The reasons for this shift are diverse. During the Rakhine violence and crisis, Western tourists were discouraged from traveling to Myanmar owing to ethical considerations and safety and security issues; however, in 2018 and 2019, their absence was more than replaced by the steeply rising numbers of Chinese tourists and those from other Asian nations (Bangkok Post, 2018; Dunant, 2019; Lintner, 2019).

In 2018, MoHT decided to focus on Korea, Japan, and China as part of its promotion of tourism by holding Tourism Fairs and introducing no-visa policies. Therefore, it is expected that the number of tourists from these three countries will continue to rise in the coming years. Furthermore, China's Belt-and-Road Initiative is expected to contribute to this increase (Rimmer, 2018). Moreover, it was announced in 2019 that tourists from Italy, Spain, Switzerland, Germany, Russia, and Australia can obtain a visa on arrival starting on October 1, 2019, and for a 1-year probation period thereafter (MoHT, 2019c).

The average tourist in 2018 stayed in Myanmar for nine days and spent US \$122 per day, resulting in a reported total spending of US\$1,651 million; in comparison, however, two years earlier (in 2016), tourists were staying for an average of 11 days and spent on average US\$154 per day, with a total expenditure of US\$2,197.15 million (Table 11.1) (MoHT, 2019b; Kraas & Häusler, 2016). Thus, the overall number of tourists now remain in the country for fewer days and spend less than in the previous years. Of course, this decline is linked to the Rakhine crisis and the focus of marketing activities on the Asian market predominantly.

In particular one finds criticism over the fact that, on average, Chinese tourists tend to have shorter stays (less than four days) compared with other tourists and they often spend less money per day than Western visitors do. The expression 'zero-dollar tourism' is now frequently used to describe Chinese package tours (Zeyar Hein, 2019b), which seem to be more or less controlled by Chinese businesses, including overnight stays in Chinese-owned hotels and visits to Chinese restaurants.

Development of tourism policies in Myanmar

Immediately after the political opening of Myanmar in 2012, MoHT expressed the intention to develop tourism in a responsible and sustainable way (Mascontour, 2012). In 2012, the *Policy on Responsible Tourism* summarised the results of discussions that took place during a series of 10 seminars involving more than 350 participants from the public and private tourism sectors. This policy contains a strategic vision, nine overall aims, and 58 specific action points for the implementation of sustainable tourism practices (Häusler & Baumgartner, 2013). Specifically, the strategic vision includes the improvement of living standards, economic empowerment of local communities, conservation of cultural and natural resources, and the responsible behaviour of all tourism stakeholders (MoHT, 2012, p. 6).

The responsible tourism policy has nine overall aims:

1) to make tourism a national priority sector;
2) to promote broad-based local socio-economic development;
3) to maintain cultural diversity and authenticity;
4) to conserve and enhance the environment;

5) to compete on product richness, diversity, and quality, not just on price;
6) to ensure the health, safety, and security of visitors;
7) to strengthen institutions which manage tourism;
8) to create a well-trained and well-rewarded workforce; and
9) to minimize unethical practices.

In response to the demand for greater integration of local communities into the tourism sector, a second policy regarding community involvement was formulated that focuses on capacity-building through community-related activities in tourism.

Building on these two policies, the Myanmar Tourism Master Plan was introduced (MoHT, 2013b). This plan stressed the need to achieve sustainable tourism development with a focus on the following aims:

1) strengthening the institutional environment (Ministry, associations);
2) building human resource capacity and promoting the quality of services;
3) strengthening safeguards and procedures for destination planning and management;
4) developing quality products and services;
5) improving connectivity and tourism-related infrastructure; and
6) building the image, position, and brand of 'Tourism Myanmar'.

Whilst the process of elaborating these two policies and coming up with a master plan in 2012 and 2013 was swift and successful, their implementation has been challenging. First, MoHT and related Ministries at the national and state levels lack trained staff, and there is currently little coordination between the national and regional actors. In 2015, after the victory of the NLD, hopes were high that a functioning and constructive government at all levels would soon be established. However, both the government and MoHT have not yet realised an implementation policy built on existing documents, policies, and master plans (e.g. conducting an investigation regarding the case of Bagan, as outlined by Myo Aung, 2019). Instead, their strategy has shifted mainly towards developing CBT projects and to increasing the volume of the Asian market. In the view of the local communities, the shift to CBT is mostly perceived as positive, because the tourism industry, and its related effects on the local transport sector, local traditional culture, and local handicraft production in particular, would contribute substantially to the growth of local income. These opportunities have been studied in detail by Zin Nwe Myint (2011, 2014, 2016) for Mrauk-U, by Zin Nwe Myint and Kraas (2017) and Lusby and Eow (2015) for Mawlamyine, by Khin Khin Soe, Kraas, and Yee Yee Than (2016) for Sagaing, by Zin Mar Than (2017) for the Indawgyi Lake area, and by Zin Nwe Myint, Kraas, and Swe Zin Theik (2017) for Mogok. Moreover, the improved acknowledgement of local cultural heritage through tourism – both tangible and intangible – is much appreciated by the local population, even though some have raised the issue of a potential transformation and alienation of cultural practices once they are 'discovered', commodified, and commercialised by the tourism industry (Zin Nwe Myint, 2016).

Finally, in 2018, a new Tourism Law was enacted that focused on decentralisation, responsible tourism, and CBT. Chapter 2 of this law mentions its objectives, such as '(f) to promote responsible tourism activities' (although the term 'responsible tourism' is not defined) and '(g) to support community tourism-related businesses and SMEs and to create regional economic opportunities for communities as well as the development of community-based tourism' (Union of Myanmar, 2018). In accordance with this law, three new committees were established: the Central Committee (see Chapter 3 of the law), the Tourism Working Committee at the national level (see Chapter 4 of the law), and the State or Regional Tourism Working Committees (see Chapter 6 of the law) (Table 11.2).

As the time this chapter is being written, the implications of the new Tourism Law, which focuses on the decentralisation of tasks and, in particular, authorises the issuing of licences at the regional level, remain to be seen, because the transfer of these tasks and responsibilities and the creation of regional tourism committees is ongoing. In any case, this law is an interesting step towards the overall decentralisation policy. If the State or Regional Tourism Working Committees fail to function in a professional way, and if there is no proper coordination among these three recently established committees, the new decision-making structure for planning and managing tourism in Myanmar could lead to a lack of progress and even stagnation.

New trends in tourism development since 2015

The messages from MoHT about Myanmar's tourism planning are conflicting, in that they hope to promote CBT, Asian tourism, and opportunities for casino gambling all at the same time. On its website, MoHT promotes 24 CBT sites that either have already been implemented or are in the process of being implemented (MoHT, 2019d). Yet the challenges to this development are twofold.

First, because a clear definition for CBT in Myanmar is still lacking, there is room left for interpretation. For example, outside investors may see it offering a simple lodge (two rooms, with mattresses on the floor) within a community, but they fail to gain a deeper understanding of the meaning of CBT or an appreciation for the challenges that come with trying to involve community members. These challenges can be related to:

a   power issues, such as external pressures, issues of governance, conflicting agendas, and jealousy, which are quite often linked to internal power struggles;
b   the often underestimated role of social capital in a community;
c   the level of transparency and participation skills among the community members; and
d   the overall role of the community culture including kinship, gender and spirituality.

Table 11.2 Overview of membership, leaders, and tasks of the Central Committee, Tourism Working Committee, and State or Regional Tourism Working Committees

Committee	Membership	Principal tasks
Central Committee, chaired by Vice-President of Myanmar (should meet at least twice a year)	Minimum 25 members, among them 14 chairmen of the states and regions, three private-sector representatives, and three tourism experts	• Guiding and supervising the development and implementation of tourism master plans, strategies and projects, especially providing guidelines to promote community tourism-related businesses and CBT • Developing policies and plans to achieve and promote responsible tourism
Tourism Working Committee, chaired by Union Minister of Hotels and Tourism (should meet at least twice a year)	Minimum of 32 members, among them 14 chairmen of the State or Regional Tourism Working Committees, 10 private-sector representatives, and five tourism experts	• Implementing policies and guidelines as set up by the Central Committee • Providing guidance to the State or Regional Tourism Working Committees • Coordinating with relevant government departments for national and international investment • Coordinating with relevant government departments on matters of environmental conservation and to help safeguard Myanmar's cultural heritage
State or Regional Tourism Working Committees chaired by State Minister (should meet at least once a month)	Minimum of 12 members, among them six public-sector representatives, three private-sector representatives, and one tourism expert	• Implementing policies • Carrying out all tasks related to the licencing of hotels, guides and tour operators • Developing new destinations • Enhancing the quality of standards and services; protecting the culture and environment of Myanmar • Developing human resources

Source: Author's compilation, based on Tourism Law, Union of Myanmar, 2018

Such oversight can lead to stakeholders having different expectations, as well as to a non-cooperative atmosphere (Häusler, 2017).

Second, the target groups of most CBT projects in Myanmar are not clearly defined. Most entrepreneurs seek to attract Western tourists, especially backpackers with a limited financial budget for accommodation and food. MoHT's approach contradicts this view, focusing its promotional efforts on China, Korea, and Japan instead, without having actually analysed the demand for CBT and limited receptivity for CBT among these Asian tourists.

Furthermore, research needs to be undertaken to get a better understanding of the linkage between CBT and domestic tourism as Myanmar citizens seem to be more interested in meeting other ethnic groups and staying with them for one or two nights.

However, with the launch of the 'Community-based Tourism Standards' (MoHT, 2019a), the quality of the existing CBT projects can improve, as more training might be offered in achieving this standard, and the criteria set for CBT may help prevent misunderstandings of the term 'community-based tourism' for ASEAN (Novelli, Klatte, & Dolezal, 2016). Furthermore, the government is pressing for permission to open casinos in order to attract more Asian tourists, especially from China and Thailand (DFDL, 2019). So far, Myanmar and Thailand are the only two Southeast Asian countries that do not officially have casinos, although some are already operating illegally in areas of Myanmar that border Thailand and China. It is hoped that the legalisation of casinos will provide support in terms of tax revenue and will set rules and regulations to systematise their operation. Whilst Myanmar citizens will be allowed to do business and accept employment at the casinos, they might not be permitted to gamble (Kyaw Ye Lynn & Dunant, 2019; Chan Mya Htwe, 2019). However, concerns have been expressed by a few local NGOs that permitting casinos could negatively impact tourism owing to the potential for human trafficking and child prostitution, especially in the border areas.

Nevertheless, numerous positive steps are being taken as a result of local sustainable tourism initiatives over the past few years. These include:

a   the establishment of the Myanmar Responsible Tourism Institute (MRTI) in 2016, which offers training in various fields of sustainable tourism, and the establishment of the annual Myanmar Responsible Tourism Award;
b   an annual conference on 'Tourism and Communities', organised by MRTI, the Hanns-Seidel Foundation (HSF), and the Myanmar Centre for Responsible Business (MCRB);
c   the establishment of the Sustainable Tourism Network (formerly the CBT Network), which meets on a regular basis to exchange information; and
d   the publication of Dos and Don'ts by Tourism Transparency and partner organisations.

Still missing, however, are clear strategies – to be set forth by the government and the private tourism sector (such as the Myanmar Tourism Federation, as the umbrella organisation for all tourism associations) – that will link all these initiatives and mainstream them, including a comprehensible marketing strategy.

For sure, more effective coordination among the local organisations, the development partners, and the private-sector associations at their annual or biannual national meetings would provide a more constructive and beneficial way to overcome certain challenges. Although selected members of the private sector are invited to join the Central Committee of Tourism, led by the Vice President with MoHT as secretary, once a year, neither the development partners nor the civil society organisations have been invited to join as members or even as observers.

Current challenges to tourism development

The challenges to tourism development in Myanmar are manifold, and although the following descriptions cover the main problems, this list is not complete.

1) For many years the rise in the number of visitors to Myanmar has had certain negative impacts on the environment within the country, such as a decrease in biodiversity and an increase in the illegal trade of flora and fauna (Nijman & Shepherd, 2014; Zhang, Gouveia, Qin, Quan, & Nijman, 2017; Phelps & Webb, 2015; Zin Mar Than, 2017). However, not enough action has been taken to at least minimise these detrimental effects. Destinations such as Bagan, Inle Lake, and the Golden Rock (Kyaikhtiyo) are already experiencing environmental problems resulting from inadequate waste disposal and wastewater management (MCRB, 2015). Comparable problems exist at almost all the tourism sites in the country. Even in Mrauk-U, which is visited by only a few tourists, more than 90% of the total responses to a questionnaire indicated that improvements in the drainage and waste disposal systems are urgently needed (Zin Nwe Myint, 2014).

2) Increasingly vocal complaints have revealed the negative impacts of planned large-scale investments in hotel zones, particularly the displacement of local communities and the inadequate compensation paid by investors.

3) Rising land prices and conflicts over use of the land, as well as resource conflicts (e.g. concerning the use of water), are becoming a pressing issue.

4) Even though policies and a master plan exist, their implementation has often not been carried out in a structured or systematic way (for Mawlamyine, see Lusby and Eow, 2015). For example, a destination management plan was created for Inle Lake (MoHT, 2014), but the initial practical measures for its implementation were not undertaken until late in 2015 and were limited to a series of workshops at which MoHT defined preliminary responsibilities and activities in conjunction with local stakeholders. The implementation stage is still a long way off, owing largely to the lack of local experts with in-depth knowledge of destination planning and management.

5) Service and safety standards for hotels, guesthouses, and transportation vehicles need to be defined and controlled (see also Zin Nwe Myint, 2011).

6) Many local people lack preparedness and an awareness about the consequences of tourism and are not adequately informed about how to deal with and treat tourists, particularly foreign visitors (Zin Nwe Myint,

2011; Lusby & Eow, 2015). Concerns about culturally inappropriate behaviour towards their local hosts on the part of foreign tourists, especially young people, need to be taken seriously. Also, local government institutions, such as the General Administrative Department (GAD) and the police force, have not been trained and are not yet well prepared to handle tourists, a need that is recently being addressed through special training programmes offered by MoHT.

Future challenges and priorities for tourism development

Based on the priorities framed by MoHT and the main institutions responsible for tourism development in Myanmar, and based on the results of our own empirical research, we would recommend that tourism development policies focus on the following challenges and priorities:

1) Integrated, sustainable destination management planning and development for these regions, including environmental and social impact assessments and the introduction of innovative environmental technologies, should be supported. This will require cooperation between MoHT and international experts. Practical training courses on the planning and implementation of local destination management plans should be established.
2) Tourism-related education needs to be improved in both secondary and higher educational institutions, including its comprehensive integration in school and university curricula.
3) After the development of the Responsible Tourism Policy (MoHT, 2012), there were calls for more intensive local community involvement in tourism, and a policy on Community Involvement in Tourism (CIT) has been developed (Häusler, 2014). Still pending is the question of whether the degree of participation is adequate. Representatives from neither civil society organisations nor local communities have joined the tourism committees that have recently been set up at both the national and the regional levels.
4) The promotion of tourism as a regional development tool and as a means of reducing regional disparities is already producing visible successes – specifically, income and net foreign exchange (NFE) earnings are increasing, jobs are being created and maintained, regional and social inequalities are being lessened, out-migration has been curbed, improvements in healthcare and education have received a fresh impetus, and the demand for local goods has been boosted. The lack of capital resources can still be offset by labour inputs, resulting in considerable direct and indirect employment effects, not least in the informal sector. Local communities will see additional gains as a result of infrastructure expansion, and improved regional integration and connectivity as a result of better trade and transport links will also bring benefits to communities.

5) Tourism should also be taken seriously as a route toward peace and conflict resolution if all the stakeholders involved are willing carefully and transparently to join in a continuing co-development of tourism sites (Häusler, Zin Mar Than, & Kraas, 2019). Problems such as the connections among entertainment and casino tourism, prostitution, and human trafficking need to be dealt with effectively.

6) The commercialisation of certain elements of Myanmar's traditional culture can harness endogenous growth potential, with the 'discovery' of culture being seen as an economic resource. This view can in turn help preserve and strengthen the production and trade of traditional crafts (e.g. souvenirs). Nevertheless, to prevent negative effects on the local communities, these steps deserve careful attention, and members of these communities need to be included in the planning and development of tourism.

Conclusion

As Myanmar opens up to the world, the growing options and opportunities are also leading to greater regional and societal disparities. A lack of transparency in the planning and development of new destinations may soon cause conflicts within and between communities, local authorities, and investors (MCRB & HSF, 2015b), thus making Myanmar less attractive for future investment. As local communities sense that foreign and large-scale investments might deny them the benefits of growing tourism, discussions are under way to avoid potential conflicts. Nevertheless, the participation of and careful consultation with the local population in both established and emerging tourism sites will be crucial.

Future developments in Myanmar's tourism industry will need to take into account innovations and trends in the broader regional context of the growing competition for tourism in Southeast Asia, especially since the 'exotic novelty' of Myanmar as a destination is likely to fade over time. For example, the current potential of nature tourism based on the unique selling point of Myanmar's national parks and nature reserves – and hence the appeal and value of these assets – will decline with the growing demand for tourism and the inevitable impact of use, similar to what is happening in other countries in this region (Trupp, 2018), such as in Thailand. Spiritual and meditation-based tourism is also enjoying a surge in popularity, particularly among domestic tourists, since it is not only the growing middle classes that can afford weekend and short vacation trips. However, as international values and demands begin to influence and alter not only the local communities but also the daily practices of social and religious life, the originality and authenticity of this type of tourism is also likely to lose some of its appeal.

Moreover, national and international tourism are bound to diversify further with respect to both supply and demand: among the new trends are wellness, sports, and medical tourism; MICE tourism; educational/summer course tourism; and cross-border and trade-related tourism. These trends point to opportunities for regional segmentation to become much more diversified and, in some cases, for growing specialisation of the tourism potential.

Lastly, against the background of Myanmar's burgeoning international engagement, it is clear that new investors will contribute to a more diversified tourism offering (e.g. by introducing low-budget but also high-end price segments into the market). Furthermore, new customers will want their specific expectations and demands to be met. It is often said that tourism destroys the very assets on which the industry itself depends and thus destroys itself, and it is feared that this may soon hold true for Myanmar. This risk can be mitigated only through carefully crafted strategies and sustainable, systematic planning and development processes that are based on the principle of fairness and that involve a wide range of knowledgeable and farsighted decision-makers and stakeholders.

Acknowledgements

This research project was possible through the generous cooperation of experts and citizens in numerous tourism areas in Myanmar. The paper emerged from the long-standing and close cooperation among the Department of Geography, the Centre of Excellence (CoE) on Urban and Regional Development at the University of Yangon, and the Institute of Geography at the University of Cologne/Germany.

References

Bangkok Post (2018, February 22). Myanmar sees rise in tourism despite Rohingya crisis. Retrieved from: https://www.bangkokpost.com/world/1416390/myanmar-sees-rise-in-tourism-despite-rohingya-crisis.

Carruthers, M. (2018, May 25). Myanmar goes from undersupply to oversupply of hotels. *TTG Asia*. Retrieved from: https://www.ttgasia.com/2018/05/25/myanmar-goes-from-undersupply-to-oversupply-of-hotels.

CBI, Ministry of Foreign Affairs (2018, April 12). Tourism value chain report: Myanmar. Retrieved from: https://www.cbi.eu/sites/default/files/vca-_study-tourism-myanmar.pdf.

Chan Mya Htwe (2019, March 31). Casino operations to be legalised under new gabling law. *Myanmar Times*. Retrieved from: https://www.mmtimes.com/news/casino-operations-be-legalised-under-new-gambling-law.html.

Cheesman, N., Skidmore, M., & Wilson, T. (Eds.) (2012). *Myanmar's transition: Openings, obstacles and opportunities*. Singapore: Institute of Southeast Asian Studies (ISEAS).

DFDL (2019, May 10). Myanmar legal alert: New gambling law permits casinos to operate in Myanmar. Retrieved from: https://www.dfdl.com/resources/legal-and-tax-updates/myanmar-legal-alert-new-gambling-law-permits-casinos-to-operate-in-myanmar/?fbclid=IwAR1HC1M_j7O8dduWa3fg_GOvsFIwV1jYHNzyGA67HIx7iNs_8PsFTtXJoas.

Dunant, B. (2019, April 25). Why is Serge Pun betting on tourism? *Frontier Myanmar*. Retrieved from: https://frontiermyanmar.net/en/why-is-serge-pun-betting-on-tourism?fbclid=IwAR1iEDitPC_LCqrn1ywaNQWHkZBJ3A0Qar-rQ5pZ-kg4BKka hdJJUvPC-RA.

Ei Ei Thu (2018a, November 15). Growth of 'Zero-dollar tours' for Chinese worries local operators. *Myanmar Times*. Retrieved from: https://www.mmtimes.com/news/growth-zero-dollar-tours-chinese-worries-local-operators.html.

Ei Ei Thu (2018b, November 16). Hotel investments continue to rise despite lower tourist arrivals. *Myanmar Times*. Retrieved from: https://www.mmtimes.com/news/hotel-investments-continue-rise-despite-lower-tourist-arrivals.html.

Ei Ei Thu (2018c, December 18). Looking to cruise ships to boost tourism. *Myanmar Times*. Retrieved from: https://www.mmtimes.com/news/looking-cruise-ships-boost-tourism.html.

Ei Ei Thu (2019, January 3). Tourist arrivals rise 3.15% in '18. *Myanmar Times*. Retrieved from: https://www.mmtimes.com/news/tourist-arrivals-rise-315-18.html?fbclid=IwAR1 fyso1ra6O54GvIOMAtqGQAqYQhAYEJq2otB8NFdsjHTNONlrcCx0lWiE.

Ei Ei Thu, & Kean, T. (2015, January 19). Why Myanmar's tourist numbers don't add up. *Myanmar Times*. Retrieved from: https://www.mmtimes.com/in-depth/12828-why-myanmar-s-tourist-numbers-don-t-add-up.html.

Egreteau, R., & Robinne, F. (Eds.) (2016). *Metamorphosis: Studies in societal and political change in Myanmar*. Singapore: NUS Press.

Hall, M.C., & Ringer, G. (2000). Tourism in Cambodia, Laos and Myanmar: From terrorism to tourism? In M.C Hall & S.D. Page (Eds.), *Tourism in South and Southeast Asia: Issues and cases* (pp. 178–194). New York: Butterworth-Heinemann.

Häusler, N. (2014). Nachhaltiger Tourismus in Myanmar: Erste wichtige Schritte? In U. Köster, P. L. Trong, & C. Grein (Eds.), *Handbuch Myanmar: Gesellschaft, Politik, Wirtschaft, Kultur, Entwicklung* (pp. 293–303). Berlin: Horlemann.

Häusler, N. (2017). *Cultural due diligence in hospitality ventures. A methodological approach for joint ventures of local communities and companies*. Cham: Springer.

Häusler, N., & Baumgartner, C. (2013). Myanmar on its way to responsible management: The important role of stakeholder dialogues. In C. Wohlmuther, & W. Wintersteiner (Eds.), *International handbook on tourism and peace* (pp. 181–198). Klagenfurt: Drava.

Häusler, N., Zin Mar Than, & Kraas, F. (2019). Tourism as a tool for peace? Between the lines - Thandaunggyi in Kayin State, Myanmar. In R.K. Issac, E. Cakmak, & R. Butler (Eds.), *Tourism and Hospitality in Conflict-ridden Destinations* (pp. 84–103). Abingdon: Routledge.

Henderson, J.C. (2003). The politics of tourism in Myanmar. *Current Issues in Tourism* 6(2), 97–118.

Hudson, S. (2007). To go or not to go? Ethical perspectives on tourism in an 'outpost of tyranny'. *Journal of Business Ethics* 76, 385–396.

Ingelmo, I.A. (2013). Design and development of a Sustainable Tourism Indicator based on human activities analysis in Inle Lake, Myanmar. *Procedia – Social and Behavioral Sciences* 103, 262–272.

Ishida, M. (2013). Epilogue: Potentiality of border economic zones and future prospects. In M. Ishida (Ed), *Border economies in the Greater Mekong subregion* (pp. 299–331). Basingstoke: Palgrave Macmillan.

Kesinee, S., Suthep, N., & Pairach, P. (2015). An investigation and evaluation of cross-border truck transportation from Mae Sot-Myawaddy to Yangon. *International Journal of Supply Chain Management* 4(4), 102–107.

Khin Khin Soe, Kraas, F., & Yee Yee Than (2016). Economic development potentials of Sagaing region: Perception on crafts and handicrafts of Sagaing Town. *Taungoo University Research Journal* 7(1), 29–38.

Ko Ko Thett (2012). *Responsible tourism in Myanmar: Current situation and challenges.* Prague: Burma Center Prague.

Kraas, F. (2014). Tachileik/Myanmar und Mae Sai/Thailand: Grenzstädte im Transformationsprozess. *Thailand-Rundschau* 27(1), 18–23.

Kraas, F. (2016). Rubine und Saphire: Zur Entwicklung der Bergbaustadt Mogok/Myanmar. In *Die Welt verstehen – eine geographische Herausforderung. Eine Festschrift der Geographie Innsbruck für Axel Borsdorf.* Innsbrucker Geographische Studien 40, 95–118.

Kraas, F., & Häusler, N. (2016). Tourismusentwicklung in Myanmar. *Geographische Rundschau* 68(9), 52–57.

Kraas, F., Spohner, R., & Aye Aye Myint (2017). *Socio-economic atlas of Myanmar.* Stuttgart: Franz Steiner Verlag.

Kraas, F., & Zin Mar Than (2017). Socio-economic developments in the Indawgyi Lake Area, Kachin State, Myanmar. *Journal of the Myanmar Academy of Arts and Science (Geology and Geography)* XIV(5), 281–299.

Kraas, F., & Zin Nwe Myint (2015). Potentials for sustainable tourism development in the Taunggyi Area, Myanmar. *Journal of the Myanmar Academy of Arts and Science* 13(6), 237–254.

Kraas, F., Zin Nwe Myint, & Khin Khin Soe (2016). Urban developments in Hakha and Falam, Chin State/Myanmar. *Journal of the Myanmar Academy of Arts and Science (Geology and Geography)* XIV(5), 301–318.

Kudo, T. (2013). Border development in Myanmar: The case of the Myawaddy-Mae Sot border. In M. Ishida (Ed), *Border economies in the Greater Mekong Subregion* (pp. 186–205). Basingstoke: Palgrave Macmillan.

Kyaw Ye Lynn, & Dunant, B. (2019, February 27). Casino tycoons' stake hopes on legislation. *Frontier Myanmar.* Retrieved from: https://frontiermyanmar.net/en/casino-tycoons-stake-hopes-on-legalisation.

Lintner, B. (2019,July 31). As West retreats, China surges in Myanmar. *Asia Times.* Retrieved from: https://www.asiatimes.com/2019/07/article/as-west-retreats-china-surges-in-myanmar.

Lusby, C., & Eow, K. (2015). Tourism development in a new democracy: Residents' perceptions of commmunity-based tourism in Mawlamyine, Myanmar. *Journal of Tourism and Recreation* 2(1), 23–40.

Mascontour (2012). Impulse. Myanmar: On the road to responsible tourism. Nr. 3. Berlin. Retrieved from: https://www.mascontour.info/images/PDF/newsletter/Newsletter_Impulse_09.2012_English.pdf.

MCRB (Myanmar Centre for Responsible Business) (2015). *Myanmar tourism sectorwide impact assessment.* Yangon: MCRB.

MCRB & HSF (Hanns-Seidel-Foundation) (2015a). Mobilise, Market, Mentor, and Monitor: How to Support Community Involvement in Tourism. Nay Pyi Taw: MCRB & HSF. Retrieved from: http://www.myanmar-responsiblebusiness.org/news/community-involved-tourism.html.

MCRB & HSF (2015b). Tourism in Myanmar Needs More Local Involvement. Nay Pyi Taw: MCRB & HSF. Retrieved from: http://www.myanmar-responsiblebusiness.org/news/tourism-myanmar-needs-more-local-involvement.html.

Michalon, M. (2017). Tourism(s) and the way to democracy in Myanmar. *Asian Journal of Tourism Research* 8(1), 150–176.

MoHT (Ministry of Hotels and Tourism) (n.d.). *Policies.* Nay Pyi Taw: MoHT. Retrieved from: https://tourism.gov.mm/policies.

MoHT (2012). *Responsible Tourism Policy.* Nay Pyi Taw: MoHT.

MoHT (2013a). *Policy on Community Involvement in Tourism (CIT).* Nay Pyi Taw: MoHT.

MoHT (2013b). *Myanmar Tourism Master Plan 2013–2020.* Nya Pyi Taw: MoHT.

MoHT (2014). *Destination Management Plan for the Inlay Lake Region 2014–2019.* Nay Pyi Taw: MoHT.

MoHT (2018). *Tourism Statistics 2017.* Nay Pyi Taw: MoHT. Retrieved from: https://tourism.gov.mm/wp-content/uploads/2019/03/Myanmar-Tourism-Statistics-2017-Final.pdf.

MoHT (2019a). *Community-based Tourism Standards.* Nay Pyi Taw: MoHT.

MoHT (2019b). *Tourism Statistics 2018.* Nay Pyi Taw: MoHT. Retrieved from: https://tourism.gov.mm/wp-content/uploads/2019/08/Myanmar-Toursim-Statistics-2018.pdf.

MoHT (2019c). *Visa on Arrival.* Nay Pyi Taw: MoHT. Retrieved from: https://tourism.gov.mm/visa-requirements/visa-on-arrival.

MoHT (2019d). *Community-based Tourism.* Nay Pyi Taw: MoHT. Retrieved from: https://tourism.gov.mm/community-based-tourism.

Myo Aung (2019). Strategies to survive and thrive of Myanmar tourism GDP: Case study of Bagan tourism. *International Journal on Recent Trends in Business and Tourism* 3(1), 16–21.

Nijman, V., & Shepherd, C.R. (2014). Emergence of Mong La on the Myanmar-China border as a global hub for the international trade in ivory and elephant parts. *Biological Conservation* 179, 17–22

Novelli, M., Klatte, N., & Dolezal, C. (2016). The ASEAN community-based tourism standards: Looking beyond certification. *Tourism Planning & Development* 14(2), 260–281.

Phelps, J., & Webb, E.L. (2015). "Invisible" wildlife trades: Southeast Asia's undocumented illegal trade in wild ornamental plants. *Biological Conservation* 186, 296–305.

Philp, J., & Mercer, D. (1999). Commodification of Buddhism in contemporary Burma. *Annals of Tourism Research* 26(1), 21–54.

Phyo Thu (2015, June 2). Ministry to tap MICE tourism through new website. *Myanmar Business Today.* Retrieved from: https://mmbiztoday.com/ministry-to-tap-mice-tourism-through-new-website.

Rich, A.-K., & Franck, A.K. (2016). Tourism development in Bagan, Myanmar: Perceptions of its influences upon young peoples' cultural identity. *Tourism Planning & Development* 13(3), 333–350.

Rimmer, P.J. (2018). China's Belt and Road Initiative: Underlying economic and international relations dimensions. *Asia Pacific Economic Literature* 32(2), 3–26.

Suntikul, W., & Rogers, P. (2017). Myanmar opening for tourism. In R. W Butler & W. Suntikul (Eds.), *Tourism and political change* (pp. 123–137): Oxford: Goodfellow Publishers Ltd.

Su Su, & Win Kyaing (2016). 2,000 Years of urban continuity in Sri Ksetra-Pyay. In F. Kraas Mi Mi Kyi & Win Maung (Eds.), *Sustainability in Myanmar* (pp. 307–318). Southeast Asian Modernities 15. Berlin: LitVerlag.

Trupp, A. (2018). Tourismus in Südostasien. Entwicklung und trends. In K. Husa, R. Korff & H. Wohlschlaegl (Eds.), *Südostasien* (pp. 274–291). Vienna: New Academic Press.

Union of Myanmar (2018, September 17). Myanmar Tourism Law. Union of Hluttaw Law. No. 26/2018.

Worrachaddejchai, D. (2019, April 19). Thailand, Myanmar agree to cooperate. *Bangkok Post*. Retrieved from: https://m.bangkokpost.com/business/tourism-and-tra nsport/1663652?refer=http%3A%2F%2Fm.facebook.com%2F&fbclid=IwAR2 SHUzl4l1Pegnh0c5PC54zSacze1sQ6YGLDSUhMp7Xz7ubfVqXLo7eWRI.

Zeyar Hein (2019a, April 29). Mogok attracts more tourist in six months since opening to foreigners. *Myanmar Times*. Retrieved from: https://www.mmtimes.com/news/mogok-attracts-more-tourists-six-months-opening-foreigners.html?fbclid=IwAR2zlm4Wwjih1 WSzNdcqsImJkva-60WvJon6z2KuTtX3blL5QZBLI3KVsYk.

Zeyar Hein (2019b, June 12). Authorities urged to take action against growing zero-dollar tourism. *Myanmar Times*. Retrieved from: https://www.mmtimes.com/news/a uthorities-urged-take-action-against-growing-zero-dollar-tourism.html.

Zhang, M., Gouveia, A., Qin, T., Quan, R., & Nijman, V. (2017). Illegal pangolin trade in northernmost Myanmar and its links to India and China. *Global Ecology and Conservation* 10, 23–31.

Zin Mar Than (2017*). Socio-economic development of Indawgyi Lake Area, Kachin State, Myanmar*. Urban and Regional Development in Myanmar 1. Stuttgart: Franz Steiner Verlag.

Zin Nwe Myint (2011). Host perceptions on tourism development of Mrauk-U, Rakhine State. *Journal of Myanmar Academy of Arts and Sciences* IX(6), 175–194.

Zin Nwe Myint (2014). Heritage, culture and tourism development of Mrauk-U: Perception of local community. In *Cultural Traditions* (pp. 1–20). Yangon: SEAMEO Regional Centre for History and Tradition.

Zin Nwe Myint (2016). Drivers of cultural tourism in Mrauk-U, Myanmar. In F. Kraas, Mi Mi Kyi & Win Maung (Eds.), *Sustainability in Myanmar*. Southeast Asian Modernities 15 (pp. 319–345). Berlin: Lit Verlag.

Zin Nwe Myint (2017). Managing tourism under strain in Myanmar. *Journal of National Research Council of Thailand* 3(2), 40–52.

Zin Nwe Myint, & Kraas, F. (2017): Tourism development potentials of the Mawla-myine Area Myanmar. *Journal of the Myanmar Academy of Arts and Science* XV (5), 253–273.

Zin Nwe Myint, Kraas, F., & Swe Zin Theik (2017). Gemstone picture production in Mogok: Opportunities and challenges. *Journal of the Myanmar Academy of Arts and Science* XV(5), 235–251.

12 Community-based ecotourism development and destination governance in Cambodia

A comparative analysis

Sabine Müller, Jitka Markova and Sindhuri Ponnapureddy

Introduction

Cambodia can be considered a developing country according to the UN Human Development Index[1] (ranked 146 in 2017) and therefore is highly dependent on aid (Sothan, 2018). This is one of the reasons why the support of international agencies and institutions is essential for the country (UNCTAD, 2018). With financial and technical support from international agencies, in addition to internal efforts, the Cambodian economy is undergoing a transformation from a strong focus on agriculture to a growing importance of industry and service sectors. Light industry (in particular garments), the construction industry and tourism are among the most important economic subsectors (Hor, 2015; WTTC, 2018). Nevertheless, the agricultural sector is rather fragile (USAID, 2019) as it is highly vulnerable to climate change and natural resource degradation is exacerbating rural poverty. Compared to urban regions, the economic development of Cambodia's rural areas lags behind, which also results in significant socioeconomic disparities. The Royal Government of Cambodia (RGC) tried to tackle this issue by developing the Strategic Framework for Decentralisation and Deconcentration Reforms (RGC, 2005), which comprises a means of reducing such disparities by fostering local economic development.

Tourism is one of the most important sectors in Cambodia and is used as a tool for regional rural development (Mao, Grunfeld, DeLacy, & Chandler, 2014). Cambodia was, for example, the first country in Southeast Asia to establish a nature reserve and in 1925 the land around the temple complex of Angkor was declared a national park (archaeological/historical in nature), now a key tourist zone of the country (Sanderson & Islam, 2007; Winter, 2008). Today 43,000 km² or 25% of the country are under environmental protection (Ray & Robinson, 2008), though they remain threatened by the development of settlement areas, illegal deforestation and the demand for animal organs for traditional medicine. The above might also be the reason why the government of Cambodia has called tourism 'green gold', indicating the status which the government has assigned to tourism as a source of income generation. In fact, tourism is one of the key sectors in the government's Rectangular Strategy for Growth, Employment, Equity and Efficiency (RGC, 2004). Equally important is the sustainable management of natural resources (RGC, 2004) – both of which are addressed in Cambodia's Community-based ecotourism (CB(E)T) development plans. In addition, CB(E)T is fostered to create income opportunities in rural areas. The RGC has acknowledged though that until now CB(E)T development with respect to economic growth for rural areas lags behind (RGC, 2012).

According to the literature, economic growth in community-based tourism (CBT) can be achieved through different paths: (1) organic (spontaneous, market-led growth); (2) induced (mix of regulated and market-led growth); and (3) incremental (regulated) (Dangi & Jamal, 2016). As Cambodia is a centralised country with strong regulations, the questions addressed in the present chapter therefore are: could a stronger public involvement, particularly with financial aid, help emerging CB(E)T enterprises in Cambodia to become successful tourism entities? Or, rather, do CB(E)T's that have grown organically[2] out of tourists' demand have a better chance to be successfully sustainable? What kind of role do non-governmental organisations (NGOs) or public institutions, such as district, provincial authorities and governments play in CB(E)T development of a region?

Community-based tourism development

Regional tourism development in Asia is recognised as having great market potential for international but also intraregional travel (UNWTO, 2017). Especially in many rural communities entering the tourism sector for economic growth is seen as a pathway when other natural resource-based industries such as logging, mining, or fishing are in decline. CBT as a tourism concept has been at the forefront of the promotion of regional development, both in developed countries and in the developing world (Honey, 2008; Hummel & van der Duim, 2012; Spenceley & Meyer, 2012). CBT as a means of enhancing community development, poverty alleviation, and conservation is increasing in a variety of geographical contexts, particularly in Southeast Asia. Here, where a large proportion of the population lives in rural areas and often struggles with economic inequalities, CBT is an important way of contributing to rural development. Furthermore, CBT can be used as an alternative tourism strategy to mass tourism to empower rural communities (Dolezal, 2014). Typically, Cambodian CBT as a product consists of different aspects, including activities (ox-cart rides, fishing, weaving, rice field treks) and specialist accommodation with locals (e.g. homestays) – all depending on the geographical area. In order to distinguish CBT from other forms of tourism which have significant benefits for local communities, CBT is defined as tourism owned and/or managed by communities and intended to deliver wider community benefits and often also to conserve the environment (Dodds, Ali, & Galaski, 2018). Recognising a 'need to promote both the quality of life of people and the conservation of resources' (Scheyvens, 1999, p. 246) and to differentiate between forms of eco-tourism, the term 'community-based ecotourism' was introduced (Belsky, 1999; Fitton, 1996; Timothy & White, 1999) and has been adopted by various development agencies.

CB(E)T refers to ecotourism entities that are owned and managed by the community and implies that a community takes care of its natural resources in order to gain income through operating a tourism enterprise and using that income to better the lives of its members (Mbaiwa & Stronza, 2010; Su, Wall, & Xu, 2016). Therefore, CB(E)T involves conservation, business enterprise and community development (Mtapuri & Giampiccoli, 2019) and often faces the challenge of balancing economic development with cultural, heritage and nat-ural resource preservation. It is critical that national governments recognise this tourism potential and initiate supporting policies to ensure sustainable growth. Often, however, this CBT development emerges from the bottom-up based on locally inspired initiatives in response to a certain tourism demand. This organic growth, as opposed to growth initiated and supported by outside organisations or actors, can support learning and skill development within the community and better mitigate negative impacts while also create less dependency. Nevertheless, the majority of CB(E)T proposals rely on external technical and financial assis-tance (Scheyvens, 2002). Previous studies critically discuss the mechanisms and techniques for participation in CBT (Goodwin & Font, 2014; Mowforth, Charlton, & Munt, 2009; Okazaki, 2008). Kiss (2004) pointed out how projects that are often promoted as successful actually involve little change in e.g. existing local land and resource-use practices and rely on external funding for long peri-ods of time. Especially in rural areas where lack of skills and knowledge is widely spread, good destination governance might play a crucial role and one can argue that it might be a key success factor for CB(E)T development. The next section gives an overview of the concept of governance and its link to CB(E)T.

Governance and CBT

With increasing competition amongst established destinations, emerging desti-nations and changes in political and social structures, debates on destination governance arose, particularly in the European tourism market (d'Angella, 2010). Here, in popular 'hot spot' destinations with many inhabitants and a large number of stakeholders, the destination marketing organisation (DMO) func-tions as an institution that markets the area and supports local tourists (Beritelli, Bieger, & Laesser, 2007). Given the unstable political situation in Cambodia[3] and the lack of DMOs, the relevance of networks and the establishment of clear communication channels is essential for tourism development in rural areas. As many of the CB(E)T spots are located in remote areas, do not always have access to latest information and are not always aware of decisions made by the gov-ernment, informal networks are useful. To create better conditions for success, communities should actively form and manage governance structures and their mechanisms.

Governance concerns the many ways in which public and private actors from the state, the market and civil society govern public issues on multiple levels, autonomously or in mutual interaction (Beaumont & Dredge, 2010). It is pertinent for tourism development since it involves decision making, planning and management processes (Farmaki, 2015). The effectiveness of the organisational structures and processes as well as the available resources determine the capabilities of local tourism organisations and their effectiveness in local destination governance (Beaumont & Dredge, 2010).

Destination governance facilitates the understanding of the dynamics within a destination (Nordin & Svensson, 2007), including the interests of actors and interactions between private and public institutions (Nordin & Svensson, 2007). Further, it identifies the often-difficult power asymmetries and politics as additional elements that make governance of tourist destinations difficult. The tourism sector is fragmented which hampers the governance of destinations (Scott & Marzano, 2015) – all of which impacts on the sustainable development of a destination.

According to the OECD's Development Assistance Committee's (DAC) Principles for Evaluation of Development Assistance, maintaining consistent governance involves the participatory development of all stakeholders to encourage sustainable economic growth and promote sustainable development (OECD, 2015). Participatory development creates a favourable climate and conditions to enable good governance. In addition, the success of the different networks depends on knowledge sharing and trust amongst stakeholders, which varies according to the background of the destination, institutions and individuals involved (Beritelli et al., 2007).

Governance under CBT involves the participation of local communities in the management of tourism, ultimately seeking a power equilibrium, facilitating environmental stewardship, social justice, well-being and sustainable local livelihoods. However, CBT as a tool for development has also been critically viewed by scientists and donor organisations, especially in terms of financial viability, poor market access and poor governance (Kiss, 2004; Lucchetti & Font, 2013). As mentioned before, different governance models exist relating to how CB(E)T can be executed. In addition to government regulations, the influence of donor organisations or NGOs plays a major role regarding CBT development. The next section compares and contrasts two of these, the CBT model with strong NGO support and the one without NGO support.

CBT with strong NGO support: Strengths and weaknesses

When developing CB(E)T, it is important for communities to work in partnership with national NGOs and international organisations (Sproule, 1996), particularly for the provision of financial support. To support local communities, a variety of donors of aid exist, including multilateral (World Bank, United Nations Development Programme, Asian Development Bank, European Union) and bilateral donors (national cooperation/development aid agencies), NGOs, and foundations. Donor agencies prefer short term finance, target driven projects; however, effective aid usually requires core funding over a longer period to facilitate local empowerment (Goodwin & Font, 2014). Clear planning with objectives, goals and quality management groups can be considered pre-determinants amongst these kind of organisations (Tieng, 2016).

At the same time, the dependency on donor funding often leads to problems regarding the long-term financial sustainability of CB(E)T. To highlight some further challenges, often there is no established consensus between the organisations and the nature of interactions with local projects. Issues often arise such as partners with strong voices, partial consensus on a particular issue or flow of information. In addition, there is limited assignment of roles and responsibilities which is considered a challenge leading to power asymmetries and trust issues (Juhola & Westerhoff, 2011).

Other setbacks are linked to different levels of commitment in regard to ability and willingness to contribute finances, environmental sustainability or the availability of resources amongst parties, which makes it more difficult to collaborate in business (Vernon, Essex, Pinder & Curry, 2005). These challenges arise in encouraging CBT to successfully execute an inclusive form of governance. Whether the collaborative process improves the effectiveness to capitalise on tourism opportunities in the destination and of policy coordination is a question to be answered through empirical research (Goodwin, 1998). The present research is an attempt to shed more light on this topic.

CBT without NGO support: Strengths and weaknesses

Integration of CB(E)T principles at the local level without NGO support requires the participation of local communities and the facilitation of environmental balance while contributing to their societal well-being (Dangi & Jamal, 2016). Local participation is a key principle of CB(E)T, however when local residents are involved in decision-making it can lead to a range of challenges.

Dangi and Jamal (2016) pointed out that local control through resident-driven decision making in CB(E)T might be problematic, since locals often have limited awareness of governance issues. Further, it would be difficult to gauge the visitor's perspective due to intra-community challenges, including unbalanced power relations amongst residents, lack of encouragement from local operators to develop hospitality skills and language barriers (Beritelli, 2015). Therefore, it becomes difficult for the local community to meet tourists' demands and engage in effective management, but also to create a destination identity due to different opinions and a lack of tourism promotion skills. This needs further collaborative agreement from all the stakeholders to agree on which direction to take to develop a certain destination identity and ultimately aid the success of the CBT product (Yodsuwan, Pianluprasidh, & Butcher, 2018).

Therefore, a lack of appropriate skills among locals, such as an awareness about tourism and its employment opportunity, serves as a challenge to realise the economic development opportunities that are available through tourism. After all, the success or failure of governance depends on the network and participants in a region. The present research discusses only a particular regional context, that of Cambodia. Cambodia is a worthwhile region to discuss tourism development and governance in the context of CB(E)T, which the following sections will explain.

Case studies

The Department of Ecotourism within the Ministry of Environment (MoE) in Cambodia strives to develop and promote sustainable and inclusive ecotourism development, multi-stakeholder collaboration mechanisms, ecotourism linkages, connectivity and knowledge systems between the 49 protected areas (PAs). The overall aim is to enhance environmental sustainability and community welfare in PA ecotourism destinations (RGC, 2012). This means that any ecotourism development, including all CB(E)T projects being developed within the PAs falls under the administration of the MoE. On the other hand, the Ministry of Tourism (MoT) oversees the tourism development across the country and is the key ambassador for the tourism industry. Therefore, any CBT projects that are being set up and developed outside of the PA, which are managed by the MoE, fall under the responsibility of the MoT.

However, in practice, on the local or provincial level, the Provincial Departments of Environment have limited tourism knowledge, as their main mandate is protection and management of natural resources and the environment. This lack of capacity often results in a vacuum of support for CB(E)T projects, where in some provinces the Provincial Departments of Tourism step in to provide tourism expertise and support to projects not under their direct administration. This sometimes leads to misunderstanding, insecurities and also financial discussion, which hinders positive development in the regions. The RGC has chosen four areas for the development of ecotourism in Cambodia – two of which form part of the present analysis as explained in the following sections.

Reaksmey Phoum Pir Kiri Boeng Kranhak Ecotourism Site, Kampong Thom Province

The Reaksmey Phoum Pir Kiri Boeng Kranhak CB(E)T project was set up as a part of a USAID funded project (2014–2017) – the Cambodia Supporting Forests and Biodiversity (SFB) Project implemented by Winrock International. The project aimed to empower forest communities, government officials at all levels, NGOs, businesses and communities to become champions for sustainable forest management practices. The project conducted extensive assessments to support wildlife and biodiversity within the dedicated project area, and improved planning and management of 900,000 hectares. One of the key objectives of the project was to provide forest communities with alternative livelihoods, and shift communities from illegal forest logging and animal poaching. The potential for ecotourism was identified within the Sandam district, which led to the use of CB(E)T as a development tool to bridge the gap between community needs, wildlife protection and biodiversity requirements for sustainable resource management. The initial work with local communities started in 2014, with the later establishment of the Reaksmey Phoum Pir Kiri Boeng Kranhak CB(E)T in 2015.

Product

This ecotourism site has a varied landscape (lake, forest and rice fields with water buffalos), which provides opportunities for bird watching, nature walking, cycling and possibilities to learn about local farming. The local landscape is well-preserved and unspoiled by mass tourism, however there are visible signs of deforestation outside of the immediate lake area. At the same time, the site is not home to animals such as elephants, gibbons or river dolphins or spectacular landscape such as the Cardamom Mountains in comparison with other CB(E)T sites in Cambodia. Therefore, the site's main potential is experiencing the local environment through physical activities and engaging tourists to get involved in nature.

During the USAID funded Cambodia SFB Project, Winrock International mainly focused on two main areas of the development of the CB(E)T site: capacity building of the local community (local governance of the site); and product development (developing high-end birding experiences and homestay options with the hope that the site could be included in the Sam Veasna specialist birding experiences). A local CB(E)T committee was established to oversee the development of the CB(E)T site, with representatives from the local community and the village committee (part of the Commune structure in Cambodia, non-related to CB(E)T). Due to the large financial investment by the donor in the PA and based on the current socioeconomic and political societal structures, it is likely that the selection of the committee was difficult. The traditional hierarchical social structures and a patriarchal political culture create an environment that impedes women's and young people's ability to be equal partners in public decision-making. Cultural stereotypes mean women and young people continue to be considered as subordinates who cannot participate in politics and hold senior decision-making positions. Therefore, most of the CB(E)T committee members were political appointees and those who already have a strong influence within the existing structures of the village, rather than those within the community interested in environmental or ecotourism issues. In addition, most of the members saw their primary role as an oversight of funding distributed by the international NGO, and not necessarily in delivering tourism services to visitors. In some situations, this means that once funding is finished, the CB(E)T committee lacks the motivation to continue the project.

Large investments were made to train the local community and build capacity for CB(E)T, through management skills training and homestay owners training (cooking, health and hygiene, housekeeping), however this was done with limited understanding of who the target audience was, the level of desirability of the proposed tourism products and the current level of demand.

Role of the government and international agencies

The site was developed in close collaboration with the MoE in Cambodia and provincial authorities. The SFB project provided extended technical support and training to the provincial department of environment and the district level officials. However, with very limited funding from the central government, and no money being raised through the ecotourism initiatives there is a limited possibility to continue capacity building beyond the life of the project. It is also important to note that due to the main focus of this project being environmental protection, most of the provincial and national level involvement by relevant ministries has been through the MoE and not the MoT.

Success factors and challenges

Winrock International invested heavily in supporting the development of tourism promotional material and guidebooks that could be used to showcase the fauna and flora in the PA. One of the key challenges of the project identified in the feasibility study in 2017 was the lack of connections to the tourism market: the site development focused heavily on biodiversity protection, and as a result lacked tourism focus both in terms of product design and links to the market. This disconnect from the tourism market is particularly noticeable in terms of the tourism product offer, which did not take into account other similar tourism products available locally, therefore setting up an almost identical product in an area where there are more superior and well-established tourism products available. The training of the local community also did not take into account the planned tourism segment – international tourists – as no English language classes were ever provided for the homestay families and tour guides. Even though significant financial and human resource investment has been provided to Reaksmey Phoum Pir Kiri Boeng Kranhak Ecotourism project, the site is not financially viable at the end of the funded project, and therefore was not able to create a new livelihood for locals.

Kompong Loung Floating Village, Tonle Sap lake, Pursat Province

The Kompong Luong Floating Village is the product of one man's vision and the collective endeavour of the entire community. Situated south of Tonle Sap lake in Pursat Province, this is one of the most intriguing destinations for tourists in Cambodia, as the community of Kompong Loung offers visitors the chance to experience life on the water. Houses, schools, karaoke bars, shops and even the church are all kept afloat by empty oil drums and bamboo. During the wet season, when the area floods, downstream alluvial canals enrich the area with large fish. In the dry season the village moves north to deeper waters. The people living in Kompong Loung Floating Village rely heavily on the Tonle Sap lake for their livelihoods, through fishing and aquaculture.

Tourism activities started in the local areas in the past five to seven years given growing tourism demand. The project is locally run and was established together with the commune chief, with some support of the local government, as a way to increase opportunities for locals. The site is not registered as an official CBT site with the traditional structure of a management committee and CBT members and a central management system. Instead, the model resembles a loose colla-boration between small-scale local micro-businesses who work together to offer tourism experiences to international tourists. The project is largely self-organised by local residents, without external support form NGOs or local government.

The site is situated on one of the main tourist routes from Phnom Penh to Battambang/Bangkok, which makes it popular with international tourists. The local community consists of two main villages, one Vietnamese village and a Khmer village that are working together to promote tourism.

Product

The main tourism attraction is an Asian floating village, where visitors can experience how the community adapts to their environment as well as a Vietnamese and a Khmer village. One of the most interesting collaborations between the two villages is a boat tour that visits both Khmer and Vietnamese villages and showcases similarities and differences in each culture, creating a sense of joint history for the visitors. This stands in direct contrast to the often negative stories about the historic conflict between Cambodia and Vietnam, especially the Vietnamese role in occupation of Cambodia after the end of the Khmer Rouge period.

Currently there are three floating homestays, where visitors can experience life on water. Visitors can also explore the village by boat, immerse them-selves in Khmer culture and taste locally prepared meals. The site has been popular with international tourists seeking an 'authentic' experience in a floating village, compared to the over-developed and over-priced floating vil-lages in Siem Reap. Without any strategic plan or clear tourism development strategy, the site development has been solely driven by market demand.

Role of government and international agencies

The site has been developed without external support by local or interna-tional NGOs. Some small NGOs work in the area on a short-term basis, focusing mainly on improvement in water and sanitation and improving livelihoods through fisheries. The provincial Department of Tourism provides technical assistance, however, as in many parts of Cambodia there are limited resources to offer practical or infrastructure support to local communities. In practice, this means that most of the time local communities seek approval for their actions, rather than the government taking a proactive role in developing the site.

Success factors and challenges

Without any extensive support or financial investment, this initiative has been able to financially support over 30 families. Besides community involvement, the fact that the tourism site is accessible by public transport (bus and tuktuk) contributes to the success of CB(E)T. With no marketing, no promotional material or even online presence, the site has been able to attract approximately 10 overnight visits per month for the three homestays, and an even larger number of day visitors.

The site and service growth has been organic, without any strategic planning. This has been one of the main successes of the project, but the lack of a strategic plan is also one of the major threats to the site as unmanaged tourism can impact natural resources and create conflict between those community members benefiting from tourism and those not. For example, the quality of water suffers from extensive pollution from an uncontrolled number of motorboats taking visitors to see the Tonle Sap lake, and pollution from grey wastewater from homestays impacts families dependent on fishing.

The second issue the site faces are environmental challenges, such as waste management and climate change that have a significant impact on the floating villages. With an increased river and lake pollution in Cambodia, large parts of the Tonle Sap lake have turned into a garbage dump. These issues are much bigger than the Kompong Luong Floating Village, they impact the whole of Tonle Sap lake and local communities. With little control of these issues, the local villages are in danger of losing a tourism project they have worked hard to build.

Summary and discussion

Comparing the two cases the main success factors are strong links to the tourism sector and the ability of the project to design desirable tourism products. The key to this is the CB(E)T site governance structure and level of local ownership that enables a site to develop based on tourism market needs. With respect to governance, administrative transparency, efficiency, participation, accountability, market economy, the rule of law, and equity have to be taken into consideration.

The first case presented here had a pre-agreed project plan and official CB(E)T committee responsible for the development of the site. However, those plans were developed between government officials and the donor organisation and had only limited input from community members during the design and implementation period. Consequently, local ownership was poor and financial sustainability was not achieved during and after the project delivery period, leading to almost zero progress when the donor funding stopped.

In terms of participation, the second case was more successful, as relevant stakeholders worked together through collaborative partnerships rather than

Table 12.1 Comparison of CB(E)T dimensions (Source: own research)

	Reaksmey Phoum Pir Kiri Boeng Kranhak Ecotourism Site	*Kompong Loung Floating Village, Tonle Sap lake*
Community participation	Local committee based on hierarchical and social structures	Self-organised site with small-scale micro businesses who collaborate
Benefit sharing	No information available	Financial support to 30 families
Tourism resource conservation	Focus on environment and wildlife during the project phase	Environmental challenges include waste management, and lack of water is a threat to the tourism product
Partnership and support within the community and from outside	USAID funding (2014–2017) implemented by Winrock International Limited funding from central government	Supported by local government but only to a minimal extent No external support from NGOs or other donor organisations
Local ownership	CBET committee was heavily linked to financial support of the donor.	The site is locally owned
Management and leadership	Pre-agreed project plan	No strategic planning and foresight
Communication and interaction	Lack of connection to the market	Collaborative network of business owners Communication with village chief in place as well as exchange with local government
Quality of life	No improvement or creation of new livelihoods for local people	Families benefit from tourism, but are also threatened by the increased pollution of the Tonle Sap lake
Tourist satisfaction	No data on the official website of Kampong Thom No reviews on TripAdvisor	International visitors 45 reviews on TripAdvisor, out of which 40% rate the experience excellent and 50% very good

Source: own research

rigid committees, which resulted in a more efficient and flexible set-up to respond more easily to market needs. Administrative transparency, rule of law and accountability are determined by national structure and function as a baseline for all CB(E)T sites in Cambodia. Nevertheless, the two studies clearly show that any governance structures used for management and administration of CB(E)T sites need to be flexible to respond to the market and enable tourism services to be in line with the tourism market demand. Overly administrative and rigid governance leads to the CB(E)T projects being disconnected from the market forces and demand needs. Therefore, reviewing the success of the CB(E)T sites shows that linkages to the market have to be established, confirming the existing literature on the topic.

Conclusions

This chapter discussed CB(E)T as an alternative form of sustainable tourism development – a model which enables local communities to generate income and protect the environment. It has first introduced Cambodia and the current situation regarding CB(E)T development. CBT as a tool for development has been discussed as well as the relevance of governance for CBT development. Given the lack of empirical evidence in Cambodia, two case studies have been introduced to discuss successes and failures of CB(E)T sites. Expanding community benefits from tourism in Cambodia will depend on many factors, including governance, network creation, financial sustainability, access to markets and entrepreneurial thinking. Major changes in regard to proper site development, support of communities and capacity building could be created once the different ministries responsible for CB(E)T in Cambodia establish better communication channels and a joint strategy for tourism development.

The comparison of the two cases has shown that entrepreneurial thinking, even in small businesses, can be a better driver for sustainable success compared with financing CB(E)T sites through donor aid. It can only be assumed that the development of CB(E)T sites in Cambodia would be even more successful, if both factors matched. With respect to the first case it will be a challenge for the CB(E)T project to find a mechanism for legitimate and sustainable relationships between the NGO/international agencies and the community. NGOs and donor organisations could most likely create more impact on CB(E)T development when paying attention to local conditions, needs and potential for tourism rather than choosing sites based on their target areas or other factors. The second case shows that at a certain point in the development of the CB(E)T project, strategic planning is required. Without any organisational structure and tourism destination management, the site could easily be spoiled by ill-managed development or unregulated tourism, which could result in the destruction of biodiversity and traditional way of life, both of which are main tourism selling points. In either case, as the case studies have shown, local communities have to be supported with training and skill development to enter the tourism sector effectively.

Both case studies strongly showed that two of the key factors in the success of CBT, be it with or without NGO support, are community and local participation. Only through the active participation of both residents and the communal authority can CB(E)T successfully be established and the livelihood of the community improved. Based on the findings presented here, culturally appropriate mechanisms for resident involvement in tourism development, planning and decision-making are needed to enable local control and good governance, ensuring justice, equity and fairness in the use and distribution of tourism benefits.

In summary, this chapter supports the view generated by the literature. To begin with informal collaborative networks driven by local businesses seems to be more effective than CB(E)Ts driven by government and donor organisations with rigid administrative and hierarchical structures. However, it also became evident that market-driven CB(E)Ts need to follow a more strategic approach in terms of product development, marketing and site management. It remains to be seen in the future what the opportunities for sustainable development for tourism are, particularly considering the current administrative setup in Cambodia.

Notes

1 See http://hdr.undp.org/en/composite/HDI.
2 Spontaneous, market-led growth.
3 The civil and political rights environment in Cambodia were markedly restrained in 2017 as the government arrested the leader of Cambodia's political opposition on charges of treason; this was followed by the dissolution of the main opposition party and the banishment of over 100 members from political activity by the Supreme Court.

References

Armstrong, R. (2012). An analysis of the conditions for success of community-based tourism enterprises. ICRT Occasional Paper (No. OP21), 1–52.

Beaumont, N., & Dredge, D. (2010). Local tourism governance: A comparison of three network approaches. *Journal of Sustainable Tourism* 18(1), 7–28.

Belsky, J.M. (1999). Misrepresenting communities: The politics of community-based rural ecotourism in Gales Point Manatee, Belize. *Rural Sociology* 64(4), 641–666.

Beritelli, P. (2015). *The St. Gallen model for destination management.* (1st ed.). St. Gallen: Institute for Systemic Management and Public Governance (IMP-HSG).

Beritelli, P., Bieger, T., & Laesser, C. (2007). Destination governance: Using corporate governance theories as a foundation for effective destination management. *Journal of Travel Research* 46(1), 96–107.

d'Angella, F. (2010). Archetypes of destination governance: A comparison of international destinations. *Tourism Review* 65(4), 61–73.

Dangi, T.B., & Jamal, T. (2016). An integrated approach to "sustainable community-based tourism". *Sustainability* 8(5), 475.

Dodds, R., Ali, A., & Galaski, K. (2018). Mobilizing knowledge: Determining key elements for success and pitfalls in developing community-based tourism. *Current Issues in Tourism* 21(13), 1547–1568.

Dolezal, C. (2014). Understanding the meaning and possibilities of empowerment in community-based tourism in Bali. Paper presented at ISCONTOUR 2014 – Tourism research perspectives: Proceedings of the international student conference in tourism research.

Farmaki, A. (2015). Regional network governance and sustainable tourism. *Tourism Geographies* 17(3), 385–407.

Fitton, M. (1996). Does our community want tourism? Examples from South Wales. In M.F. Price (Ed.), *People and tourism in fragile environments* (pp. 159–174). Chichester: John Wiley & Sons.

Goodwin, H., & Font, X. (Eds.). (2014). *Progress in responsible tourism* (3rd ed.). Oxford: Goodfellow Publishers Ltd.

Goodwin, M. (1998). The governance of rural areas: Some emerging research issues and agendas. *Journal of Rural Studies* 14(1), 5–12.

Honey, M. (2008). *Ecotourism and sustainable development: Who owns paradise?* Washington, DC: Island Press.

Hor, C. (2015). Modeling international tourism demand in Cambodia: ARDL model. *Review of Integrative Business Economics Research* 4(4), 106–120.

Hummel, J., & van der Duim, R. (2012). Tourism and development at work: 15 years of tourism and poverty reduction within the SNV Netherlands Development Organisation. *Journal of Sustainable Tourism* 20(3), 319–338.

Juhola, S., & Westerhoff, L. (2011). Challenges of adaptation to climate change across multiple scales: A case study of network governance in two European countries. *Environmental Science & Policy* 14(3), 239–247.

Kiss, A. (2004). Is community-based ecotourism a good use of biodiversity conservation funds? *Trends in Ecology & Evolution* 19(5), 232–237.

Klimek, K. (2013). Destination management organisations and their shift to sustainable tourism development. *European Journal of Tourism, Hospitality and Recreation* 4(2), 27–47.

Lucchetti, V.G., & Font, X. (2013). Community-based tourism: Critical success factors. Paper presented at the The International Centre for Responsible Tourism 27, Hyderabad, India.

Mao, N., Grunfeld, H., DeLacy, T., & Chandler, D. (2014). Agriculture and tourism linkage constraints in the Siem Reap-Angkor region of Cambodia. *Tourism Geographies* 16(4), 669–686.

Mbaiwa, J.E., & Stronza, A.L. (2010). The effects of tourism development on rural livelihoods in the Okavango Delta, Botswana. *Journal of Sustainable Tourism* 18(5), 635–656.

Mowforth, M., Charlton, C., & Munt, I. (2009). *Tourism and Responsibility: Perspectives from Latin America and the Caribbean.* Abingdon: Routledge.

Mtapuri, O., & Giampiccoli, A. (2019). Tourism, community-based tourism and ecotourism: A definitional problematic. *South African Geographical Journal* 101(1), 22–35.

Nordin, S., & Svensson, B. (2007). Innovative destination governance. *The International Journal of Entrepreneurship and Innovation* 8(1), 53–66.

Nunkoo, R., & Ramkissoon, H. (2011). Developing a community support model for tourism. *Annals of Tourism Research* 38(3), 964–988.

OECD (2015). DAC Criteria for Evaluating Development Assistance. Retrieved from: oecd.org/dac/evaluation/daccriteriaforevaluatingdevelopmentassistance.htm.

Okazaki, E. (2008). A Community-based tourism model: Its conception and use. *Journal of Sustainable Tourism* 16(5), 511–529.

Ray, N., & Robinson, D. (2008). *Lonely Planet Cambodia.* Singapore: Lonely Planet.

RGC (2004). *The rectangular strategy for growth, employment, equity and efficiency in Cambodia.* Phnom Penh: Royal Government of Cambodia.

RGC (2005). *Strategic framework for decentralisation and deconcentration reforms.* Phnom Penh: Royal Government of Cambodia.

RGC (2012). *Tourism development strategic plan 2012–2020. Unofficial Translation, Phnom Phen, Cambodia.* Phnom Penh: Royal Government of Cambodia.

Sanderson, J., & Islam, S.M.N. (2007). *Climate change and economic development – SEA Regional Modelling and Analysis.* New York: Palgrave Macmillan.

Scheyvens, R. (1999). Ecotourism and the empowerment of local communities. *Tourism Management* 20(2), 245–249.

Scheyvens, R. (2002). *Tourism for development: Empowering communities.* Harlow: Prentice Hall.

Scott, N., & Marzano, G. (2015). Governance of tourism in OECD countries. *Tourism Recreation Research* 40(2), 181–193.

Sothan, S. (2018). Foreign aid and economic growth: Evidence from Cambodia. *The Journal of International Trade & Economic Development* 27(2), 168–183.

Spenceley, A., & Meyer, D. (2012). Tourism and poverty reduction: Theory and practice in less economically developed countries. *Journal of Sustainable Tourism* 20(3), 297–317.

Sproule, K.W. (1996). Community-based ecotourism development: Identifying partners in the process. *The ecotourism equation: Measuring the impacts* 99, 233–250.

Su, M.M., Wall, G., & Xu, K. (2016). Heritage tourism and livelihood sustainability of a resettled rural community: Mount Sanqingshan World Heritage Site, China. *Journal of Sustainable Tourism* 24(5), 735–757.

Tieng, S. (2016). *Chi Phat: An exemplar of a successful community-based tourism destination in Cambodia.* Master's thesis, Victoria University, Wellington,

Timothy, D.J., & White, K. (1999). Community-based ecotourism development on the periphery of Belize. *Current Issues in Tourism* 2(2–3), 226–242.

UNCTAD (2018). *Division on Investment and Enterprise.* Retrieved from: https://uncta d.org/en/PublicationsLibrary/diae2018d1_en.pdf.

UNWTO (2017). *Asia Tourism Trends.* Retrieved from: https://www.unwto.org/archi ve/asia/publication/unwtogterc-annual-report-asia-tourism-trends-2017-edition.

USAID (2019). *Agriculture and food security.* Retrieved from: https://www.usaid.gov/ cambodia/agriculture-and-food-security.

Vernon, J., Essex, S., Pinder, D., & Curry, K. (2005). Collaborative policymaking: Local sustainable projects. *Annals of Tourism Research* 32(2), 325–345.

Winter, T. (2008). Post-conflict heritage and tourism in Cambodia: The burden of Angkor. *International Journal of Heritage Studies* 14(6), 524–539.

WTTC (2018). *World Travel and Tourism Council Q1/2018, European Tourism in 2018–Trends and Prospects.* Retrieved from: https://etc-corporate.org/uploads/rep orts/ETC-Quarterly-Report-Q1-2018_Public.pdf.

Yodsuwan, C., Pianluprasidh, P., & Butcher, K. (2018). Against the flow: Challenges in tourism development for a small-border town in Thailand. In Y. Wang, A. Shakeela, A. Kwek, & C. Khoo-Lattimore (Eds.), *Managing Asian Destinations* (pp. 107–123): Singapore: Springer.

13 Creative agritourism for development

Putting the 'culture' into agriculture in Thailand

Tracy Berno, Jutamas (Jan) Wisansing and Glenn Dentice

Introduction

Food, cuisine, and food traditions all have their roots in local agriculture and are among the most fundamental elements of culture. Cuisine can be used to reinforce cultural identity and economic self-sufficiency, as well as to contribute to national health and well-being. Local cuisine as a cultural tourism product and as a part of the agritourism experience can be an integral tool for sustainable tourism development. Enhancing linkages between agriculture and tourism along the value chain presents genuine opportunities: for stimulating local agriculture, artisanal food production and local artists; retaining tourism earnings; and improving the distribution of economic benefits within the local community. Additionally, as destinations increasingly seek to differentiate themselves in the market, linking distinctive local cuisines to the landscapes from which they came can be used as a tool for destination promotion. The effects of these demands can result in a variety of positive outcomes, including the enrichment of localities and economic links; more attractive, vital and viable rural areas; a more vibrant and locally distinctive tourism; and greater economic and social well-being for the host community.

This chapter considers the potential for agritourism as a tool for sustainable community development in Thailand within the context of the nation's current economic development policy, Thailand 4.0. Particular emphasis will be placed on a new way of conceptualising agritourism for development through the relationship between agriculture, cuisine, local arts, and tourism, and how these can be harnessed collectively as 'creative agritourism'. Consideration will be given to how creative agritourism can contribute to community development through promoting and using local products and knowledge, while at the same time meeting travellers' needs for an authentic, quality experience. Examples of this new way of conceptualising agritourism are also presented.

From tourism to agritourism

Thailand's popularity as a tourism destination cannot be disputed. Inbound tourist numbers have grown from just over 80,000 tourists in 1960 (Van Beek,

2017) to over 38 million in 2018 (Muqbil, 2019). Thailand is now in the top 10 destinations (ranked 10th) for international visitor arrivals (UNWTO, 2018). Tourism has become one of the fastest growing and most important sectors of the Thai economy (World Travel and Tourism Council, 2017).

Despite the unquestionable success of tourism for Thailand's economy, successive governments have continued to be concerned about rural development as it is in the rural regions that the majority of the country's poor reside (Srisomyong, 2010). Although industrial-scale agriculture has expanded in Thailand over the years, the sector continues to be dominated by small-scale producers, who represent approximately 25 percent of the population earning their livelihood in the sector (Choenkwan & Fisher, 2018). Over the years, the Thai agricultural sector has faced ongoing challenges of price fluctuations, increasing roles (and costs) of middlemen, pressures to adopt modern agricultural technologies, the rising cost of machinery, fuel and chemicals, and climate change. As a result, the country has experienced a decline in agriculturalists and those remaining in the sector have looked for means to diversify their activities and revenue streams from formerly dominant production systems toward a more variable mix of production and consumption (Songkhla & Somboonsuke, 2013; Srisomyong & Meyer, 2015). One of the diversification options available to rural communities is agritourism. Indeed, successive Thai governments have encouraged tourism growth in rural areas to stimulate rural development. Since the 1990s, this has been reflected in both the National Economic and Social Development Plans and the Tourism Authority of Thailand's tourism masterplans, which have identified a need for the development of tourism attractions in rural areas. Similarly, the Department of Agricultural Extension also developed its own strategic plans promoting tourism as a means for farmers to generate additional revenue and to stimulate stronger rural economies (Srisomyong, 2010). As a result, agritourism is increasingly recognised as a new form of agriculture in Thailand (Choenkwan & Fisher, 2018), one that provides rural people with opportunities for a second occupation in addition to their main occupation, and self-employment that requires minimal new investment (Srisomyong, 2010). Agritourism also presents the opportunity to attract new customers (i.e., tourists) for the sale of agricultural and value-added products. These direct sales also benefit farmers by eliminating the need for and cost of brokers and middlemen (Choenkwan & Fisher, 2018).

Although tourism to rural regions in Thailand existed long before 'agritourism' was identified as a specific sector, it was the Thai Rak Thai (TRT)-led government that was responsible for launching agritourism in 1999 through encouraging farmers to diversify their agricultural holdings to other businesses, such as handicraft production, food processing, and agritourism (Srisomyong, 2010; Srisomyong & Meyer, 2015). The objectives of the TRT government in promoting agritourism were to encourage farmers to generate additional income, strengthen local communities, and promote tourism in rural areas. In support of this, in 2003 the Agritourism

Development and Promotion Group (ADPG) – within the Bureau of Farming Development in the Department of Agricultural Extension – was established by the government with the aim of encouraging and supporting farmers in diversifying their farm holdings into tourism. While the ADPG focuses on planning and supporting agritourism communities and enterprises, it is the Tourism Authority of Thailand (TAT) that markets agritourism products (Srisomyong, 2010).

In 2015, the Ministry of Tourism and Sport and the Ministry of Agriculture and Cooperatives joined forces to launch the 2015–2017 agritourism masterplan (TAT, 2015a), which aimed to 'promote and develop agro-tourism destinations with an objective of boosting the economy, enhancing the quality of new tourism products, and spreading income to agriculturists and community-based tourism destinations' (para. 2). The project started with the identification of four pilot projects, with another nine projects planned for roll-out in 2016. Further, the Ministry of Sports and Tourism's *Second National Tourism Development Plan (2017–2021)* also identified agritourism as a key activity, particularly as it related to community-based tourism (CBT) development and gastronomy tourism (The Ministry of Tourism and Sports, 2017). One of the conduits for this was the articulation of the 'One Tambon ("sub-district"); One Product' (OTOP) policy with agritourism. The Thai government introduced its OTOP scheme in 2001 as a means of stimulating the rural economy (Natsuda, Igusa, Wiboonpongse, & Thoburn, 2012). OTOP aims to encourage rural development through community-based activities that employ local resources and knowledge. These aims are reflected in the policy's five objectives:

1) to create jobs and income for communities;
2) to strengthen communities to become self-sufficient;
3) to promote Thai wisdom;
4) to promote human resource development; and
5) to promote communities' creativity in developing products in harmony with the local culture and way of life (Su-Indramedhi, 2017).

Indeed, a unique OTOP offering was identified as one of six key components destinations needed for inclusion in the 2015 pilot agritourism development, discussed above (TAT, 2015a).

But just what is 'agritourism' in the Thai context? Thai agritourism has its foundations in the Thai Sufficiency Economy philosophy (SEP). Following the economic crisis in 1997, H.M. King Bhumibol Adulyadej's 'sufficiency economy' model for sustainable development came to prominence. Rooted in Buddhist economics (Prayukvong, Huttasin, & Foster, 2015), the SEP consists of a set of principles (moderation, reasonableness, and self-immunity), requiring two essential underlying conditions: knowledge and integrity (Khaokhrueamuang, 2014). One of the concepts based on the SEP is 'The New Theory of Agriculture', a form of sustainable, integrated agriculture. As part of this approach, numerous Royal Projects were established in rural areas

(Mongsawad, 2012). These later gave rise to early opportunities for agritourism (Muqbil, 2011; TAT, 2017, n.d.). The Royal Projects continue to feature as agritourism attractions in initiatives such as the publication *Agro-tourism: Green Travel in Thailand* (TAT, n.d.).

Definitions of agritourism in Thailand tend to adopt that of the Bureau of Farmers Development (2005), which defined agritourism as broadly comprising short-term tourist activities that typically involve visiting a farm, participating in farm-related activities (fruit picking for example), and staying overnight in a local village to observe and learn about traditional and contemporary rural lifestyles (Seisawatwanit, 2013; Songkhla & Somboonsuke, 2013). On the farmers' side, agritourism is primarily understood as being business-led, providing the opportunity to bring the market to their site of production, thus shifting farmers' focus from solely production to combining production with leisure and recreation (Srisomyong & Meyer, 2015). In this way, agritourism redefines rural areas as not just sites of production, but as spaces of consumption and of multi-purpose activities for visitors to the area, giving new value, notably as tourism products, to the resources in rural areas (Srisomyong & Meyer, 2015). This has contributed to transforming the overall restructuring of a subsistence-oriented rural economy to one that is more market-oriented (Choenkwan & Fisher, 2018). Over time, the understanding of agritourism has expanded to include aspects of conservation and sustainability (Peamnivesana, 2001, as cited in Seisawatwanit, 2013); the role of farmers in sharing Thai local wisdom (Thongkaew, 2005, as cited in Seisawatwanit, 2013); and, more recently, elements of creative tourism (Richards, 2015) and, by extension, community-based tourism (Richards, 2016). We argue, however, that the element missing from all these conceptualisations is the very thing that sits at the heart of agriculture – food and its various expressions through the culinary arts.

From watching to doing: Agritourism and cuisine as part of the Thai creative economy

It was the launch of the TAT's 7 Greens Concept in 2008 that marked a shift in how agritourism was being conceptualised and promoted in Thailand. A joint initiative between the TAT and the Thai tourism industry, the 7 Greens Concept took a holistic approach to environmental management with the aim of protecting and preserving the environment to help restore environmental quality. The programme was designed to provide a conceptual framework and establish practical guidelines to balance tourism with a healthy and sustainable environment through a multi-stakeholder approach (Muangasame & McKercher, 2014; TAT, 2009). As part of the 7 Greens Concept's promotion of sustainable tourism, the TAT identified agritourism and eco-tourism, along with local food supply chains and Thai cuisine, as important elements of community-based tourism (TAT, n.d.). In support of this approach, the TAT released a publication, *Agro-tourism: Green Travel in Thailand* (TAT, n.d.), in which they:

... carefully [chose] a number of exemplary destinations in the 5 regions of the country to present an expedient and diverse selection of agro-tourism experiences. 'Agro-tourism: Green Travel in Thailand' provides useful information that allows readers to plan trips to learn about local wisdom and participate in traditional Thai agricultural activities (p. 3).

Following the implementation of the 7 Greens campaign, and in line with the Thai Sufficiency Economy philosophy, the *10th National Economic and Social Development Plan (2007–2011)* emphasised a 'Creative Economy System' for Thailand. As some of its constituent components, the creative economy included both cultural tourism and traditional Thai food. Similarly, the *National Tourism Development Plan (2012–2016)* identified five strategies, one of which was tourism's contribution to the development of the creative economy (Wattanacharoensila & Schuckert, 2016). In line with this, in 2012 the TAT launched a 'Creative Tourism' campaign, which was promoted to implement the policy objective of developing a creative economy (Watta-nacharoensila & Schuckert, 2016). Subsequent to this, in 2015 Thailand launched 'Thailand 4.0' as a national economic development policy. Thailand 4.0 aims to move the country's economy from that of middle-income to high-income, promoting a new, value-based economy (Anuroj, n.d.). A key com-ponent of this development policy is to drive creativity and innovation through high-value services and experiences, including creative tourism (Suf-ficiency Economy Philosophy, n.d.).

Creative tourism is a form of host-guest (producer-consumer) experience that embraces local wisdom, through which it finds ways to express local identities. These can be used as an innovative tool to develop intergenerational exchanges of arts, history and stories of places. The concept of creative tourism was first formulated by Richards and Raymond (2000, p. 19), who defined it as 'tourism which offers visitors the opportunity to develop their creative potential through active participation in learning experiences which are characteristic of the holiday destination where they are undertaken'. Key attributes that differentiate creative tourism from other forms of tourism include active engagement; acquisition of skills and tacit knowledge; and embedding in the destination. Creative tourism, compared with traditional tourism, offers a more active and engaged role for both tourists and hosts, with both groups being involved in the transfer and development of creative knowledge and skills. Creative tourism emphasises relationships rather than economic transactions and producing (i.e., making and doing) rather than just consuming. It differs from cultural tourism in that 'cultural tourism tends to be based on exploiting the past as a resource' (Richards, 2015, p. 4). Creative tourism, on the other hand, emphasises the contemporary use of cultural knowledge and skills to develop future creative potential (Richards, 2015).

As part of its ongoing tourism campaigns, in 2015 Thailand launched 'Amazing Thailand', which identified 'Thainess' (*kwam pehn thai*) as a key fea-ture of the country's unique context. In essence, Thainess is a well-constructed collective Thai identity shaped by the need to be loyal to the Thai language, religion, and monarchy (Laungaramsri, 2003). This is underpinned by 12 socio-cultural values that are inculcated broadly across Thai society (Farrelly, 2016). In launching 'Amazing Thailand' in 2015, the prime minster referenced the centrality of Thainess to the campaign when he stated:

> The Thai government appreciates TAT, the Ministry of Tourism and Sports and all stakeholders for helping to promote the country's unique cultural treasures and the Thai way of happiness to be passed onto international visitors. At the same time, this campaign will help strengthen the pride of the Thai people, and encourage stronger participation in the preservation of our heritage and culture for the coming generations (TAT, 2015b, para. 4).

In considering the TAT's use of Thainess as part of this campaign, Farrelly (2016, p. 331) suggested that 'This foreigner focused marketing initiative matches an internal drive that encourages the Thai people to defend their heritage. These are both politically charged efforts'. Consistent with the ethos of creative tourism, this was part of the government's strategy to promote the distinctive character of the Thai people and their unique culture as a tourism attribute (Muangasame & Park, 2019). This, Muangasame and Park (2019) suggest, was the beginning of CBT in conjunction with creative tourism development that targeted second-tier (or smaller) tourist destinations in Thailand. Within this new approach, the Thai government placed more emphasis on developing new agritourism products, (authentic) local cuisine, and food supply and related activities (Muangasame & Park, 2019). The seeds for creative agritourism had been sown.

Creative tourism: Putting the culture into agriculture

Thailand's Creative Tourism campaign provided a means to link the various components of Thainess by grounding Thai creativity in the geography of 'place' (Berno, Dentice, & Wisansing, 2019). In this sense, through creative tourism, rural landscapes become more than a visual backdrop to be photographed, but a space in which landscape, culture, and creativity are linked; in essence, it becomes a foodscape where culture and creativity are grounded in the place and landscape in which the agricultural roots of the food products are found.

A foodscape centres around a food environment comprising the institutional arrangements, cultural spaces, and discourses that mediate our relationship with our food (MacKendrick, 2014). At its most fundamental definition, foodscapes are 'cultural, economic, historical, personal, political, or social landscapes that, in one way or another, are about food' (Adema, 2007, p. 3). Broadly conceived, foodscapes represent the relationship between food and landscape, but more specifically, they refer to the foods that are particular to the locality and/or people that live there. However, foodscape refers to much more than just the physical manifestation of food; it also references the intangible association between a particular place and its food.

Foodscapes play an important part in forming a place-based identity. Food is also a key component of sense of place, and one of the ways in which this is manifested is through terroir. Typically associated with wine-growing regions in France, the term 'terroir' is now commonly used to describe a range of food and wine products internationally. The notion of terroir is complex and incorporates not just environmental aspects such as climate, water and soil, but also integrates the agronomic, social and cultural dimensions of the location, with each of the individual components of terroir interacting dynamically. Taken as such, terroir is more than the place itself, it is also the relationship that exists between the land and the people that work it. In essence, land becomes terroir through the valorisation of agricultural production (Deloire, Prévost, & Kelly, 2008; Fusté-Forné & Berno, 2016). The UNWTO (2012, p. 11) has recognised this relationship between land, agriculture, food and culture suggesting that terroir is the foundation of all gastronomic offerings. When a product with terroir association is consumed, both the physical product as well the psychological representation of the terroir are also consumed. In essence, it is both the tangible and intangible aspects of a place that are consumed through terroir (Deloire, Prévost, & Kelly, 2008).

Agritourism, as an expression of creative tourism, provides a platform through which a visitor can be engaged more deeply with a destination through its food. Understanding the systems within which agricultural practices engage in the shaping of a local culture and cuisine, and how both culture and environment interact within a defined social and geographical space, provides opportunities for visitors to experience a deeper understanding of the culture at hand. Berno, Laurin and Maltezakis (2014) suggest that local foods that are supported by local agriculture are critical for rural tourism development because agriculture is the prerequisite for food. All cuisines have their origin in seeds, which themselves are the foundation of all agriculture (Berno, 2019). Thus, the agri-tourist who eats local cuisine that originated from a seed planted in a particular locale is not only incorporating the nutritional characteristics of the food, but is also 'tasting' its symbolic features: nature, culture and the identity of the area. Consuming regional specialities at their point of origin:

> is an act of complicity with the place, a way of becoming a part of the intimacy of that place and of the other, a symbolic consumption of a land, a region, a province, its climate, its history, its scenery ... embodying it in a real sense (Bessière, 2001, p. 117).

Conceptualised as such, creative agritourism puts the culture into agricultural, and provides a unique platform through which creative agri-tourists can genuinely discover Thainess.

Yet creative agritourism is about more than tourists just watching agricultural activities and eating local foods. Creative tourism engages tourists more deeply with culture by providing opportunities for them to learn. These may include hands-on agricultural experiences such as picking and/or shopping for fresh ingredients on-farm, or visiting markets and participating in cooking classes. In addition to contributing to fulfilling tourists' desire for authenticity, these creative agriculture-tourism-cuisine linkages can also reinforce local communities' cultural identity and economic self-sufficiency by stimulating local agriculture and artisanal food production, retaining tourism earnings and improving the distribution of economic benefits to the community. An additional benefit of this approach is that it can also promote tourism within the community as a means of supporting sustainable community development (Wisansing, 2018). This is consistent with the Sufficiency Economy approach, Thailand 4.0, the aims of OTOP and the goals of Creative Tourism (Berno et al., 2019). Essentially, these tourists are engaging in what can be considered 'creative rural gastronomy', which, we argue, is an integral part of creative agritourism. Conceptualised as such, gastronomy becomes an essential part of creative agritourism, which in turn can be an integral tool for sustainable CBT. Indeed, Richards (2016, p. x) has suggested that Thailand's model of creative tourism can 'actually be seen as a model of community-based tourism, because the central thrust of the program is based on sustainability and local creativity'. In other words, Thainess is communicated through creative agritourism as a total process that includes production (visits to farms, fruit picking, etc.), preparation (cooking classes, food preparation processes, etc.), and consumption (eating and dining experiences, etc.). In doing so, it lays the foundation for a more meaningful experience for both hosts and guests. This type of creative agritourism becomes the start of a unique and memorable experience for both hosts and guests, one that combines the creativity of local wisdom together with what the rural environment has to offer, along with the cultural, social and economic interconnections that come with it (Berno et al., 2014, 2019; Richards, 2015).

From three pillars to four: Extending the scope of creative agritourism to the arts

In extending the conceptualisation of agritourism to that of creative agritourism, 'creative rural gastronomy' has been incorporated as an integral component. This gives effect to Wisansing and Vongvisitsin's (2017) suggestion that discovering Thainess within the context of creative tourism comprises three pillars: nature (landscapes), life (society and culture), and art (the culinary arts/gastronomy). Wisansing and Vongvisitsin (2017, p. 2), however, went beyond these three pillars to consider how the linkages between tourism and Thainess can be expressed specifically through the 'art of food'. They define the art of food as not only including the culinary arts, but also the 'aesthetic presentation of food through forms of visual art ... food can be viewed as the new art incorporating a holistic experience, such as tastes and smells, food design and decoration, cooking simulation or performing arts' (ibid., 2017, p. 5). Specifically, 'the links between agriculture, senses of place and how to create a pairing of food and local performing arts' in which pairing art with gastronomy formed the foundation for a simulation of value creation for 'Tourism with Thainess' were explored (Wisansing & Vongvisitsin, 2017, p. 13). To operationalise this, local food menus were designed by artisan chefs, following which the stories behind the dishes were interpreted through performing arts. The conclusion was that through this pairing of the culinary and performing arts, 'senses, stories and sophistication were all integrated into one identity' (Wisansing & Vongvisitsin, 2017, p. 1). They concluded that Thai food, with its origins in local agriculture, can increase the value of a destination, as well as increase the value of local identity as expressed through the art of food.

Berno and Wisansing (2019) have suggested that local cuisine, as a manifestation of the culinary arts, is uniquely placed to bring together a diverse range of activities from agriculture through to the arts in a synergistic way that creates benefits for both tourists and host communities. The way in which they define gastronomy tourism positions it as a central element of creative agritourism:

> Gastronomy and tourism comprise an integrated, networked and holistic approach to food and food culture that spans the continuum from production through post-consumption. This includes landscapes, place, agriculture and food production, food traditions, food presentations, hospitality, eating, culture and heritage, lifestyle, destination development, sustainability and importantly, their synergistic relationship between gastronomy as an expression of the culinary arts and creativity, innovation and design (Berno & Wisansing, 2019, p. 23).

The link between gastronomy, agritourism and the creative industries is an important but often neglected relationship in tourism. The United Nations Industrial Development Organisation (UNIDO, 2017, p. 5) have identified what they refer to as a 'huge potential of linkages and synergies among the agro-food, tourism and the creative industries', suggesting that it is the integration of these various sectors that are key to fostering the socioeconomic development of a region. Indeed, UNIDO suggests that food and gastronomy are a form of artistic and cultural expression and one of the most salient examples of the expression of the contemporary tourist experience. UNIDO refers to the integration of these experiences as an 'integrated cluster approach' (UNIDO, 2017, p. 5). In taking this integrated cluster approach, territorial assets, including cultural, heritage and historical traditions (food, crafts, folklore, visual arts, drama, literary references, and historical sites), and natural resources (landscapes, flora, fauna, physical, and social spheres of production), come together in a place-based approach that capitalises on the distinct local characteristics that define a particular place.

Building on the concepts introduced through the three pillars of Thainess, it has been suggested that there are four pillars of gastronomy tourism in Thailand. These pillars are: 1) farming systems, 2) the story of food, 3) the creative industries, and 4) sustainable tourism (Berno & Wisansing, 2019). These four pillars are experienced as a 'journey' co-created by the tourist and the host community in which they come together in a place-based approach that captures local character. As discussed above, it is the way that culture is communicated through cuisine as a total process including production (agritourism, visits to farms, etc.), preparation (cooking classes, food preparation processes, etc.), and consumption (eating and dining experiences, etc.) that presents the foundation for a co-created, meaningful experience for both host and guest. This journey has at its foundation the philosophies of both creative rural gastronomy as well as creative agritourism; that is, the integration of place, food production, cuisine and artistic expression. Specifically, farming systems underpin the food system; they are the source of all cuisine. Cuisine is more than just food, however, it is an expression of culture and identity. By telling the story of local food (through sharing cuisine, cooking classes, etc.), host communities share Thai knowledge and wisdom with their guests, creating a deeper and more meaningful experience. As an expression of culture, the stories of food and cuisine can also be expressed and experienced through art, literature and music. Taken in their entirety, these create sustainable tourism experiences that contribute to community development, local pride and an enhanced tourism experience for both tourists and locals.

Rice tourism: A taste of Thainess

An example of how this creative agritourism is beginning to manifest in Thailand is through recent initiatives around 'rice tourism' (Berno et al., 2019). Rice is both an agricultural commodity and food. However, in the Thai context, rice is more than this. Rice is inextricably interwoven with the life cycle of Thai people in terms of landscape, consumption, religious belief and ritual practice (Siriwan, n.d., p. 2). For Thais, rice is a sacred food, divinely given and integrally intertwined with human life. With its seasons of birth, death and rebirth, the life cycle of rice is aligned with that of humanity; rice also becomes pregnant, gives birth and dies (Barnes, 2003). Rice is believed to have its own soul, which manifests through *Mae Posop*, the goddess and mother of rice. To demonstrate their deep respect and gratitude to *Mae Posop*, rice is blessed at every stage of its life cycle. Even the King has a connection to rice. As 'owner and protector of the land' and, by association, the 'protector of rice farms', the King oversees the annual Royal Ploughing Ceremony, a ritual performed for more than 700 years (Gomez, 2001, p. 3). Rice is essential to the Thai economy; it also forms the basis for many Thai festivals, rituals and customs. Rice has shaped Thailand's very landscape. '[Rice] has created a society, culture and cuisine that are uniquely Thai ... Rice has made the Thai' (Thompson, 2002, pp. 98–99).

The current 'Amazing Thai Taste' tourism campaign, which was launched in June 2017, is a collaborative initiative involving 45 public and private sector organisations that are working collectively to promote agriculture-tourism linkages through Thai cuisine (Amazing Thai Taste, 2018). Within this campaign is a focus on the role that rice plays in Thai culture, but it focuses on more than just rice as cuisine. The campaign invites tourists to participate in rice-centric activities that go beyond just eating and include co-created activities across the four pillars of gastronomy tourism. As part of this campaign, two YouTube video clips promoting 'Amazing Thai Rice' were released. In the first of these, 'Amazing Thai Rice Introduction', two tourists are seen participating alongside locals in a range of rice-related activities including a cooking class, eating rice and visiting a rice paddy where they plant and harvest rice. The relationship between agriculture, rice and society is emphasised throughout the clip (Amazing Thailand, 2017a). The second video, 'Amazing Thai Rice Route', extends the idea of rice as more than just a side dish by describing it as being expressive of 'life and Thainess'. The video invites tourists to 'Discover each region of Thailand through the enchanting culture of Thai rice' and to 'Enjoy the unique experience of [the] Thai way of life and way of rice' (Amazing Thailand, 2017b). The video clip again depicts tourists participating in rice-centric activities, but they are extended to include more than just participation in cooking and eating. Activities are broken down by region and are themed: rice and art, where 'rice stimulates creativity to create an artwork' (Northern); rice and festivals (North Eastern); rice and cycling (Central); rice and learning (Eastern); and rice and happiness (Southern). Evident throughout is a strong emphasis on the relationship between agritourism, culture and rice as part of the creative Thainess experience. The 'Amazing Thai Rice Route' has an accompanying downloadable brochure further detailing the activities depicted in the video (Amazing Thailand, 2017c).

Although these Amazing Thai Rice initiatives invite tourists to discover Thainess through the articulation of agriculture, cuisine and art, they do not fully reflect the integration of the three pillars of Thainess within the context of creative tourism as identified by Wisansing and Vongvisitsin (2017) and the four pillars of creative agri- and rural gastro-tourism as suggested by Berno and Wisansing (2019). A recent event, the Association of Southeast Asian Nations (ASEAN) Gastronomy Tourism Fair and Forum 'The Art of Sustainable Food Network' held in Bangkok in 2019, did so, establishing a platform on which agritourism can be reconceptualised as part of a more holistic approach to creative tourism that better reflects its potential within the Thailand 4.0 economy. Organised by Thailand's Ministry of Tourism and Sports and with support from the TAT the Fair aimed to highlight the unique combination of the four pillars through ingredients (farming), story (heritage), the creative industries, and taste of place (tourism). Starting with the poster used to advertise the event, the articulation of agriculture, cuisine, the arts and sustainable tourism can be seen (Figure 13.1).

Figure 13.1 Poster advertising the ASEAN Gastronomy Tourism Fair and Forum, 2019
Source: Artist Weerawut Kangwannavakul

The poster, a truncated version of an original woodcutting by Thai artist Weerawut Kangwannavakul, was titled simply 'Gastronomy Journey'. The artwork reflects the four pillars as being experienced as a 'journey', co-created by the tourist and the host community in which they come together in a place-based approach that captures local character. Central to the artwork are a tourist and host depicted as coming together in an agricultural setting in which various forms of sustainable food production can be seen as part of a cultural landscape. In the original artwork, an airplane traverses the sky, flying above a bright orange sun flanked by a fork and a knife, further reinforcing the linkages between agriculture, tourism, cuisine and art.

As delegates at the Forum entered the venue, they did so through a traditional 'market' setting, where stall holders plied their wares – local organic foods, agricultural products, handicrafts and artworks. Over the two days, agricultural producers, chefs and artists shared stories of their relationships with the land, food, art and tourism, as did government officials, academics and industry professionals. On the first day, delegates were invited to express their relationship with food through 'serious play', creating expressive artworks and storytelling through the use of Lego. On the second day, starting with the story of organic farming and its relationship to sustainability, food and tourism (https://sampranmodel.com/en/), delegates commenced a journey that spanned the continuum from production through to post-consumption, and in doing so, gave effect to the four pillars. Presentations were interspersed with expressions of agriculture and food through art: a dance troupe depicting the life cycle of rice; a pop-up art gallery of pieces that expressed the linkages between agriculture, food and tourism; even a couture outfit that depicted the rice harvest worn by a delegate.

The ASEAN Gastronomy Tourism Fair and Forum had at its core the aim of challenging current thinking and 'pushing the boundaries' of what comprises creative tourism, particularly as it relates to agri-foods. It was designed as an experiential showcase to highlight the potential linkages and synergies between agritourism, gastronomy and the creative industries. In this way, the whole of agritourism becomes larger than its constituent parts, and goes further in addressing the development outcomes targeted through the Thailand 4.0 economy, which are to drive creativity and innovation through high-value services and experiences, inclusive of creative tourism. By extending the conceptualisation of Thainess within creative tourism (the three pillars) and purposively integrating agriculture, the story of food, the creative industries and sustainable tourism along the entire value-chain (from production through to post-consumption), the four pillars approach to tourism development extends the potential benefits of tourism for both producers and consumers. In essence, the four pillars approach to agri- and gastronomy tourism introduces what is potentially a new generation of creative tourism.

Conclusions

Thailand has been highly successful in building a strong tourism sector. This has been reflected in an exponential growth in arrivals since the early 1960s. 2018 saw record numbers of tourist arrivals, with tourism expenditure of just over 2 trillion baht (US$64.7 billion) generated (TAT, 2019). Despite Thailand's success with tourism, many of the rural agricultural regions of the country are yet to see the benefits, and rural regions continue to be some of the poorest in the country. Successive governments have developed policies and strategies to stimulate economic development in the regions, often using tourism as the tool for development, but with mixed results.

In the mid-1990s, the Thai government started to promote agritourism as a means for economic development in rural areas. However, it was not until 1997 with the introduction of the SEP, that the early forms of agritourism began to emerge through the 'royal projects'. This change in approach was reflected in how tourism to rural regions was conceptualised as a tool for development. From its initial conceptualisation of being tourism focused on farm and village visits, agritourism evolved over time to reflect more global directions taken by Thai tourism such as sustainable tourism, creative tourism and tourism for community development, particularly in rural areas. Along with these there has been a gradual incorporation of related aspects such as cultural attributes (for example, 'Thainess' and 'local wisdom'), the OTOP initiative, and cuisine and gastronomy. Over time, this shift has redefined rural areas as not just sites of production but as spaces of tourist consumption and of multi-purpose activities for visitors to the area. This has given new value (socio-cultural and economic), notably as tourism products, to the resources in rural areas.

In order for agritourism to continue to be an effective tool for sustainable development, one that broadens the net of beneficiaries in rural regions, the way in which agritourism is conceptualised and operationalised in these rural areas needs to continue to be challenged. We argue that it is the relationship between agriculture, cuisine, local arts and tourism, and the creative ways in which these can be harnessed collectively as 'creative agritourism' that has the potential to effect these changes.

References

Adema, P. (2007). Foodscape: An emulsion of food and landscape. *Gastronomica: The Journal of Food and Culture* 7(1), 3.

Amazing Thai Taste (2018). Mission. Retrieved from: http://amazingthaitaste.com/index.php?page=content&contentId=48.

Amazing Thailand (2017a). Amazing Thai rice introduction [video file]. Retrieved from: https://www.youtube.com/watch?v=_TvladWPjlE.

Amazing Thailand (2017b). Amazing Thai rice route [video file]. Retrieved from: https://www.youtube.com/watch?v=F__xJW6aKfk.

Amazing Thailand (2017c). *Amazing Thai rice*. Bangkok: Tourism Authority of Thailand. Retrieved from: http://tourismproduct.tourismthailand.org/detail/308.

Anuroj, B. (n.d.). *Thailand 4.0 – a new value-based economy*. Bangkok, Thailand: Thailand Board of Investment. Retrieved April 20, 2019, from https://www.boi.go. th/upload/content/Thailand,%20Taking%20off%20to%20new%20heights%20@% 20belgium_5ab4e8042850e.pdf.

Barnes, C. (2003). The art of rice. *Humanities* 24(5), 42–45.

Berno, T. (2019, April 9–10). Expert roundtable: The four pillars of gastronomy. Invited panel presentation at the ASEAN Gastronomy Forum, Bangkok, Thailand.

Berno, T., Dentice, G., & Wisansing, J. (2019). Kin kao laew reu young ('have you eaten rice yet')?: A new perspective on food and tourism in Thailand. In E. Park, S. Kim & I. Yeoman (Eds.), *Food tourism in Asia* (pp. 17–30). Singapore: Springer.

Berno, T., Laurin, U., & Maltezakis, G. (2014). The special role of agriculture in food tourism. In E. Wolf & W. Lange-Faria (Eds.), *Have fork will travel: Handbook for food tourism* (pp. 105–114). Portland: World Food Travel Association.

Berno, T., & Wisansing, J. (2019). *The development of ASEAN gastronomy network and region of gastronomy master plan*. Bangkok: Ministry of Tourism and Sports, Thailand & Perfect Link Consulting.

Bessière, J. (2001). The role of rural gastronomy in tourism. In L. Roberts & D. Hall (Eds.), *Rural tourism and recreation: Principles to practice* (pp. 115–118). Wallingford: CABI International.

Bureau of Farmers Development (2005). *The handbook of agro-tourism development*. Bangkok: Department of Agricultural Extension.

Choenkwan, S., & Fisher, M. (2018). Agrarian transformation in Thailand-commodities, landscapes, and livelihoods. *Forest and Society* 2(2), 112–172.

Deloire, A., Prévost, P., & Kelly, M. (2008). Unravelling the terroir mystique: An agro-socioeconomic perspective. *Perspectives in Agriculture, Veterinary Science, Nutrition and Natural Resources* 3(32), 1–9.

Farrelly, N. (2016). Being Thai: A narrow identity in a wide world. *Southeast Asian Affairs* 2016(1), 331–343.

Fusté-Forné, F., & Berno, T. (2016). Food tourism in New Zealand: Canterbury's foodscapes. *Journal of Gastronomy and Tourism* 2(2), 71–86.

Gomez, K. (2001, September 20). Rice, the grain of culture. Paper presented at the Siam Lecture Series, The Siam Society, Bangkok, Thailand.

Khaokhrueamuang, A. (2014). The characteristics of agricultural practices in Bang Kachao area, the Bangkok metropolitan fringe. *International Journal of Tourism Sciences* 7, 1–10.

Laungaramsri, P. (2003). Ethnicity and the politics of ethnic classification in Thailand. In C. MacKerras (Ed.), *Ethnicity in Asia* (pp. 157–173). London: Routledge.

MacKendrick, N. (2014). Foodscape. *Contexts* 13(3), 16–18.

Mongsawad, P. (2012). The philosophy of the sufficiency economy: A contribution to the theory of development. *Asia-Pacific Development Journal* 17(1), 123–143.

Muangasame, K., & McKercher, B. (2014). The challenge of implementing sustainable tourism policy: A 360-degree assessment of Thailand's "7 Greens sustainable tourism policy". *Journal of Sustainable Tourism* 23(4), 417–516.

Muangasame, K., & Park, E. (2019). Food tourism, policy and sustainability: Behind the popularity of Thai food. In E. Park, S. Kim & I. Yeoman (Eds.), *Food tourism in Asia* (pp. 123–142). Singapore: Springer.

Muqbil, I. (2011). Thailand's unique royal projects. Retrieved from: https://www.tra vel-impact-newswire.com/thailands-unique-royal-projects.

Muqbil, I. (2019). The best analysis of Thailand's record-breaking visitor arrivals. Retrieved from: https://www.travel-impact-newswire.com/2019/02/the-best-analysi s-of-thailands-2018-record-breaking-visitor-arrivals.

Natsuda, K., Igusa, K., Wiboonpongse, A., & Thoburn, J. (2012). One Village One Product – rural development strategy in Asia: The case of OTOP in Thailand. *Canadian Journal of Development Studies/Revue canadienne d'études du développement* 33(3), 369–385.

Prayukvong, W., Huttasin, N., & Foster, M.J. (2015). Buddhist economics meets agritourism on the Thai farm. *International Journal of Culture, Tourism and Hospitality Research* 9(2), 183–199.

Richards, G. (2015, November 5). Recipes for sustainable creative tourism. Keynote presentation at the 3rd Business Management International Conference, Pattaya, Thailand.

Richards, G. (2016, August 5). The development of creative tourism in Asia. Keynote address presented at the Arte-Polis 6th International Conference, Institut Teknologi, Bandung, Indonesia.

Richards, G., & Raymond, C. (2000). Creative tourism. *ATLAS News* 23(8), 16–20.

Seisawatwanit, P. (2013). An approach to efficient management models for agritourism businesses in eastern region of Thailand. *PSAKU International Journal of Interdisciplinary Research* 2(1), 114–129.

Siriwan, S. (n.d.). *Rice, ritual and performance: Thai identity in the green field.* Unpublished manuscript. Retrieved from: https://www.academia.edu/8876327/Rice_ Ritual_and_Performance_Thai_Identity_in_the_Green_Field.

Songkhla, T.N., & Somboonsuke, B. (2013). Interactions between agro-tourism and local agricultural resources management: A case study of agro-tourism destinations in Chang Klang District, Southern Thailand. *Discourse Journal of Agriculture and Food Sciences* 1(4), 54–67.

Srisomyong, N. (2010). *Agritourism, rural development and related policy initiatives in Thailand.* Unpublished doctoral dissertation. Sheffield Hallam University, England.

Srisomyong, N., & Meyer, D. (2015). Political economy of agritourism initiatives in Thailand. *Journal of Rural Studies* 41, 95–108.

Sufficiency Economy Philosophy (n.d.). SDG 8: Promote sustained, inclusive and sustainable economic growth, full and productive employment and decent work for all: Transforming industry through creativity. Retrieved from: http://www.mfa.go.th/sep 4sdgs/contents/filemanager/images/sep/8.pdf.

Su-Indramedhi, S. (2017). *Rural socio-economic development: Sustainable agriculture dependent on utilizing regional resources comparing Japan and Thailand.* Unpublished doctoral dissertation. Mie University, Tsu, Japan.

The Ministry of Tourism and Sports (2017). *The second national tourism development plan (2017–2021).* Bangkok: The Ministry of Tourism and Sports.

Thompson, D. (2002). *Thai food.* Berkeley: Ten Speed Press.

TAT – Tourism Authority of Thailand (2009). *7 Greens kits.* Bangkok: Tourism Authority of Thailand.

TAT – Tourism Authority of Thailand. (2015a, August 17). Thailand launched four pilot agro tourism destinations. *TAT Newsroom.* Retrieved from: https://www.ta tnews.org/2015/08/thailand-launches-four-pilot-agro-tourism-destinations.

TAT – Tourism Authority of Thailand (2015b, January 14). Thailand invites international travellers to "Discover Thainess" with year-round activities. *TAT Newsroom.* Retrieved from: https://www.tatnews.org/2015/01/thailand-invites-international-tra vellers-to-discover-thainess-with-year-round-activities.

TAT – Tourism Authority of Thailand (2017). Make a real connection to Thailand through the Royal Projects. *TAT Newsroom*. Retrieved from: https://www.tatnews.org/2017/10/make-a-real-connection-to-thailand-through-royal-projects.

TAT – Tourism Authority of Thailand (2019). As Chinese visitors bounce back, Thai tourism income crosses two trillion Baht Available. *TAT Newsroom*. Retrieved from: https://www.tatnews.org/2019/01/as-chinese-visitors-bounce-back-thai-tourism-income-crosses-two-trillion-baht.

TAT – Tourism Authority of Thailand (n.d.). *Agro-tourism: Green travel in Thailand*. Bangkok: Tourism Authority of Thailand.

UNIDO – United Nations Industrial Development Organisation (2017). *Agro-food, tourism and creative industries: An integrated cluster approach*. Vienna: UNIDO.

UNWTO – United Nations World Tourism Organisation (2012). *Global report on food tourism: AM reports* (Volume 4). Madrid: UNWTO.

UNWTO – United Nations World Tourism Organisation (2018). *UNWTO tourism highlights: 2018 edition*. Madrid: UNWTO.

Van Beek, S. (2017). *Thailand tourism: The early days*. Bangkok: Dusit Thani Public Company.

Wattanacharoensila, W., & Schuckert, M. (2016). Reviewing Thailand's master plans and policies: Implications for creative tourism? *Current Issues in Tourism* 19(10), 1045–1070.

Wisansing, J. (Ed.). (2018). *Creating creative tourism toolkit*. Bangkok: Designated Area for Sustainable Tourism Administration (DASTA).

Wisansing, J., & Vongvisitsin, T. (2017). *Mechanisms for the art of food: Tourism with Thainess and multi-stakeholder participation approach*. Barcelona: International Institute of Gastronomy, Culture, Arts, and Tourism. Retrieved, from: https://igcat.org/wp-content/uploads/2017/03/MECHANISMS-FOR-THE-ART-OF-FOOD-TOURISM-WITH-THAINESS-AND-MULTI-STAKEHOLDER.pdf.

World Travel and Tourism Council (2017). *Thailand: How does travel and tourism compare to other sectors?*London: World Travel and Tourism Council.

14 Tourism and development in Southeast Asia

Concluding remarks and future outlook

Claudia Dolezal, Alexander Trupp and Huong T. Bui

This volume has discussed the important and ever-growing role of tourism as an engine for development in the region of Southeast Asia. While the contributions to the current volume varied in scope and geographical focus, overall they formed part of four major thematic streams: theoretical/methodological foundations, protected areas, local communities, and governance. Authors of this edited volume shared conceptual approaches and empirical evidence that accentuated the regional importance of tourism as a livelihood for people and an ever-growing engine for development in the future. However, at the same time, challenges were noted in all of the chapters – tourism might be contributing to development, but what kind of development, and can it really contribute to sustainable development for the Southeast Asian region? What is the future of tourism for development in the region?

Tourism: A viable engine for sustainable development in Southeast Asia?

The majority of contributions in the present book are based on a participatory and community-empowerment ethos, strongly emphasising that tourism can only be successful if based on true community participation – no matter what governance model it may follow (Müller, Markova, & Ponnapureddy – Chapter 12). Kausar, Darmawan, and Firmansyah in their study on a national park in Indonesia (Chapter 6) even argued that tourism has the potential to empower local communities and feel a sense of ownership, however, most of it will remain at the level of Pretty's (1995) 'functional participation', given that outcomes and objectives are often predetermined by other parties. The external drive and management of tourism initiatives that should benefit local communities has indeed been a point of criticism for a long time and needs to be urgently addressed so that communities do not occupy the position of the less powerful actors and mere recipients in tourism schemes—even if they might be of collaborative nature. Phommavong and Müller (Chapter 7), however, reminded us that even pro-poor tourism (PPT) has essential work to do to really benefit those in need, i.e., the poorest of the poor. Rather than offering financial support, PPT marginalises those further that are most in need of help, and hence is not in line with the UN Sustainable development Goals' (SDG) tagline of 'leaving no one behind'.

The contributions in this book also pointed toward urban-rural relationships, such as Kausar et al.'s research on national parks at the outskirts of the Indonesian capital Jakarta (Chapter 6) or Trupp's research (Chapter 8) on highland ethnic minorities in urban areas in Thailand. Particularly the latter offered a valuable insight into how those that are marginalised carve their own niches and find their way in tourism to turn it into a new livelihood. At the same time, however, he also showed that urban contexts often marginalise indigenous people and ethnic minorities further, therefore leaving them at the fringes of urban tourism business. Tourism, nevertheless, is seen as a key livelihood for many of those that have few other options available. However, as shown by Lasso and Dahles (Chapter 9), tourism becomes problematic when it replaces existing livelihoods and creates further dependence. Both of these cases demonstrate that, while tourism may be a new and viable livelihood for many communities, particularly in rural areas in Southeast Asia, it may not be the most sustainable livelihood of all.

Nevertheless, tourism does have the potential to transform the lives of people and to contribute to conservation. Pham and Bui in their research on ecotourism and protected areas in Vietnam (Chapter 4) have reminded us of the power of tourism, specifically alternative tourism, which, unfortunately is often underused. Issues like weak governance, information problems and lack of coordination between stakeholders in developing countries often create obstacles to successful, and above all sustainable, tourism ventures. In a similar vein, Jones and Syura questioned whether park rangers really offer stewardships for sustainability in Langkawi, Malaysia (Chapter 5), and argued that there is a long way from 'green washing' to sustainable tourism given current constraints from administrative capacities. While the outcome of tourism often does not match its potential, this book has demonstrated that tourism remains a driver for good – beyond economic income and diversification into the social and environmental spheres.

On a more conceptual level, this book has contributed to the discussion of how tourism for development is approached as a research subject. Many of the contributors ask for a dissolving of binaries in our research, such as Dolezal, Trupp, and Leepreecha (Chapter 3), who argue for the need to break down distinctions between research at home and away and, rather, to dedicate ourselves to how we reflect on the challenges we encounter in the field. After all, it was shown that there is not one ideal or comfortable position from which to do research in Southeast Asia. In addition, it was made clear that we need to start rethinking the mass versus alternative tourism divide, accepting mass tourism in Southeast Asia as a reality and asking questions about the sustainability of tourism, rather than only its size (Bui & Dolezal – Chapter 2). Rather than seeing tourism in categories, thinking outside the box might be what is needed.

After all, Southeast Asia is experiencing rapid changes and the categories initially created might no longer be of use for the research we do (Husa, Korff, & Wohlschlägl, 2018). Yotsumoto's work in this volume (Chapter 10) offered a valuable insight into how modernity, globalisation, and wider development affect rural areas in the Philippines by questioning in how far traditional ways of life can be preserved under these various impacts that villages experience while also actively engaging in and become a part of processes of modernisation and globalisation. The question that therefore remains here, is what does the future for Southeast Asian tourism for development hold?

The future of Southeast Asian tourism for development

Despite the wide range of topics covered in this book, these are only some of the issues towards the future of tourism for development in Southeast Asia that can be discussed in such a volume with a regional focus. Kraas, Myint and Häusler (Chapter 11) pointed specifically to the future of tourism in Myanmar, a rising destination in the Southeast Asian region. The authors state that the appeal of nature might fade as the structures and characteristics of tourism change. Among the new trends are wellness, sports, and medical tourism; meetings, incentives, conferences, and events (MICE) tourism; educational/summer course tourism; and cross-border and trade-related tourism. These trends point to opportunities for regional segmentation to become much more diversified and, in some cases, for growing specialisation of the tourism potential.

Part of the tourism trends in the Asia-Pacific region are the experience economy (Pine & Gilmore, 2019) and activity-oriented travel (Tolkach, Chon, & Xiao, 2016). Berno, Wisansing, and Dentice in this volume (Chapter 13) show how agritourism in Thailand, when aligned with principled of creative tourism, provides opportunities for visitors to be engaged more deeply with a destination through its food. Also, Yotsumoto (Chapter 10) pointed to the experiential potential of tourism through active participation in activities, enabling a more fluid understanding of authenticity through 'authentic experiences' rather than the idea of an authentic, oftentimes static culture. This frees local residents from the pressures of having to appear or act authentic, with culture perceived as stuck in time and space, a challenge that often conflicts with ideas of development and striving for a more modern way of life for villagers.

We are aware of a number of important topics that have not been included in the collection. For example, the importance of transportation networks including the developments of an increasing number of airports and railways, the expansion of low-cost carriers (LCCs), and how these impact environment and local communities. Moreover, the growth and role of new source markets from emerging world regions (Cohen & Cohen, 2015) (particularly but not exclusively from Asia) and other forms of tourism, such as cruise tourism, casino tourism (particularly in Singapore and Cambodia) or MICE tourism require further critical examination. Geographically, studies of tourism for development in Brunei, Singapore and Timor-Leste are missing from our edited volume.

Overall, international tourism arrivals to Southeast Asia are expected to grow by 5.1% a year between 2010 and 2030 (UNWTO, 2016). Changing global trends as well as demographic, economic, and social changes in the region will continue to pose a challenge to tourism and development in Southeast Asia. The structural changes of tourist arrivals in the region have yet to be thoroughly analysed, but what we already know is that China plays an increasingly important role in Southeast Asian tourism, both as source market for many destinations and as economic and political power in the region. At the same time, overdependence on the East Asian market comes with certain risks, which have become particularly visible when the novel coronavirus pandemic broke out in the main source markets for the region, including China. As also highlighted in several chapters of this volume, Asian and domestic tourism are key drivers of Southeast Asian tourism (Winter, Teo, & Chang, 2009) – with the latter potentially playing an even stronger role in current times of uncertainty, risk and decreased intra-regional, if not global, mobility. Given the current challenging times that the industry is facing, it was therefore important to secure contributions from authors within the region, not only to balance Western academic gazes but also to enhance collaboration, discussions, and dialogues across geographical and political borders.

Finally, future research in the region could more systematically examine the linkages between tourism development and the SDGs, either by focusing on one particular SDG or the overall SDG framework. This has yet to be applied specifically to the region of Southeast Asia and a tourism context. As shown by Bui and Dolezal in this volume (Chapter 2), development theory has come a long way since the 1950s – and while mass tourism and modernisation are still a reality for Southeast Asia, sustainable development is increasingly embraced. The question that remains is whether this is the most suitable way forward to really contribute to the kind of development through tourism that local communities envisage, or whether alternatives to development per se, inspired by post-development thinking, would carve out a more positive future. Social enterprises are on the rise and de-growth has become a powerful emerging concept (Higgins-Desbiolles, Carnicelli, Krolikowski, Wijesinghe, & Boluk, 2019), however, very little research has been done to date on alternatives to development that work outside the dynamics of capitalism and stem from the region of Southeast Asia itself, particularly in relation to tourism.

This book has made a contribution to the ambiguous relationship between tourism and development in Southeast Asia in the 21st century. Bearing in mind future challenges that the region and industry are facing, this book provides a fertile ground for researchers with the potential to inform policy making, consultants and academics in using tourism as an effective tool for regional sustainable development. Most importantly, this volume has not only shed a realistic light on the issues of tourism, but also on the obstacles that keep destinations from using tourism more effectively – an industry that is oftentimes mismanaged but also whose power as an engine for sustainable development is regularly underestimated.

References

Cohen, E., & Cohen, S.A. (2015). A mobilities approach to tourism from emerging world regions. *Current Issues in Tourism* 18(1), 11–43.

Higgins-Desbiolles, F., Carnicelli, S., Krolikowski, C., Wijesinghe, G., & Boluk, K. (2019). Degrowing tourism: rethinking tourism. *Journal of Sustainable Tourism* 27 (12), 1926–1944.

Husa, K., Korff, R., & Wohlschlägl, H. (Eds.). (2018). *Suedostasien. Gesellschaften, Raeume und Entwicklung*. Vienna: New Academic Press.

Pine, B.J., & Gilmore, J.H. (2019). *The experience economy* (2nd ed.). Brighton: Harvard Business Review.

Pretty, J.N. (1995). Participatory learning for sustainable agriculture. *World Development* 23(8), 1247–1263.

Tolkach, D., Chon, K.K., & Xiao, H. (2016). Asia Pacific tourism trends: Is the future ours to see? *Asia Pacific Journal of Tourism Research* 21(10), 1071–1084.

UNWTO (2016). *UNWTO Tourism Highlights: 2016 Edition*. Madrid: UNTWO. Retrieved from: https://www.e-unwto.org/doi/pdf/10.18111/9789284418145.

Winter, T., Teo, P., & Chang, T.C. (Eds.). (2009). *Asia on tour: Exploring the rise of Asian tourism*. Abingdon: Routledge.

Index

Note: Information in figures and tables is indicated by page numbers in *italics* and **bold**.